ALSO BY CYNTHIA LINDSAY

I Love Her, That's Why
    (with George Burns)

Mother Climbed Trees

Home Is Where You Hang Yourself—
    or How to Be a Woman—and Who Needs It?

The Natives Are Restless

DEAR BORIS

DEAR BORIS

THE LIFE OF WILLIAM HENRY PRATT

a.k.a. BORIS KARLOFF

BY CYNTHIA LINDSAY

ALFRED A. KNOPF   NEW YORK   1975

THIS IS A BORZOI BOOK PUBLISHED BY ALFRED A. KNOPF, INC.

Since this page cannot legibly accommodate all permissions
acknowledgments, they can be found on page *viii*.

Library of Congress Cataloging in Publication Data

Lindsay, Cynthia Hobart.
Dear Boris: the life of William Henry Pratt.
Filmography: p.
1. Karloff, Boris, 1887–1969. I. Title.
PN2287.K25L5   791.43′028′0924 [B]   74–21295
ISBN 0–394–47579–8

Manufactured in the United States of America

FIRST EDITION

Special thanks to the researchers,
Rowena Ross, Monty Arnold, Bongo Wolf, and Richard Brooke.

FOR DEAR BORIS

"To live in the hearts we leave behind is not to die"

and for Evie,

Sara Jane,

Michael, and David

CONTENTS

PREFACE /
THE GREAT KARLOFF
DETECTIVE STORY

How *does* one write the life of a close and beloved friend of thirty-six years, whose daughter is one's godchild, when, faced with assembling material, one realizes one knows almost no facts? Memories are endless, diverse, and heartwarming. His sense of nonsense—each year at Christmas or birthdays my gifts arrived, for some reason known only to him, in large galvanized iron garbage cans tied with huge satin ribbons; Boris in impeccable tweeds strolling through the garden followed by innumerable dogs, one a lamb-like Bedlington terrier named Agnus Dei, the group trailed by a huge sow named Violet, wearing a dreadful multicolored sweater I had given Boris as a joke. Or his passion for serious gardening—pitchfork, spade, or hose in hand, stomping about the property clad only in ghastly elastic swimming trunks called "wickies" and a proper tall black opera hat. Or his knowledge of literature—evenings of his articulate discussion of new books, old books, and his great love, Joseph Conrad. His sense of tradition and ceremony—at home, Boris in dinner jacket surrounded by friends, at attention as pipers piped in the New Year; Boris weeping openly at a child's Christmas carol, or falling down roaring at an outrageous joke; Boris in freezing temperature standing in a graveyard, his arm around me, literally holding me up at my husband's burial. Boris as the friend who was there when you needed him, before you knew you needed him. Boris the man no one ever referred to as anything but "dear Boris," as if it were one inseparable word.

Remembering him, one remembers being *with* him, loving, respecting, and giggling at him. But facts? Next to none. I never saw a Karloff film until later years on television and in projection rooms. In all the years of closeness, I never thought of him as a "movie star," only as a woolly friend. And there *is* a tactile memory of him that *is* woolly, the good soft tweeds and the silvery gray hair that had always been shaved for some monstrous role and for which, as it grew furring in, he charged fifty cents a feel. In

Boris at ease with Agnus Dei.

advance. (Beards were a dollar. They were rarer.) One was never aware of it, but Boris was a most secret man. His business was his own business, and yours was yours. One did not pry. And I would always have respected his great sense of privacy.

Obviously, however, "A Life" must be properly researched, not just full of personal memories. When it came to the portions of Boris's life I had never known about and which he had never mentioned to anyone—not even to his wives or his daughter—it was necessary to instigate a search for obscure records made more obscure by Boris having deliberately covered his own tracks. The only available information on his past lay in old studio biographies that were inaccurate at worst and scanty at best, plus a few family facts and pictures in Evie Karloff's (his widow's) possession. One of the mysteries in The Great Karloff Detective Story, incidentally, is why he never kept in touch with any member of his family. As the clues came in, one thing became perfectly clear: When Boris closed a door on a part of his life, it stayed closed.

Among the contributing difficulties in research was the fact that this attitude appears to have been shared by other members of the far-flung family. The major portion of the family records was housed in Sir John Pratt's (Boris's brother's) flat at the Temple in London, an office totally obliterated during the Blitz. The following day he viewed the rubble and sniffed: "That's that. Now I can get on with my work." So much for the family records.

In 1971, when Evie started her end of the digging for this book, in England, she found only one of Boris's nine siblings alive: Richard Septimus Pratt, aged 89, living in Bristol. She wrote him regarding Boris's childhood, and he replied: "I'm afraid my memories of Billy are nil." So much for familial research.

Then when enough material had come to light so Evie was able to tell Richard Septimus Pratt things he had never known about his own family, he started to search for things himself and came up with scraps of paper, a daguerreotype, a baptism certificate. Richard Septimus and Evie (who have never met) now conduct an affectionate running correspondence, and he is on the alert for any new information.

I myself continued the search, flying from England to Canada, to which Boris had migrated in 1909 at the age of twenty-one. No clues. He had played in stock companies. The companies and most of the theaters in which he appeared no longer exist. But I did find a student of the theater who was a Karloff fan, and left him working on the meager information I had been able to acquire. (One researcher I had employed was already at work in London.)

At the Library of the Performing Arts of the New York Public Library I found another bright, professional researcher, also a Karloff fan. He went to work in the East and I returned to California. At home I was soon surrounded by piles of material from everywhere. Some duplications, some contradictions—from Evie, from the three researchers. I was in the middle of a giant jigsaw puzzle, and clearly many of the pieces were permanently missing. So that reassembling Boris's life—that part of it constituting all we will ever know—has not been easy. But it *has* been a labor of love.

CYNTHIA LINDSAY

OPPOSITE: *Boris age two with friend.*

It's moving! It's alive! It's moving! It's *alive!*"

It is doubtful if William Henry Pratt, also known as Boris Karloff, was greeted with as much hysterical enthusiasm at his first birth in Dulwich, England, in 1887, as he was at his second in Universal City, California, in 1931, when as Dr. Frankenstein's Monster he rose, bewildered, from the operating table and reached wonderingly for a shaft of sunlight.

Billy's father's marriage to his mother, Eliza Sarah Millard, had been preceded by divers marriages to other ladies with resultant progeny from all. From his first marriage, to Julianna Campbell, a girl, Emma Caroline, was born in 1850. The same year a boy, Edward, was born and died at birth; Julianna died shortly thereafter. From the next marriage, to a lady named Charlotte (no traceable last name), another daughter, Eliza Julia, was born sometime around 1855, but there is no record of what ever became of her. Charlotte died around 1860, and in 1864 Eliza Sarah became the third Mrs. Edward John Pratt. In the course of the next twenty-three years, nine children were born of this union: Edward Millard, George Marlow, Charles Rary, Frederick Grenville, David Cameron, Julia Honoria, John (Jack) Thomas, Richard Septimus, and William Henry.

Being the youngest by five years of a family of eight brothers and one sister (plus one half-sister) whom he by no means knew well, Billy was virtually an only child. His mother was frail and ill and his government-servant father a tyrant when at home—which was seldom. Billy's entire association with his brothers and his father took place when one or another of them, returning from somewhere or other, observed him as if under a microscope and muttered, "Something's got to be done about that boy!" No one agreed on *what* should be done, so apparently nothing was, and he went his own way and found his friendships elsewhere. One of the elsewheres was the home of Noel Hearns, now Mrs. Noel Horsey. Living with her in the mid-1890's—they were then both little girls—was her cousin from India, Winifred Cumming, now Lady Cocke.

In 1972 I had the privilege of meeting these ladies in the sunlit living room of Evelyn Karloff's cottage, "Roundabout," in Bramshott, Hampshire. Lady Cocke zipped into the living room in an Irish fisherman's sweater reaching below her knees, followed by Mrs. Horsey in serious tweeds. As Evie served us tea, Lady Cocke said:

"Well now, let's see . . . what can I tell you about Billy? It's been a bit of a while, you know. . . ." (Lady Cocke was then eighty-four, Mrs. Horsey, eighty-seven.) "I'll tell you one thing, though. Actually, Billy had a pretty stiff time. His was a strange, uncommunicative family."

"He was very shy," said Mrs. Horsey, "and no wonder. He was, I think, a very lonely little boy. We had a large house, full of young people— he liked that. He loved our house because he was always welcome. His brothers were never at home, his mother was so ill—and his father was a very severe man. He found something with us, and we enjoyed having him. Billy was an awfully good-natured boy. He had to be to put up with all of us as well as his treatment at home. We had great games—he loved games, and he was terribly good at them."

"Wouldn't you rather say 'keen'? He was *terribly* keen!" said Lady Cocke.

"No, I wouldn't. I say he was *good*. I expect far better than he thought —he was very modest, you know!"

"What sort of games?" I asked.

"Oh, let's see . . . 'Up Jenkins.' . . ."

". . . and 'Down Jenkins.'. . ."

"And 'Mumbledy Peg' and 'Crawlers' and 'Bangers,' " said Lady Cocke. "And we could cycle over and play hockey in the brickfields in front of Wormwood Scrubs Prison. Believe me, mixed hockey is the most danger- ous game ever invented. As I say, Billy was *very* keen!"

"I can still smell those brickfields," said Mrs. Horsey. "And charades —we played a lot of charades. Our mother and father had brought clothes from India and we dressed up. I remember I was Fatima. Billy particularly enjoyed charades and was *definitely* good at them."

"Especially Bluebeard," said Lady Cocke. "We did a beautiful Blue- beard. We cut holes in an old sheet to stick our heads through and put red paint under the holes for where our heads were chopped off by Bluebeard."

She paused, with her head poised like one of the birds which we'd been watching in the birdbath outside the window. "I'll bet you'd like me to say Billy played Bluebeard, wouldn't you? Well—he *didn't*. But you can say so."

Evie asked, "Did you ever see him *away* from your home? I mean outside of the playing fields of Wormwood Scrubs?"

"Oh *quite*," said Lady Cocke. "Billy took me to the opening of the two-penny tube. It was the *first* tube—went from Shepherd's Bush to the Bank . . . that's the Bank of England, you know."

"And we went to the theater," added Mrs. Horsey. "Billy adored the theater. He worshipped his brother George, who was the only one who was good to him. George was an actor. I expect possibly that's why Billy always wanted to be one. We saved every penny to buy seats way up in the gods. Remember? We saw Lewis Waller play Monsieur Beaucaire."

"Remember? How could I forget it?" answered Lady Cocke. "I was dressed in white satin and wore a hat with a nest of robins in it that kept falling into my eyes. Billy couldn't see the play for laughing!"

Evie said, "If life was so miserable at home, I'm surprised he never mentioned it to me. But I suppose it was a part of that characteristic of his —never grumbling. How lucky he was to have had you to go to!"

"We loved him. Admired him for being such a good sport," Lady Cocke said. "He never showed any sign of rejection—he just made a joke about the family, never moaned about his rotten childhood."

"He was put down a lot," said Mrs. Horsey. "In fact, he was downright squashed. His mother was frail and he was very much on his own— then one or another of his brothers would return home from somewhere or other and bully him. He was a generous boy—he never seemed to hold it against them, just sort of got on with it."

Lady Cocke said, "I know all the brothers did very well later on. Edward was a judge on the High Court in Bombay when I was there."

"Yes," Evie said, "Boris always joked: 'All my family was brilliant—I was the only one with no brains.' "

"He was wrong about that," said Mrs. Horsey. "He was *very* bright. All the Pratt boys were. You know, Evie, I didn't even know he had sisters until you told me the other day."

"He did, of course, although one was only a half-sister," Evie said. "But I was surprised that you, having been such close friends, knew as little of his later life as I did of his early one."

"Well," Lady Cocke said, "one felt awkward. Billy being such a star —one hesitated to call."

"What a pity," Evie said. "He would have adored seeing you. Anyway, Boris did go to live with his half-sister, Emma, after his mother died. She was about the same age as his mother. She never married and ultimately left Boris everything in her will—this being a hundred pounds a year, but it came at a time when he needed it desperately. His other sister, Julia Honoria, married Arthur Donkin, the Vicar of Semer, Suffolk. Boris admired the vicar tremendously, because, although Arthur was Church of England, he allowed Julia Honoria to convert to Catholicism and he even entertained the local priest at his church because he said that what she did was quite her own business, 'as long as you do your duty to the parish.' Boris considered this to be a very civilized attitude."

"How amazing that at such a time a man of the cloth would allow his wife those liberties," said Mrs. Horsey.

"Let me ask you," Evie said, "when Boris was very young, did he stammer?"

"Oh definitely," said Lady Cocke, "and the lisp—he never quite got over them, did he?"

"No. He frequently had to rephrase dialogue to encompass them."

"Interesting—he never outgrew being bowlegged either, did he? We used to tease him about it."

"No—and a crime, too. These days they break and reset a child's legs. That's one of the reasons the arthritis became so agonizing later on," said Evie quietly.

Suddenly I thought: Of course—the strange rolling gait of the Monster, not a characterization, but a necessity, like a large ship at sea being forced from side to side by the tides. He had no control over this movement.

As we talked, some of the pieces had started to pull together. His trademarks: the rolling gait; the studied delivery of lines; the quiet, gentle, endearing, "Mustn't grumble" personal attitude. They all sprang from the boy who had played and found comfort with these very ladies when they were little girls in Dulwich, almost eighty years ago.

OVERLEAF: *Boris about age five in school uniform. The lady is probably his half-sister or perhaps his teacher. (From the Dorothy Stickney collection.)*

Except for portraying a demon king in the Enfield parish church play, Boris followed the childhood pattern set by his brothers. But this one tangent may have set the course for the future. As he always said of this performance: "It fired my blood for it." After a time at the Merchant Taylors' School, he entered Uppingham School, then—1903—as now, one of the finest of British public schools. The present Bursar of Uppingham kindly compiled and contributed Boris's unremarkable scholastic record, from which we learn that his house was Fircroft and that his housemaster was the Rev. T. E. Raven, who was succeeded in 1904 by R. N. Douglas, later Headmaster of Giggleswick. That he went from next-to-last in his form to second to fourth to tenth. And that at Christmas 1905 he won a prize for "Music and Choir" and in the summer of 1906 an award, on Speech Day, for German. Also: "In term III 1903, he played forward for the second side of the 8th Rugby Football game. They won eleven games." His record of modest achievement in sports continues through his three remaining years at school.

Boris himself, although he didn't frequently discuss his school days, once contributed the fact that the Rev. T. E. Raven was known to the boys as "The Old Bird" and the two housemistresses were lovingly referred to by them as "Big Bum Ada" and "Pee Drawers Elsie."

Selwyn Jepson, the well-known British author, discussed with me the importance of Boris's school experience. He knew Boris well in his last years —Selwyn and Tania Jepson's house is close to the Karloff cottage in Bramshott—and admired him deeply. Jepson also shares the same educational background, although he attended St. Paul's rather than Uppingham.

"One or two points come to mind," Jepson said about Boris and his schooling. "I think it is a vital point that he did not go to Uppingham as a boarder until he was somewhere about fifteen or sixteen, and up to that age had been a day-boy there and at his previous schools, living at home with all its advantages in social and opposite-sex contacts. Thus, by the time his traditional-minded brothers decided he needed discipline, it was too late for the change to being a boarder to do him much harm. He was by then already set in character and temperament. I can imagine those brothers were bothered by, and even unconsciously resentful of, his independence of spirit, resulting from a broader education than they had had themselves, and from which, of course, sprang his courage and adventurousness in facing adult life, his superior qualifications for surviving in it. I am pretty sure, too, that his talent owed much to his early escape from an 'un-family' existence in a boarding school. The wider experiences in those formative years would have developed understanding and observation of people, on which an actor calls for his interpretations of the roles he has to play; and not least his—in Boris's case—immense adaptability.

"Boris's circumstances were appalling. Appalling, because at a crucial time in the development of his spirit—at the age when he needed the stability of family background—all he got from his brothers was: 'That boy needs discipline.' Ultimately, Boris rejected their disciplines of old-fashioned Victorian schooling and the demagoguery of family belief that he should follow in his father's profession in the diplomatic corps. But he maintained his own innate personal discipline indefinitely. Because of it, he could have done anything he had chosen to do—he chose to act."

During this period, no young Englishman stood a chance of becoming a "gentleman" without attending a "decent public school." One did not necessarily need brains, but one needed at least a façade of "breeding," and, more importantly, facility in games—primarily on the cricket field.

The impact of this background stayed with Boris in what Selwyn Jepson refers to as "his exile." Boris's devotion to the sacred game of cricket, in which he referred to his abilities as "a first-rate enthusiast, but a rabbit," was second only to his dedication to the theater, through the rest of his life. Another continuing characteristic was that although he was the most liberal of men, he was essentially a snob. But a special type of snob: He invariably chose the company of the movie crew to that of the men in the front office, because his own brand of snobbism was based on a regard for a man's abilities and professionalism, not his position. He had no tolerance for the phony at any level.

The qualities of bearing, the regard for manners forced on him—conceivably with the aid of a birch rod—never left him, nor did his love for England. No matter where he lived—California, New York, anywhere—he was a "proper English gentleman." As he always said, "I would have made a hell of a Little Lord Fauntleroy—I was trained for it."

Asked about his childhood and schooling in an interview with Arlene

Boris age six. Figure at left is unidentifiable.

and Howard Eisenberg in the *Saturday Evening Post*, November 3, 1962, Boris was quoted:

> Actually I am assured that I was a quiet infant and a gentle boy. No whipping by cruel step-parents scarred my childhood. No sadistic governesses read me horror tales by flickering candlelight. My childhood as William Henry Pratt in the serene London suburb of Enfield was extraordinarily tame. Both my parents died during my childhood. I was reared by one amiable stepsister [the half-sister] and seven stern older brothers, who knew exactly what I was to be—a government servant in the family tradition. However, my scholarship or lack of it, during four years at Uppingham in 1902–1906 [really 1903–1907], bespoke my disinterest in any profession based upon higher learning. Actually, my macabre career was already settled. At the age of nine I had appeared in

a Christmas play version of *Cinderella*. Instead of playing the handsome Prince, I donned black tights and a skull cap and rallied the forces of evil as the Demon King. From then on I resolved to be an actor.

What about the stern father and the lonely little boy Lady Cocke and Mrs. Horsey remember? Did Boris choose to forget, or was he as usual "telling the members of the press what they want to hear"?

While he was in school, Boris's interest in the theater continued to overshadow his interest in his classes. There are scanty records of academic accomplishments of the time, but he maintained a clear impression of what he saw on the stage in the opening years of this century. In a syndicated newspaper interview given in 1950, when he was appearing in *Peter Pan*, he said:

When I was an impressionable youngster in England, I was taken to the Duke of York's Theatre—to see a play that was enchanting all of London. It was an incredible and novel adventure—children flew about the stage, pirates and Indians fought to the death, mermaids, a crocodile, a large Newfoundland dog, an invisible fairy who signaled her comings and goings by flashes of light—it was James Barrie's *Peter Pan*.

More than by the adventures of Peter and the Lost Boys, I was fascinated even that long while back by the figure of Gerald du Maurier as that ace of scoundrels, Captain Hook. As one who has been in the business of frightening children for the past two decades, it would be easy to look back now and say that Gerald started me off on an evil life. Perhaps he did; at any rate, the memory of that actor in that role is very much with me, for after forty-six years I, too, am playing Hook in *Peter Pan*.

After Uppingham, Boris went on to King's College of the University of London, but only for a short time, after which came the period of exile mentioned by Selwyn Jepson. Whether Boris's decision to leave England was prompted by his family, which was disappointed in his lack of application to a diplomatic future, or by his own desire to get away, there is no way of knowing. The fact remains that he turned his back on family tradition. At the time, British nonconformists had two havens to which they could flee: the new frontiers of Australia and Canada. Conveniently, when he was twenty-one years old, Boris's half-sister, Emma, died, leaving him a small sum of money. While collecting his inheritance in the solicitor's office, he tossed a coin to see which new frontier he would storm—heads: Canada; tails: Australia. It came up heads, and he packed for Canada, his coffers swelled by the brothers who wanted him out of sight instead of outraging them by hanging about not being a diplomat. In May 1909 Boris, age twenty-one, sailed from home on the *Empress of Britain*.

It took a good deal of courage to set out alone for an unknown country. On board ship he summoned up even more courage, and attempted to take himself a bride. And here starts the search for the mysterious, seldom-mentioned lost wives.

The records of the *Empress of Britain*'s May 7, 1909, passage to Canada show an application for marriage certificate. There is a space stating: "Name in full of both parties: Man, Woman." Under "Man, Christian or other Forenames": "William Henry." Under "Surname": "Pratt." Under "Woman": Nothing. No name. Blank. In the space for signature of applicants is written: "No records of marriage at sea."

What happened? Did he change his mind? Did they wait until later and did she become one of his wives at some other time?

The ship sailed on for Montreal and there is no record of anyone going overboard.

OVERLEAF: *Transatlantic liner entering Montreal Harbor, 1909, perhaps the very ship on which Boris arrived.*

3 / PRATT TO KARLOFF

On May 17, 1909, the *Empress of Britain* landed in Montreal. From the time Boris (still Billy Pratt) disembarked, he laid a trail as difficult to follow as if he had deliberately obliterated it. Obviously, this was not his intention, if only because he did not believe that anyone would ever be interested in tracing his movements.

At the time, Canada had an immigration program aimed at bringing people from England. The period was comparable to the opening of the American West, and the Canadian West was equally wild and woolly. Billy had made an arrangement in England at the offices of the Canada Company for employment in the New World as a farmer; he was to go to the corresponding office in Toronto for assignment. When he arrived at the office, he was directed to Hamilton, Ontario, to the farm of one Terrance O'Reilly. He hitched a ride with a horse and buggy and traveled eight miles to a little farm in the country. Boris later said: "I arrived all smiles and blushes—but the fellow had never heard of me, wasn't expecting anybody, didn't want anybody. Farmer O'Reilly and I just looked at each other—I had only pennies left, no way to get back to Toronto. Thank God it was spring and work on the farm was beginning. O'Reilly finally said, 'All right, you can stay.' I stayed three months at ten dollars a month—and what a rough ride! O'Reilly would get me out of bed with a pitchfork at four in the morning to go catch the horses in the fields and bring them in. I'd never known a horse personally before and knew nothing about them. . . . I soon learned."

After the stint at horsebreaking, Billy headed west for Banff—but work was scarce, so he stayed only a short time, though long enough to have had the beauty of the place indelibly stamped on his memory. He mentioned it frequently in later years.

His trail can next be picked up in Vancouver, British Columbia, in 1910. Ostensibiy, he was working only to keep himself alive at the time, and barely making it. He was not consciously striving toward any particular goal, but his primary interest always remained the theater.

One day in Vancouver, Billy was walking down the street and was startled by a cry of: "That must be a Pratt!" and he was embraced by an old friend of his brother Jack's from England, Hayman Claudet. Claudet said, "I knew that had to be one of you! There aren't any other heads in the world shaped like yours! What are you doing here?" "Starving," Billy answered.

Claudet took him under his wing immediately, gave him food, money, advice, and even better, secured him a job in a real estate office. When this kind man died many years later in 1955, Boris wrote to Claudet's widow:

I can never forget what a good friend he was to me and how kind you both were to me in my early days in Vancouver. I was so completely at a loss as to what to do, and Hayman gave me exactly the right advice—and not content with that, he implemented it by getting me my first job, keeping an eye on me and helping me in so many ways. . . . I always think that true immortality lies in the love and the memories that are left behind in the hearts of those who knew you. Hayman's immortality is safe.

Evie Karloff so loved these final sentiments that she placed the words "To live in the hearts we leave behind is not to die" under Boris's death notice in the London papers.

The real estate job in Vancouver didn't last, and Billy next worked for the British Columbia Electric Company. He dug ditches, laid streetcar tracks, cleared land, shoveled coal, and worked on survey parties with at least a monetary promotion. He was now earning two dollars and fifty cents a ten-hour day instead of ten dollars a month.

Any time off from labor for the Electric Company, Billy devoted to approaching, with no success, local touring stock companies in hopes of his first break. The stories regarding how it finally came vary from the one about a copy of *Billboard* flying out of a train window, Billy picking it up, seeing an advertisement for a leading man for the Jean Russell Players in Kamloops,* B.C., to Billy working at wrapping freight and seeing the ad in the wrapping paper, to even more unlikely stories.

Boris's version was: "I was off on a survey party in the brush about seventy miles from Vancouver when I got this letter from an agent I had called in Seattle—Walter Kelly I think his name was—representing myself as an experienced English actor in Canada on a visit, who might be available,

---

* Apropos of nothing, Kamloops is named after a fish as hard to catch as the Loch Ness monster. It is classified as a salmon trout, runs to six feet in length, requires thousands of dollars worth of equipment to catch, and exists only in extremely deep water. A single fish is called a "kamloops." One assumes the plural is the same.

would deign to take work, et cetera. I'm sure the agent saw through the story, but actors were hard to get at the time. He referred me to the Jean Russell stock company in Kamloops, a small town somewhere in British Columbia. I left my axe in the middle of a tree and got the first train to Kamloops."

The decision to leave steady employment for this ephemeral job was a big one. Having made the first decision with no hesitation, Billy, while on the train, plunged into a second. Somewhere between Vancouver and Kamloops, William Henry Pratt changed his name to Boris Karloff. Although Boris may very well have *thought*—as he was later to say—that " 'Karloff' was a family name on my mother's side," research as far back as three generations has not unearthed anyone with this name.

Research does, however, prove that for a while Boris's mother's family, the Millards, lived in Bombay at the same time as did the family of one Lazarus Kholoff. Is it possible that Boris's mother knew Lazarus Kholoff? If so, how well? Well enough to have mentioned the name in later years? Frequently enough for the name to be embedded in Boris's memory so that when he chose a new name for himself it came forward—if not accurately, closely? On the other hand, as he said, he picked "Boris" from the cold Canadian air. Is the "cold Canadian air" equally responsible for "Karloff"?

Or where *did* it come from? Lazarus Kholoff! What a name on a marquee!

OVERLEAF: *Early stock (1912). By the look of it, when his salary dropped from thirty dollars a week to fifteen.*

oris's impersonation of "an experienced English actor" may or may not have fooled the management of the Jean Russell Players. But in his desperation, penniless, and his "blood fired for the stage," he must have given a superb performance—they *did* hire him. (As Boris said later, "At the time actors were so scarce, all you needed to be employed was two legs and a head.") The play was Ferenc Molnar's *The Devil*, and Boris, aged twenty-two, played a sixty-year-old banker, his hair covered with cornstarch and his face wrinkled by lines drawn with streetcar paint. When the curtain went up on his performance, he was earning thirty dollars a week. When the curtain came down, he was getting fifteen. However, in spite of his inexperience, he kept his job.

The repertory of the Jean Russell Players consisted of eighteen plays, and Boris had to be up on the lines of all of them, as well as functioning as assistant stage manager. When not on stage or carrying props, he was studying. Learning what to do and what not to do; when to cross upstage or downstage; memorizing lines, and practicing to control the stammer, to eliminate the lisp.

Press stories have Boris at this time with "The Jean Russell Players" and "The Ray Brandon Players." It is possible these troupes either were one and the same or were later combined. There is a review of a vaudeville act— "Jean Russell who is appearing with Ray Brandon in the feature act of the new vaudeville bill at the Arcade Theatre"—in the Toledo (Ohio) *Blade*, January 22, 1915. Boris always referred to the group as "The Jean Russell Players," and for a year he toured all of Western Canada with them, playing such vintage pieces as *East Lynne* and *Charley's Aunt*.

In 1912 the company was playing in Regina, Saskatchewan, a frontier outpost between Winnipeg and Calgary. The town's sidewalks were wooden planks and practically everything else mud. A militant Social and Moral Reform League characterized one side of Regina society, while gambling and opium dens run by Chinese and thriving bordellos run by Scots defined the other. Also there was the added fillip of visiting curling teams, whose presence inspired the splendid extracurricular sport of whirling chamberpots down the hotel corridors.

As far as theater was concerned, the Regina citizenry was addicted to

Sophie Tucker, Buffalo Bill And His Circus, and Barney Oldfield And His Racing Car. Rather heavy competition for a touring stock company whose "leading man" was a fifteen-dollar-a-week actor with no previous experience. However, the troupe was a wild success and Boris had reached the first rung of the ladder. Then the ladder was blown out from under him by one of the worst tornadoes in Canadian history.

On July 31, 1912, preceded by an oppressive, sultry day and a crimson sun in the sky, a ghastly huge green funnel sped through Regina at a speed of five hundred miles per hour, viciously sucking up and tossing out everybody and everything in its path. The town was destroyed, twenty-eight people were killed outright, thirteen victims later died of injuries, three hundred were maimed, and three thousand were left homeless. The tornado sliced down blocks of houses, cut buildings in half, tossed horses and cows into the air like popcorn, and twisted steel girders into pretzels.

The tornado passed, leaving the people of Regina prostrate with shock. When they came to, they started clawing through the ruins for the screaming people entombed inside.

Meanwhile, the members of the Jean Russell Players, having fled the heat, were at Lake Wascana some miles away on a boating picnic. They returned to find the city leveled, the people in a state of panic, death and destruction everywhere, and their theater a heap of rubble.

The company took an ad in a local paper announcing that it would stage a benefit performance of the comedy *The Real Thing* at the still standing Regina Theater, one half the receipts to be donated to the relief of the sufferers. But apparently there was little appetite for comedy, and the Jean Russell Players disbanded.

Boris, blown out of the theater, optimistically went to work cleaning up rubble, making just enough money to enable him to eat.

With interim laboring jobs, he next made his way to Prince Albert, Saskatchewan, where he joined the Harry St. Clair Players, with whom he first toured for fifty-two weeks—not only in Canada but also in the northern United States.

He increased the number and quality of the parts he played, because the actor who was the fastest study was rewarded with the best parts. Boris had already committed to memory *Way Down East, Bought and Paid For, What Happened to Jones, Baby Mine, East Lynne, Paid in Full, Charley's*

Aunt, and *Why Smith Left Home*. He loved his work, and had nothing but admiration for Harry St. Clair, who was, Boris said, "A truly honest man. When he had the money he paid us. When he didn't—he didn't have it."

When St. Clair "didn't have it," starvation was waiting in the wings, but Boris was ingenious in the art of survival. His two suits were bought for five dollars apiece from cleaning establishments where they had been left by customers and never picked up. At the end of the day, Boris stretched his suit out under the mattress of the bed in the cheap boarding house and slept on it to keep it in press. His meals in the "no cooking allowed" room consisted of one egg cooked on the surface of an inverted traveling iron, or half a can of mulligatawny soup. Mulligatawny because it had chunks of meat in it and hence made two meals: the soup number one, the meat number two.

After the tornado of July 1912, the town of Regina, Saskatchewan, and Boris's theatrical career were in ruins.

Boris stayed with the Harry St. Clair Players, traveling back and forth to the United States, until 1916. Many press stories have him becoming an American citizen in 1913, but this was not the case. He never became a citizen at all and never legally changed his name. All official documents, including his death certificate, read: "William Henry Pratt a.k.a. Boris Karloff." He was admitted to the United States on October 12, 1913, at Portal, North Dakota, as an "Immigrant for Permanent Residence, United States Department of Justice, Immigration and Naturalization Service, Alien Registration Receipt Card No. 2–064–509."

Now, somewhere between October 12, 1909, and October 12, 1913, he probably married. There is no official record on file in any place in Canada where he had been, but there are oral reports of an actress named Olive de Wilton who "spoke of her days of starvation as the wife of Boris Karloff" at approximately this time.

All this raises again the discrepancies between written records and hearsay—and in this instance adds to the mystery. According to the records, Olive de Wilton was born in 1898, which would make her at this time at the most fifteen, at the least eleven. People did marry at extremely early ages in those days, but even fifteen seems unlikely. Possibly they were married at a later date and in the United States, which would account for no Canadian records of the union. On the other hand, neither have any American records come to light.

Brian Doherty, the founder of the Shaw Festival in Ontario, who earlier had his own stock company, knew Miss de Wilton well. He says she was the most dedicated woman he has ever known, to the theater and to "a daughter who was supposed to be gifted on the piano." Doherty says Olive de Wilton spoke of Boris with no animosity but with considerable affection and a strong memory of near starvation. She was dark and sallow, dressed strangely, wore no makeup, and was, according to an actor who knew her, "an almost Charles Addams character."

Again according to Doherty: "I have not seen her in years and the last address I had for her was in Montreal. I have just checked the Montreal telephone book and she is not listed, which doesn't prove anything, as she was usually stony-broke. She could even be dead."

She is dead. She died in the early 1970's, about three years before this writing. The search for her daughter began. Was she Boris's? With his propensity for closing doors, he might never have mentioned it to anyone.

In a biographical dictionary of Canadian actors, we found the following: "de Wilton, Olive (Edith Doreen de Wilton) actress, radio artist. b. Rodley Hants, Eng. 25 March 1898, daughter Capt. Gerald Sussex (Royal Scots Greys) and Edith Juliet (Holloway) de Wilton. Married Richard Meadows-White (marriage dissolved). One daughter, Rosalind E.C." This was followed by a long list of her theatrical activities. *One* "marriage dissolved" to Richard Meadows-White. And *no* mention of Boris whatsoever!

The next piece of information from Canada: The daughter, Rosalind Meadows-White, was known by some people who had known Olive de Wilton. She was a recluse who lived with a great many cats in the country outside Montreal. Then a moment of triumph. The address was found and I sent a letter to Rosalind Meadows-White containing condolences on the loss of her mother, an explanation of what I was doing, and a plea for any knowledge she might have of Boris. I sent it registered mail. The letter came back marked "No such person at this address."

OVERLEAF: *More early stock (1914). Cornstarch to whiten hair.*

Minot, North Dakota, continued the experience of what Boris always referred to as "years of bitter oblivion." Minot was then a town of eight or nine thousand people at a divisional point of a railway.

In 1957, while talking to a man who purported to be a magazine writer but who in reality was a researcher for Ralph Edwards's "This Is Your Life" TV show, Boris said: "We played in an upstairs Opera House over a large hardware store, and we had no money to do anything with—we just got by. We were up in about eighteen plays and we played those in the first three weeks. So with no money to move on, we had to stay there and start expanding the repertoire. We did two new plays a week for fifty-three weeks. Three rehearsals and you were on! It was rugged, but good training, and it stood me in good stead. I was forced to become a fast study—or starve to death.

"I think we were really a very good company actually. Of course, frequently we would leave out an entire act and no one noticed, so maybe the audiences were just not paying attention. I'll say one thing for them, though: The audiences of the sticks were in no way unintelligent. When at the end of a run we'd ask for repeat requests, they invariably chose the best plays."

In 1914, when World War I was declared, Boris volunteered for service in the British army but was rejected on account of a "heart condition." This must have been a major misdiagnosis. The great heart thumped regularly and efficiently through bitter cold, hardship, near starvation, backbreaking physical labor, thwarted ambition, and emotional crisis for eighty-one years, and even then didn't give up easily. In fact, in one of his last films, when he was in his late seventies, the studio was unable to get production insurance without the star's electrocardiogram. The doctor's medical report accompanying the results was: "Photograph this, you may not see another like it . . . and put all your money behind him!"

In 1916 Boris quit the Harry St. Clair Players and left, with his life's savings of sixty dollars in his pocket, for Chicago—the nearest "show town" —because he felt the need to "stretch out."

He found a furnished room with a gas hot plate for four dollars a week. By the time he was able to get a job, the life's savings were down to twenty-five cents. The job entailed leaving Chicago for Virginia, where he played in a very small stock company for ten weeks. Then he returned to Chicago with a new bankroll of fifty dollars, which rapidly dwindled to a dime.

Boris never forgot, but with his usual optimism overcame, the depression of those Chicago days. Many years later he said: "It was terrifying. Alone, no help, no one to turn to, no food, and rent to be paid. I never got over my terror of the place. Years later I played there in *Arsenic and Old Lace*, staying in total luxury at the Ambassador, and still later in *Peter Pan*, for which we broke every record including *South Pacific*, but I couldn't get over my feeling. Chicago has always given me the willies—the knife is really at your throat there."

After Chicago, he joined the Billie Bennett Company—a traveling troupe playing *The Virginian*—and traveled with it through Minnesota, Iowa, Kansas, Colorado, and Nevada, finally landing in Los Angeles, where around 1918 he joined another repertory theater which toured along the San Joaquin Valley, ending up in San Francisco. From San Francisco he joined the Maude Amber Players in Vallejo, a small northern California town. There a flu epidemic closed the theater, and the company disbanded.

"Being addicted to roughly three meals a day," Boris said, "I went to work for the Sperry Flour Mills, waiting for the flu scare to be over so the theater could reopen."

By the time the scare died down, there was no company and Boris returned to San Francisco, where he joined the Robert Lawrence Players, a small company that performed in a mission. Then he made his way to San Pedro on a lumber freighter because it was the cheapest form of transportation. He never forgot the voyage: "There was no place for anything on deck except this great load of lumber. No place to sit, or lie; below decks was so filthy you couldn't go there and the sea was too rough anyway." He joined a San Pedro stock company and toured Southern California for a few weeks, leaving the company in Los Angeles about 1918.

· · ·

A scene from another Evelyn Brent film, Forbidden Cargo *(1925). Here, Boris is still in the "pool" of actors. (Photograph courtesy of Miss Brent.)*

In those days the City of the Angels was still a small but sprawling town. The orange groves had not been bulldozed, freeways didn't exist, and the brilliant California sunlight could still penetrate the smogless air. The film industry, in this perfect atmosphere, was in its healthy infancy. Camera trucks clattered down shady pepper-treed lanes, and Hollywood Boulevard was "Main Street." There were no sidewalks intaglioed with brass stars blazoning the names of present and departed greats, and the only footprints preserved for posterity were those of the dinosaurs in the La Brea Tar Pits, not the stars' in the forecourt of Grauman's Chinese Theater. (In later years, incidentally, his agent suggested that Boris go through the ceremony of placing his footprints in that forecourt. Then Boris was notified that the cement work was the actor's responsibility and would cost him five hundred dollars. "Forget it," he said.)

In Boris's first days in Hollywood, directors really did wear puttees, turn their caps backward, and shout "Action!" through megaphones, and cameramen cranked away with no fear of the noise they were making, because those were the days of the silents. Theatrical training was not requisite to success in films, which were, at the time, an extension of the art of pantomime. Resonant voices and trained projection were nonessentials. The wide gesture, staring eye, and mobile eyebrow were the order of the day. Was this possibly an advantage to a young Karloff who had not yet conquered the lisp, the stammer? Actually, his manner of speech was probably inconsequential because he was back on the bottom rung of the ladder and destined to remain in crowd scenes as an extra for quite some time.

Boris's first move on arriving in Los Angeles was to find lodgings. He moved into a rooming house at the top of Angel's Flight, a marvelous bright orange funicular which lifted passengers from the street below to the summit of Bunker Hill. Angel's Flight has since been torn down, like everything of interest in this strange city of Los Angeles except the famous Watts Towers, which the authorities tried to knock down, but which refused to fall. Angel's Flight, at least, was not demolished. It is packed away in mothballs to be relocated in a more suitable place (undoubtedly Disneyland—up the side of the "Matterhorn," possibly).

Once in residence, Boris proceeded to knock on studio doors. In interviews later on, he stated that after months of futile approaches, he finally landed his first job in pictures: as an extra in a Douglas Fairbanks film, *His Majesty, the American*, released in 1919. Boris had a bit part as a soldier in a South American army.

"For a week," he said, "I chased Fairbanks all over the back lot. It was heaven. I was in films, I was making five dollars a day, and I worked for a solid week. I'm not at all sure that that wasn't more money than I earned in all my ten years in the theater in any one week. I thought I had made my fortune!"

Why he stated, unless he simply forgot, that the Fairbanks picture was his first film is another mystery. According to the dates of the films, the first one in which he appeared was *The Dumb Girl of Portici*, released in 1916, and starring, of all people, Anna Pavlova. Then to confuse still further the issue of which was his first film, Boris also occasionally mentioned that his first job was in a crowd scene in an unnamed Frank Borzage film at Universal.

He also forgot, and they are unlisted in *any* filmography (we could identify only two, *Forbidden Cargo* and *Lady Robin Hood*, in ours), several films in which he worked that starred Evelyn Brent. I had the great pleasure of meeting Miss Brent shortly before she died.

She was still an enchanting, humorous, and very beautiful woman. She said, "Boris was just one of a pool of actors who would hear of a film being shot, then go and stand in front of the studio and the director would come out and say, 'Okay, you,' and grab one. I saw Boris picked that way twice. He worked, I think, in about three films with me." I asked her which, and she laughed, "Lord—I don't know! I used to make two pictures a day—one in the day and one at night—I couldn't possibly remember the titles of any of them!" She did remember, however, that Boris was a charming, gentle man, and she contributed the marvelous sinister stills used here.

But how could he have forgotten Pavlova? Was proximity to greatness so overwhelming that he simply blocked out the memory, or was it because, the Pavlova film being only one day's work and the Fairbanks a full week's, the joy of steady employment and a suddenly full stomach obliterated all other recollection?

In investigating the history of *The Dumb* (that is, mute) *Girl of Portici*, I found it was based on D. F. Auber's opera of the same name, and that, fortunately, there exists a print of the film in the dance department of the Library of the Performing Arts at Lincoln Center in New York. My intrepid (and ruthless) editor, Robert Gottlieb, and I went to view the film. We ran it through a Moviola, which, if you are not aware of same, is a machine ordinarily used by film editors for cutting a film. The reels run through a lighted magnified screen approximately six inches square.

Bob and I squinted through the tiny screen in an intense search for Boris in the crowd scenes. We were so overcome by laughter at the film itself, however, that the search was difficult. Mme. Pavlova's performance could not have been surpassed by a combination of Harold Lloyd, Buster Keaton, the Marx Brothers, and the Keystone Kops. It seems she had this thing about her scarf! She clutched it, she fondled it, she tossed it into the air, and then three other ballerinas joined her in holding it above them in admiration as they formed a frieze from a Grecian urn. She flung it over her head and batted her eyelashes through it at her unfortunate lover, who comes to No Good End. Then for some inexplicable reason she races to the beach and into the water with it, and still loves it—dripping wet.

In the meantime, the Peasants Rise, Tyrants Are Torn From Their Palaces, there is Rioting In The Streets. Pavlova, the poor peasant girl, runs through the battling crowds searching for her lover, still carrying her Security Blanket. There is burning, battling, and stone-throwing. And in the foreground one angry peasant stone-thrower: Boris? Beyond this, one of the soldiers at the gate holding back the crowds is terribly bowlegged: Boris? Both look like him. Possibly a dual extra role? You guess. Anyway *she* died scarf in hand.

OVERLEAF: *Boris in his "actor pose."*

29 · *"Bitter Oblivion"*

In 1919 Boris worked in two serials, *The Masked Raider* and *The Lightning Raider*—both also before *His Majesty, the American*. He continued to do extra work, piecing out a living with any other odd jobs he could find. By this time he had worked himself up to seven and a half dollars a day as an extra. "A great promotion," he said. Well—if not great, it was a fifty percent jump.

Later in 1919 he rose in status to bit player, and he was employed by an independent producer to play a small part in a film starring William Desmond, *The Prince and Betty*, at Pathé. This was followed by *The Deadlier Sex*, starring Blanche Sweet, also at Pathé, in which he played his first substantial part, a French-Canadian trapper, which started a succession of bits as French-Canadian heavies, until the public became bored with the backwoods and, finding himself type-cast, Boris was back on his uppers.

There followed another rough period, accentuated by the fact that because of his name, casting directors thought he was Russian and called him only when they were filling up the court of the Czar. But he plowed along, until by 1923 he had raised his salary to $150 a week. Unfortunately the weeks were few.

In discussing this period with a fellow actor later in his career, Boris said: "I was faced with a decision: I was known to casting directors as a $150 a week available actor—too available. In order to eat, I could have gone back to the extra ranks and probably would have gotten work. But I felt if I did that, it would 'put paid' to everything, because once you play parts and then go back to being an extra—you're dead.

"So I got myself a forty-cents-an-hour job on the other side of town as a guard in a building material yard at Western and Slauson in downtown Los Angeles. Being a 'guard,' for some reason, meant loading and unloading boxcars of cement, gravel, rock, and other materials—it was heavy work." It was also undoubtedly a contributing factor to all the serious and agonizing problems he had with his back in later life.

A considerable amount of local subdividing and building was in progress and work was plentiful in the yard—so Boris stayed on. A fellow Englishman named Curtis worked in the yard at the same time. He was employed by the owners of the company on a commission basis to run a dump truck that he owned. He wanted to put on another truck, and one day asked Boris if he wanted a job driving it.

"I immediately said yes," Boris said, in the interview with the bogus magazine writer, really a Ralph Edwards researcher, "even though I had never driven anything in my life, had had nothing to do with automobiles—ever. But I had a friend who owned a car and he took me out on Sunday afternoon to a big vacant lot and tried to show me something about driving: how the gearshift worked, which was the starter, how to turn around, and so on. By the end of the day, he practically gave me up in despair. However, Monday morning, bright and early, I faced that awful truck—a smelly hideous thing with its engine under the seat, running on two cylinders, which always fouled up and you had to crank the thing. I drove it out the door, sailed up Slauson Avenue, traffic scattering in all directions—and drove the damn thing for a year and a half. Never did get a driver's license. I didn't try to because I knew I'd never be able to pass the test."

Boris not only drove the truck, but loaded and unloaded it daily. Hundred-pound sacks of cement, three-hundred-pound sacks of lime putty —wet—which he had to lug fifty yards from the truck to the building sites.

One day he received a telephone call. There was a small bit in a film being made in San Francisco. "I think it starred Anita Stewart," he said in the Edwards interview. "I can't remember. I know it was directed by Maurice Tourneur.* I asked for a week's leave of absence from the trucking. Curtis, who was a nice fellow, gave it to me and I left for San Francisco on location. What a windfall! We got five dollars a day for meals, stayed at the Palace in twenty-five-dollar-a-day rooms. I was rich! Then I returned to report back to my job on the truck. My leave of absence was for one week and we were gone three so they had replaced me. I was pitchforked back into films."

Later, when recalling the next few years, Boris said, "It went on like this. Let's see, the trucking period was 1923, then nothing much happened until 1930, when I got the part in *Criminal Code*."

Which brings us to another plot-thickener. Was his reference to "nothing much happened until 1930" intended to mean only that professionally he was not advancing? Or was it a deliberate smoke screen to cover what else

* It was *Never the Twain Shall Meet*, released in 1925.

did happen? Or did he feel that what happened was no one's business, or of no interest to anyone else, or both? The fact remains that during those years Boris was married and divorced. As we know, he may also have been married and divorced *twice* before that, but he seldom mentioned this to anybody afterward.

And yet another reason why his statement, "nothing much happened," is odd: In 1926 he played with Lionel Barrymore in *The Bells*, which he frequently mentioned as one of the greatest experiences of his young life.

OVERLEAF: *Boris and Dorothy at Toluca Lake.*

The mystery of the no-mention-marriages is unfathomable because, after the explosive stardom of *Frankenstein*, the press was cluttered with "The Man Behind the Monster" stories and Boris was in a constant state of siege by reporters. Either they all did a surface job, or Boris successfully kept the door to the past clanged shut. He gave gracious inteviews about his English childhood, Canadian hardships, extra work and ditch-digging on the road to fame, but the traveler was "I," not "We."

One of the early post-Frankenstein stories claimed: "Karloff has been married twice." At the date of the column he was married to his fourth wife, Dorothy—who, incidentally, never knew until years later that she *was* Number Four.

The press story reported that Boris's first wife was one Helen Vivian Soule—professional name, "Polly"—who was a dancer with the Fanchon and Marco Company. At approximately the same time, a fan magazine compared a woman called Pauline Karloff (allegedly Boris's first wife) with Josephine Dillon, the ex-wife of Clark Gable: "The Forgotten Wives of Stars." Pauline was quoted as having nothing against her ex-husband, she just never saw him, and refused lucrative offers to sell the story of her life with Boris to magazines. Olive de Wilton, *presumably* wife Number One, also had nothing against him.

Were Pauline and Polly and Helen Vivian one and the same? Pauline was referred to as a sculptress. Was she also the former dancer, Polly? Or were there a Pauline *and* a Polly?—and a Helen Vivian? Let us assume them as only one, otherwise it gets too difficult.

Then a Sidney Skolsky column in the New York *Daily News*, December 19, 1932, a column devoted solely to Karloff: "It was while driving a truck and doing extra work that he met the blond Pauline, a Fanchon and Marco dancing girl. He prefers blonds [not true]. Then one day Polly packed up to go to Panama. She had a job there in a café, dancing. A divorce followed. That was a little over three years ago."

Skolsky had Polly and Pauline one and the same, but the entire column was so inaccurate that this may be likewise. For instance, the final paragraph: "He sleeps alone in a double-sized bed. He wears black and orange pajamas and snores. Say, come to think of it, he looks like Frankenstein."

He looked nothing of the kind. Besides, Frankenstein was the scientist, not the Monster. I have no knowledge of whether he slept alone in a double bed and snored, but I know damned well he *never* wore black and orange pajamas. If anyone had ever suggested such a thing, he would have said, "Don't be so *common!*"

Boris must have done a superb snow job on the journalists, because they simply didn't look for anything more than what he told them. In two years of research into all available printed material on Boris's life, be it fan magazine junk, legitimate interviews, gossip columns, studio releases, or unauthorized "biographies," I have literally filled a room with pile on pile of boxes containing hundreds of thousands of words covering one subject: Karloff. And yet in all those years of reporting it occurred to no one to check the hall of records in any one of the places Boris lived and worked.

All journalists must have taken at face value the dubious proposition that former marriages never mentioned never existed. A trip to the Los Angeles Hall of Records would have straightened them out. It would also doubtless have infuriated Boris as an impertinent act. Now, the marriage to Olive de Wilton (in whose biographical note, one remembers, Boris was never mentioned) is not listed in the records. But since Miss de Wilton was quoted as saying they were married, and since she later married someone else, there must have been a divorce, although research has failed to locate a record of it either in Canada or the United States.

Nevertheless, the facts of Boris's varied marital states once in Hollywood, though never brought to light by journalists, *are* available in the Los Angeles Hall of Records. These archives reveal the following:

ENTRY: *July 1920.* MARRIED: Montana Laurena Williams, aged 24, of Phillipsburg, Montana, born in New Mexico, employed as a musician. PARENTS: William R. Williams and Annie Keeler. To: William Henry Pratt, aged 32. WITNESSES: Charlotte Garbor, Holland F. Burr.

No intervening record of divorce from Montana Laurena. It might have been obtained out of state.

ENTRY: *February 3, 1924.* MARRIED: Helen Vivian Soule, aged 23, of Massachusetts, born in Maine, employed as actress on stage. PARENTS: Greenwood E. Soule and Etta Rich. To: William Henry Pratt, aged 36. ADDRESS: 951

Venego Avenue, Los Angeles. J. Walter Hanby, Justice of the Peace; Harry S. Sheket, Witness.

No intervening record of divorce proceedings.

ENTRY: *December 5, 1928.* Plaintiff, Helen V. Pratt versus William Henry Pratt, Defendant. A court order for the appearance of William Henry Pratt to "then and there show cause why he should not be found guilty of contempt of court for failing to pay Plaintiff the sums set forth in this court's order of November 20, 1928."

No intervening record of divorce proceedings or any other sort of proceedings.

ENTRY: *July 10, 1929.* "Helen V. Pratt, Plaintiff, versus William Henry Pratt, Defendant. Stipulation for order; in re attorney's fees and alimony."

After pages of legal whereases and heretofores, the lawyers' names and therefores, the defendant was ordered to pay the plaintiff $100 cash and an additional sum of $240 at the rate of $50 a month. It was further stipulated that the defendant pay the plaintiff $15 a week for fifty-four weeks plus payment of all community bills. The court then made an order, "that upon signing of said order the order to show cause in re contempt be dismissed."

At the time, even these paltry preinflation sums must have been tough for Boris, which is probably why he reneged on the first court order.

Why, in all of the years of Boris's fame, wealth, and success, did none of these women ever show herself, attempt contact with him, or desire to become part of the fame? Or perhaps they did, and he simply never mentioned it?

By the age of forty-one, he had been married and divorced at least three times, as confirmed by a comment he made to me much later. One would assume he would have been wary of matrimony. But the same unconquerable spirit and "get on with it" attitude which left him undefeated by hunger, poverty, and professional disappointment must have sustained him maritally, because, undaunted, he stomped right out and married again.

OVERLEAF: *Boris in his "English actor pose"—complete with tea.*

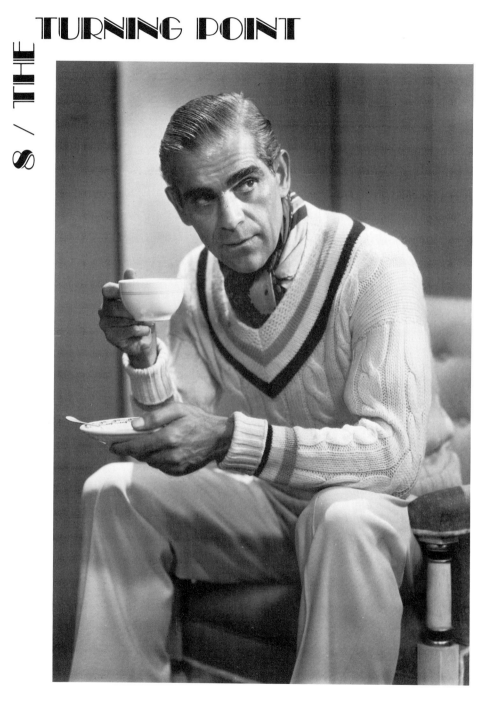

When Boris met Dorothy Stine at a dinner party in 1929, she was working for the Los Angeles City Library Central Supply System in charge of distribution of textbooks to the City School System. An impressive, rather dowdy title. At the time someone *must* have said to her: "Funny, you don't *look* like a librarian." I didn't meet Dorothy until years later, but she was then, is now, and must have been when he met her, a strikingly attractive, outgoing, intelligent woman, full of fun and rich humor and determination—one does not tangle with Dorothy.

Having known her well through all my younger years, and then not having seen her for twenty-five intervening ones, it was a strange experience "interviewing" her about Boris.

Dorothy has been married during this time to Edgar Rowe, a San Francisco attorney, a delightful man who virtually reared Sara Jane, Boris's daughter, who adores him. When we met again at last, Edgar, Dorothy, and I gossiped about Sara Jane and her young sons, Michael and David. We had a very good time, indeed, and then Edgar left "so the two of us could talk." We both immediately got the giggles, and it wasn't easy forcing myself into the role of "Brenda Starr, Reporter."

Still: When Dorothy met Boris, he was doing extra work and bit parts. Dorothy was living with her mother. After their meeting at the dinner party, the courtship was short. They were married in the Hollywood Presbyterian Church.

Dorothy said: "I really can't remember much about the wedding, except it was total confusion. Somebody got lost or drunk or something, there wasn't any money for a honeymoon, so we drove Boris's old wreck of a car back to his shack—and I do mean shack—in Laurel Canyon. We lived there for two years. I continued working, he was doing bits. There was very little money and it was Prohibition, but we always loved to entertain, so we made beer in the bathtub. Nobody could ever wait for it to ripen, or whatever you call it, so we'd all gather around and drink the green beer through straws right from the tub—wonder it didn't kill us—but we were young and strong—and we had an awfully good time."

· · ·

In 1930, while still living in the shack, Boris landed a part in the Los Angeles Belasco Theater's stage production of Martin Flavin's *The Criminal Code.*

"It was a small part, but a showy one," Boris said later. "The character was a trusty in a prison. He was the killer; had only four scenes in the play, but they were key scenes.

"I remember thinking then, Here, by golly, I go." ("By golly," incidentally, was one of Boris's stronger expletives.) "I'll show these chaps! I always left my dressing room door open after opening night expecting all the producers and agents in town to come pouring in, but not a soul came near me. I got some nice notices, but I didn't get any work, which was discouraging, because in those days that was the show window. I thought, Well, I've shown them, but nobody's paid any attention."

But somebody had—somebody from Columbia Pictures, and Boris was signed for the same role in the film version of the play.

Frankenstein has always been referred to as the "turning point" in Boris's career. It is much more likely that *The Criminal Code* did the trick. It was a fine film directed by Howard Hawks, starring Walter Huston, Constance Cummings, and Phillips Holmes. It may have done little, however, to make Boris more recognizable. He played his most important scene with his back to the camera, as he had done to the audience in the play. He felt the device would enhance the scene's suspense, an action typical of Boris, who invariably had more concern for the effectiveness of the vehicle than for his own advancement.

Howard Hawks was kind enough to see me and talk about Boris. He said: "Boris was one of the few grateful actors in the business. Actors are funny people—suddenly, they make it, and the Lord tells them they did it all on their own. They start telling me which is the better side of their face photographically, and I know I'm in trouble. I've got a story to tell, got no time for that sort of thing. Boris was a different breed of actor. He was self-effacing, he never talked about himself, he was completely charming, and he always knew his lines. With *Criminal Code* I gave him a face." I found this interesting in light of how much time the face was turned *away* from the camera. Hawks continued, "Boris had played the part on the stage and knew what he was doing, but he had no form. I've always said that if an actor had a face you couldn't caricature, he'd never be a star. Look at Gable, Bogart, Cooper—even Carole Lombard—easy caricatures. Boris had that kind of face.

BORIS KARLOFF

‽□‽

"GALLOWAY"
in
"The Criminal Code"
Howard Hawks
Columbia

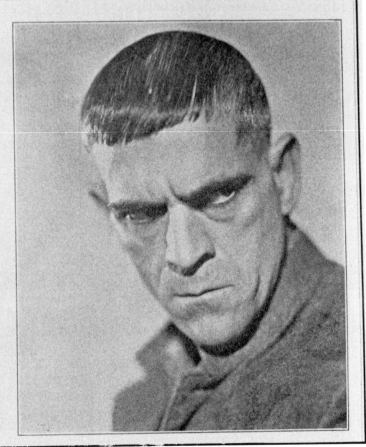

"That's the trouble with the screen today—too many faceless actors. Do you know, there's an actor who's a very big star today just because he doesn't annoy anybody?

"In *Criminal Code* I gave Boris stance. I wanted that huge menacing figure, and Boris wasn't really tall, as you know, so I shot the scene from the rear."

I interrupted to ask if he recalled whether it was Boris's idea to play the scene as he had in the play.

"I don't remember," he answered. "But I know if Boris had made a suggestion I would have listened to it because I had a great deal of respect for him. Anyway, because I wanted him to appear so huge, I ended by shooting a part of the scene through his legs."

I laughed. "Not difficult when they were that bowed."

"That did help!"

Then I told Hawks of the time when I was very young and working in a skiing film in Sun Valley. Boris had given me a bon voyage present (wrapped, as usual, in a garbage can tied with pink ribbons). The present was what he referred to as "me fats." The "fats" were symmetricals, or tights (to be worn under other tights) with padding in places to compensate for any deficiencies in the God-given shape of the actor's limbs. These had all the padding on the inside to fill up the "bow" and were a lovely pale baby blue. Boris had worn them in stock, and he must have been a glorious sight in them.

About symmetricals, Hawks said, "Barrymore wore them."*

Boris was so grateful to Hawks for *The Criminal Code* that he insisted, even if there was no good part for him, that he be in every picture Hawks made afterward. Hawks doesn't remember exactly how many of his films Boris played in, but he was unrecognizable in all of them. "We dressed him up and made him up and nobody ever knew."

There is no record in any filmography of Boris's appearance in a Hawks film during this period, so the disguises must have been tremendously clever. To Boris, a nonsuperstitious man, the appearances became a good luck fetish until Hawks put a stop to them.

"I just said, 'Look, Boris—this has gone on long enough. Wait until I have a vignette that's important enough for you, and you're in.' "

The "vignette" came in *Scarface*. This magnificent, ferocious film remains the definitive gangster picture. When Hawks was directing the film, he had several technical directors who had been involved with serious, no-kidding-mobsters. After the film was released, Hawks was visited by the Biggest-No-Kidding-Mobster of the time.

"Where did you get the story about the guy who shot Feroni?" he asked.

---

* Well, I wore them too—in bed. It was fifty below in Sun Valley and all that padding was nice and warm. They were like a cross between a teddy bear and Dr. Denton's, because they had feet in them.

Hawks answered, "From my technical advisor. He told me the story. He said he knows it's true."

"He should know," said the gangster. "He's the one who shot him."

Scarface starred Paul Muni, Ann Dvorak, Karen Morley, Osgood Perkins, Boris Karloff, and George Raft. Raft was new to pictures but had had some acquaintance with no-fooling-around-gangsters. "He couldn't act at all," Hawks said, "so I figured I'd better give him something to do with his hands. I'd read somewhere that a gangster was found dead with a nickel clutched in his hand. So I had Raft keep flipping this coin in the air—"

Thus, if you are a cinema buff, you realize A Star Is Born—the Raft coin-tossing became as identifiable as Ingrid Bergman's "Play it, Sam," or Lauren Bacall's "If you want anything, just whistle."

"Raft was new, and needed help; Boris wasn't, and didn't," Hawks said. "Boris had some vague communication with an audience—they knew what he was thinking. And he never overacted. He had, as I said, good taste." Boris played Gaffney, a "molester" who is gunned down in a bowling alley to pay for his sins. There was some criticism, not of his performance in general, but of the unbelievability of the overlay of American gangster jargon upon his unmistakably British accent.

From *The Criminal Code* on, Boris never stopped working. But Dorothy did, and they moved from the shack in Laurel Canyon to a house on Las Palmas Avenue in Hollywood. The house had great charm, though also the slight disadvantage of being at the top of ninety-two steps, which became a painful burden to Boris at the end of a day's work. As Karloff roles and salaries increased in importance, so did the quality of the Karloffs' homes. Boris and Dorothy moved on from the heights of ninety-two steps to the flats of the San Fernando Valley and then to Toluca Lake, where they bought a house. They were just breaking into "the business" but were surrounded by neighbors who were, or were about to become, stars: Rudy Vallee, Bette Davis, W. C. Fields, Charles Farrell, Mary Astor, Richard Arlen, Bing Crosby, and Bob Hope. Neighbors such as the Frank McHughs and writer Philip Dunne became close and long-time friends.

From Toluca Lake the Karloffs transferred to Bowmont Drive high in Coldwater Canyon in Beverly Hills. This house was a beautiful old

Mexican farmhouse surrounded by gardens and trees. Sara Jane, their daughter, was born there. Both the house and the garden rambled over all the hillside. Dorothy and I talked about the good times in the house and the beauty of it, and the fact that the present owner of the property had graciously taken Sara Jane, her sons, Dorothy and Edgar Rowe, and me on a tour of Sara Jane's birthplace, demonstrating that the beautiful estate is still loved and cherished. The parts of the property that had once contained the back gardens and the tennis court had been sold and are now covered by other houses.

I mentioned that I missed the gardens. Dorothy said, "Yes, they were beautiful. You remember John Beck?"

"The old actor friend of Boris's from the theater? The one he called 'Junior'?" I asked.

"Yes. He was always around."

"So many of the friends from the old days were."

"Yes, they were always turning up. Anyway, I can't remember whether Junior's one of the ones buried in the garden or not."

"One of the *what*?"

"One of the ones buried in the back garden—only all those houses are there now. . . ."

"Do you mean *actually* buried? Several of them?"

"Yes, their ashes, that is. They all loved to wander through the garden with Boris while he worked there—they'd talk about old times in the theater."

"I know, but *buried* there?"

She seemed surprised at my surprise.

"Why not? They were very dependent on him when they were alive —they loved the garden—that's the way they wanted it—to be in a place they loved and to be near him . . . he felt it was his responsibility to do as they wished. Pity they had to build all those ugly houses on top of them."

After I had recovered from the picture of all the old friends under the housing development, I realized it was quite possible: In Southern California houses are built on slab foundations—therefore, the ashes were never dug up. In those days the mortuary cartel had no control over what one did with one's ashes. So Boris's old boys are happily at rest where he placed them.*

* P.S.: Junior Beck wasn't one of them. He died in the Percy Williams Home for Actors in New York after Boris had taken care of him for many years.

I asked Dorothy if she had assisted in the burials and she said, "No. It was Boris's garden and they were his friends—it was none of my business."

My own shyness and sense of prying made it difficult to ask Dorothy what she knew of former wives. "Nothing," she said. "I found out only inadvertently that I was the fourth."

"Didn't you ever discuss it with him?"

"No. None of my business."

"Did you ever discuss his childhood or background with him?"

"Not really. He always said his mother was Russian. Later I met the British Consul in San Francisco. He said Boris's mother was the most beautiful Indian woman he had ever seen."*

"But didn't you have any curiosity about it?"

"Of course not. I'm sure Boris would have told me if I had asked . . . that is, if he even knew himself. One doesn't ask people about their pasts. After all, their lives before are what make them what they are *today*, and that's the only thing that's important."

Dorothy has not changed.

* Boris's coloring was very dark, which may account for his being cast as an Indian, both American and Eastern, in so many of his early films. Yet whenever it was mentioned to him, he would say, "Too much sun—out of work, you know!" Or if someone said, "How did you get such a great tan?" he answered, "A tight collar and plenty of gin!" He never mentioned any Indian blood. But neither, apparently, did another Anglo-Indian, Rudyard Kipling, who, though more than twenty years Boris's senior, was a part of the same unemancipated society—a society laced with bigotry, stifled by Victorian snobbism, and impressed by a sense of colonial superiority.

Is it possible that deep within Boris, the liberal, for-the-people, civil rights fighter, the kind and generous man, there lurked a modicum of prejudice from which, at an early age, he had run away? Or when he ran away, was it the fear of prejudice induced by this society which ran with him?

OVERLEAF: *Into* Frankenstein.

"_____"

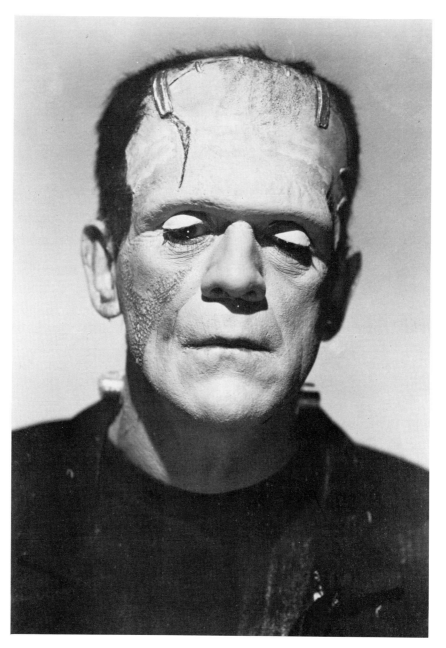

"Did I request thee, Maker, from my clay
To mould me Man? Did I solicit thee
From darkness to promote me?"

These lines from Milton's *Paradise Lost* had a strong influence on *Frankenstein*, as did Lord Byron's presence at the novel's hatching.

Byron; *Frankenstein*'s author, Mary Wollstonecraft (Shelley); her husband-to-be, Percy Bysshe Shelley; and a few rather odd close friends shared some time in Switzerland in June of 1816. Byron was writing the third canto of *Childe Harold*, and reading it aloud in the evenings to his new friends (he and Shelley had just met). Mary and Shelley spent their days walking by the lake and through the woods until the weather turned to days on end of ceaseless rain. As the group of friends became more confined, conversation lagged and it became necessary to eliminate boredom with a succession of games—some a trifle peculiar, in fact.

One of the games led to the telling of ghost stories, and then someone suggested a competition: Who could write the best ghost story? Shelley was delighted. He had always wanted Mary to fulfill her literary heritage. At the time, Mary's entire literary output consisted of a trunk full of unpublished Gothic novels she had written at the age of seventeen while sitting on her mother's grave.

Mary was the daughter of two famous literary figures, William Godwin, a social theorist, and Mary Wollstonecraft—a writer who may very well have been the harbinger of Women's Lib. Mary junior was apparently haunted by her mother's ghost after she died in giving birth to daughter Mary. Mother Wollstonecraft had had a rather racy career: she had borne an illegitimate child and had successions of lovers and mad affairs, one of which ended in her tragically leaping from a bridge into the Thames in an attempted suicide that was a dismal failure because her voluminous bloomers filled with air, and she floated away to be rescued by some fisherman down the river.

Mary's father, William Godwin, had welcomed the young Shelley—recently expelled from Oxford—and allowed him to fall in love with his daughter, despite the fact that Shelley was at the time (1814) already married and his wife pregnant. The loving couple's romance blossomed and flowered among the gravestones, and we find them a couple of years later ensconced in Dejean's Hotel in Geneva, Switzerland, with their son William. Mary's stepsister, who referred to herself as "Claire Clairmont, the actress," though she wasn't, was there because she had come to track down Lord Byron and give him the news that she was pregnant by him. After a few days Byron showed up, but he didn't care about Claire or her pregnancy, because he was in the process of forgetting an incestuous affair with his own sister, and starting another kind of affair with his personal physician and dear friend Dr. Polidori, whom he called "Polly-Dolly."

By the end of May 1816 the Shelley contingent removed to a cottage in the environs of Geneva; on June 10 the Byron group took up residence up the road a bit in the Villa Diodati. Presumably all spent a lot of time together at the Diodati if only because it was much the grander of the two residences.

Considering the intellectual level and inventive interrelationship of the friends, it is difficult to believe that time hung heavy on their hands, but it must have, because they dreamed up the ghost story competition to while away some of it.

The ghost session, on the night of June 18, did take place at Diodati. Only four people were present: Byron, Shelley, Mary, Polidori. (Authorities on the subject do not seem to have concerned themselves with the where-abouts of Claire.)

Mary Shelley (who better?) relates just what happened in her preface to *Frankenstein*:

> We will each write a ghost story, said Lord Byron; and his proposition was acceded to. There were four of us. The noble author began a tale, a fragment of which he printed at the end of his poem of *Mazeppa*. Shelley, more apt to embody ideas and sentiments in the radiance of brilliant imagery, and in the music of the most melodious verse that adorns our language, than to invent the machinery of a story, commenced one founded on the experiences of his early life. Poor Polidori had some terrible idea about a skull-headed lady. . . .
>
> I busied myself *to think of a story*—a story to rival those which had excited us to this task. One which would speak to the mysterious fears of our nature, and awaken thrilling horror—one to make the reader dread to

look round, to curdle the blood, and quicken the beatings of the heart. If I did not accomplish these things, my ghost story would be unworthy of its name. I thought and pondered—vainly. I felt that blank incapability of invention which is the greatest misery of authorship, when dull Nothing replies to our anxious invocations. *Have you thought of a story?* I was asked each morning, and each morning I was forced to reply with a mortifying negative. . . .

Many and long were the conversations between Lord Byron and Shelley, to which I was a devout but nearly silent listener. During one of these various philosophical doctrines were discussed, and among others the nature of the principle of life, and whether there was any probability of its ever being discovered and communicated. They talked of the experiments of Dr. [Erasmus] Darwin (I speak not of what the Doctor really did, or said that he did, but, as more to my purpose, of what was then spoken of as having been done by him), who preserved a piece of vermicelli in a glass case till by some extraordinary means it began to move with voluntary motion. Not thus, after all, would life be given. Perhaps a corpse would be re-animated; galvanism had given token of such things; perhaps the component parts of a creature might be manufactured, brought together, and endued with vital warmth.

Night waned upon this talk, and even the witching hour had gone by before we retired to rest. When I placed my head on my pillow I did not sleep, nor could I be said to think. My imagination, unbidden, possessed and guided me, gifting the successive images that arose in my mind with a vividness far beyond the usual bounds of reverie. I saw—with shut eyes, but acute mental vision—I saw the pale student of unhallowed arts kneeling beside the thing he had put together. I saw the hideous phantasm of a man stretched out, and then, on the working of some powerful engine, show signs of life and stir with an uneasy, half vital motion. Frightful must it be, for supremely frightful would be the effect of any human endeavour to mock the stupendous mechanism of the Creator of the world. His success would terrify the artist; he would rush away from his odious handywork, horror-stricken. He would hope that, left to itself, the slight spark of life which he had communicated would fade; that this thing, which had received such imperfect animation, would subside into dead matter, and he might sleep in the belief that the silence of the grave would quench for ever the transient existence of the hideous corpse which he had looked upon as the cradle of life. He sleeps; but he is awakened; he opens his eyes; behold the horrid thing stands at his bedside, opening his curtains and looking on him with yellow, watery, but speculative eyes.

I opened mine in terror. The idea so possessed my mind that a thrill of fear ran through me, and I wished to exchange the ghastly image of my fancy for the realities around. I see them still; the very room, the dark *parquet*, the closed shutters, with the moonlight struggling through, and the sense I had that the glassy lake and white high Alps were beyond. I could not so easily get rid of my hideous phantom; still it haunted me. I must try to think of something else. I recurred to my ghost story—my tiresome unlucky ghost story! Oh! If I could only contrive one which would frighten my reader as I myself had been frightened that night!

Swift as light and as cheering was the idea that broke in upon me. "I have found it! What terrified me will terrify others, and I need only describe the spectre which had haunted my midnight pillow." On the morrow I announced that I had *thought of a story*. I began that day with the words *It was on a dreary night of November*, making only a transcript of the grim terrors of my waking dream.

At first I thought but of a few pages—of a short tale; but Shelley urged me to develop the idea at greater length. I certainly did not owe the suggestion of one incident, nor scarcely of one train of feeling, to my husband, and yet but for his incitement it would never have taken the form in which it was presented to the world.

In 1823, when *Frankenstein* was presented as *Presumption; or the Fate of Frankenstein* (author: Richard Brinsley Peake) on the London stage, the very presumption of a man playing God caused the Monster to be billed in the dramatis personae as "———." The theme was, in fact, so bold that efforts were made to ban the play's presentation both in English and in translations in other countries. Many theatrical approaches were made to the characterization of the Monster, only two factors being consistent: He was always blue and he never spoke, he grunted. Doctor Frankenstein, on the other hand, remained something of a fool. These adaptations must have disappointed Mary Shelley, because in her original version, the Monster was not only

Half-title page from a first edition copy of Frankenstein, *autographed by Mary Shelley herself.*

articulate, he was verbose, rather more intelligent than his traumatized and confused creator.

The formalized education of the original Monster was similar to L. Frank Baum's superb Oz character, Professor H. M. Woggle-Bug, T.E. (Highly Magnified and Thoroughly Educated). This insect, under observation in a science laboratory, escaped while being magnified on a screen, and, after finding a tailor to clothe him, set forth to impress the world dressed in formal attire—top hat, striped vest, tails, and elegant pince-nez—to settle the affairs of Oz, armed with a superior intellect gained from hiding under a desk and absorbing all the knowledge available in the laboratory. Mary Shelley's Monster hid in a woodshed instead of in a schoolroom, and picked up his education by listening to the conversations of some peculiarly erudite woodsmen (actually French aristocrats reduced to a peasant-type existence), who spoke in two languages and were given to reading aloud from Plutarch's *Lives*, *Paradise Lost*, and *The Sorrows of Young Werther*, tomes the Monster could (and did—for pages) quote verbatim.

Through the years, the Frankenstein legend has been written, rewritten, written about, and misinterpreted by legions of writers—including Theodore Dreiser. In *Liberty* Magazine, June 11, 1932, Dreiser wrote a piece under the heading "The Real Sins of Hollywood." He was still in a state of rage about the film version of his *An American Tragedy*, which he considered so appalling he filed restraining proceedings against Paramount, because it had "reduced the psychology of his book so as to make it a cheap murder mystery." As an example of filmdom atrocities upon other classic literature, he wrote: "For instance, in the Universal production of *Frankenstein*, based on Mary Shelley's book, since the movies cannot see a nice hero harmed, the monster which Frankenstein the scientist creates merely batted him around, whereas in the novel, the monster finally kills the scientist." The great man should have done his research. The Monster never laid a hand on Frankenstein in the original (that is, Mary Shelley) version. Damn near talked him to death, but never touched him. Furthermore, Dreiser was really off-base in claiming that the Universal movie was based (presumably directly) on Mary Shelley's book, when in fact it *was* based, directly, on a Peggy Webling play (*Frankenstein*; London, 1927).

Boris's own Monster never turned on him, but rewarded him with thirty-eight years of a successful and lucrative career, and he was eternally grateful. And like most things in the motion picture industry, Boris's selection for the role that was finally to make him famous was a fluke. Before *Frankenstein* Boris had already made sixteen films in the year 1931. He had made about eighty in his career to that date.

OPPOSITE: *Boris as the Monster.*

52

Boris always said, "Success is simply a matter of being on the right corner at the right time." His right corner happened to be the Universal Studio's commissary, where he was lunching while playing a murderer in a film called *Graft*. Speaking of the moment sometime later, Boris recalled, "James Whale, the director, who had just come over from England triumphant from the success of his direction of R. C. Sherriff's *Journey's End*, was lunching at a nearby table. Suddenly he caught my eye and beckoned me over. I leapt—he was the most important director on the lot. He asked me to sit down. I did, holding my breath, and then he said: 'Your face has startling possibilities. . . . ' I cast my eyes down modestly, and then he said, 'I'd like you to test for the Monster in *Frankenstein*.' It was shattering—for the first time in my life I had been gainfully employed long enough to buy myself some new clothes and spruce up a bit—actually, I rather fancied meself! Now, to hide all this new-found beauty under monster makeup? I said I'd be delighted. Half a dozen actors, including Bela Lugosi, who refused it, had been tested for the part, but I ended up the lucky one—I say lucky because any one of them could have played it just as well as I did, and would have reaped the benefits that came to me.

"After Whale asked me to make a test for the Monster, the first thing I did was to go to Jack Pierce, the head makeup man at Universal. Jack was nothing short of a genius, besides being a lovely man. He was also in the inside of the studio, knew what the score was, and was in a position to stall the test. So at the end of the day's work on *Graft* I would stay, and he would stay, and nightly he worked on the makeup until we felt it was ready. People in production were constantly calling and saying, 'Aren't you ready yet?' And we would answer, 'No—we're not ready yet.'

"Of course I rushed out and bought the book—but Mary Shelley's description of the Monster would have been impossible to duplicate, so we had to devise our own approach. Jack was brilliantly inventive, but his disguise was devilish to wear. It was worth it, though. I have to give him full marks for realizing the importance of what, ultimately, was a work of art. Up to that point, the part had just meant another job but—by Jove—thanks to Jack, it kicked the goal for me."

Pierce approached the construction of the makeup in an entirely scientific fashion. In an interview in the *New York Times* in 1939, Pierce explained his creation:

> There are six ways a surgeon can cut the skull and I figured Dr. Frankenstein, who was not a practicing surgeon, would take the easier. That is, he would cut the top of the skull off straight across like a pot lid, hinge it, pop the brain in, and clamp it tight. That's the reason I decided to make the Monster's head square and flat like a box and dig that scar across his forehead and have two metal clamps hold it together. The two metal studs that stick out the sides of his neck are inlets for electricity —plugs. Don't forget the Monster is an electrical gadget and that lightning is his life force. . . .

> The lizard-eyes were made of rubber, as was his false head. I made his arms look longer by shortening the sleeves of his coat. His legs were stiffened by steel struts and two pairs of pants. His large feet were the boots asphalt-spreaders wear. His fingernails were blackened with shoe polish. His face was coated with blue-green greasepaint, which photographs gray.

Pierce then, probably unknowingly, harked back in one area to the original early theatrical concept of *Frankenstein*: The Monster was always blue. After the opening of the film and its immediate success (an early return of $12 million on a $250,000 investment), Universal started making prints of the film in a strange shade of green to add even more horror to the scene, but the process was soon discontinued because, along with making the Monster more horrible, it made all the other characters look bilious.

Whatever benefits accrued to Boris from *Frankenstein* he earned. The production was agony from beginning to end, physically and emotionally. Boris always did his own stunt work (although insisting the stunt man be hired to stand by, to spread employment). However, in this case Boris did feel that despite James Whale's intellectual brilliance as a director, he lacked any sympathy for the actor. The grotesque and painful makeup and heavily weighted clothing were necessary, but Boris never understood why Whale insisted on his carrying Colin Clive up the hill to the mill in the famous scene where the Monster dies. Whale shot the scene dozens of times, using primarily long shots in which a dummy could have been used, or an extra could

Karloff and Pierce: consultation for Frankenstein *makeup.*

have played the Monster, but Whale insisted on using Boris and Clive over and over and over.

Boris's own body was encased in a seven-foot, six-inch structure of heavy padding and putty weighing sixty-five pounds; his hands were coated with plaster; his feet dragged thirty-pound weighted boots. With the added weight of the high artificial skull, the gummy layers of greasepaint, the strips of cotton soaked in collodion on his face, his eyes stretched open with rubber lids, staggering up and down hill carrying Clive was torture. The experience undoubtedly contributed to worsening the already bad back that soon sent him to the hospital for spinal fusion.

Whale had the reputation of being an egomaniac, and Boris always felt, though he never said so publicly, that the Monster had caused such wild interest not only from the studio people, but from the press, that Whale was

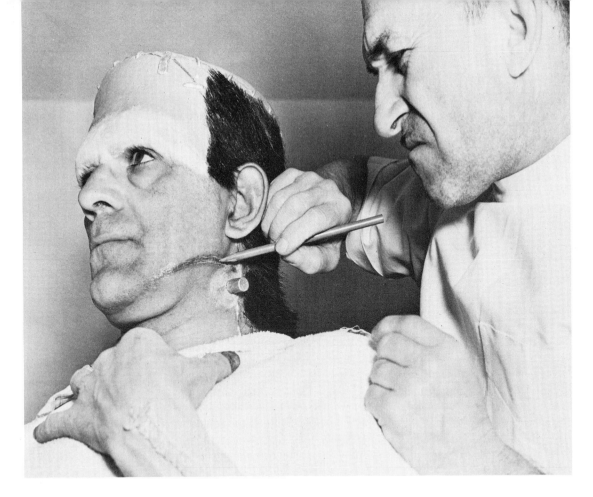

Karloff and Pierce: application of suture.

actually jealous of him and decided to punish the Monster, and inadvertently the man who created him. Not Frankenstein, but Boris.

Boris and Whale disagreed on the concept of the most important scene in the film. When the Monster comes upon the little girl (Marilyn Harris) playing by the lake, she is tossing flower petals into the water and watching them float away. She looks up and sees him, and, to his enchantment, is not repelled by him but invites him to play. He joins her, tossing the petals and laughing delightedly as the little boats sail off. Suddenly there are no more petals and he happily picks her up, thinking her another petal, and tosses her into the water to float after them. His agonized cry as she sinks instead of floating is something never forgotten. The Monster stands wringing his hands, and sobbing at what he has done.

It is not clear whether Whale and the producer or the censors cut the scene from the film because, allegedly, it was too violent. The cut was a great mistake, and Boris fought against it. In the released version, one sees only the heartbroken father carrying the body of his child, followed by the usual torch-bearing villagers out to seek revenge. The sight of only the body of the child, with no interim explanation of what actually did occur, was far more sickening than the tender scene originally filmed. This may very well have been Whale's intention.

Boris's reaction to the critical acclaim for his performance as the Monster was typical of the deeply ingrained modesty which was one of his primary characteristics. He always spoke of the Monster himself, not of his—Karloff's—interpretation of him. In talking about the role once, something he rarely did except to joke about it, he said: "I think the popularity was due to the compassion people felt for him, this poor tragic figure. His master, the only person he knew, had turned on him; he was helpless, alone, confused and terrified—how could one not feel sympathy for such a creature?"

The sympathy felt by a vast number of people for the Monster arose directly from Boris's intelligent, gentle performance. The reaction of children to the film—surprising to most people, including the studio—also came from Boris's deep understanding of the role. Though children were scared of the Monster, they also felt sorry for him. With a fundamental sense of pathos, and a certain beauty, Boris played the Monster for what he was, a child whose parent had turned on him and loved him no more. What better hero could a child have? In the jargon of today, children identified with him, and they wrote Boris thousands of letters expressing their empathy.

The surprising success of *Frankenstein* caused Universal to regret having killed off the Monster in the first film. Undaunted by their error, they resurrected him by the simple device of writing the sequel with a scene in which the Monster rises from the flooded cellar of the mill, where he had initially and quite obviously been blown to bits, perfectly fine and ready to ravage the countryside.

The Bride of Frankenstein (about which Boris said, "I met Elsa Lanchester in a scream heard round the world") was not only as successful as its predecessor, but equally as fine a film, with a remarkable dual performance by Miss Lanchester as the Monstress and as Mary Shelley in a peculiar prologue in which she bridges the gap for Lord Byron and her husband between the end of *Frankenstein* and the beginning of the new story. Boris graduated from grunts to a few words of dialogue: "Bread," "Wine," "Good," "Friends," "Alone," "Bad," and finally a coherent sentence, "Wine . . . no good." The finale of the film has the Monster so heartbroken at his bride's rejection of him that he blows up the laboratory, himself, his bride, and the evil Doctor Pretorious, after allowing Doctor Frankenstein to escape.

Despite the fact that he was constantly obliterated from the face of the earth, the Monster rose again . . . and again . . . and again. But Boris put his weighted foot down after his third Monster portrayal, in *Son of Frankenstein*, and never donned that particular makeup for films again (though he did play *in* two other "Frankensteins—*House of* and *Frankenstein 1970*— playing Doctor Gustav Niemann in the former and Doctor Frankenstein in the latter).

"I could see the writing on the wall," he said, "as to what was going to happen to the character of the Monster. There is just so much you can develop in a part of that nature, and it was a case of diminishing returns. The Monster was going to wind up as he did, a rather comic prop in the last act— and I thought, Well, this isn't any good, and I wouldn't play him anymore."

Little did Boris know that his face and his interpretation of the role would be used thousands of times over in studio ads, trick stores, and finally his entire being shaped into a children's vitamin pill. The Monster thudded straight downhill in version after ridiculous version, sporting such titles as *I Was a Teenage Frankenstein, Frankenstein's Daughter, Frankenstein Meets the Space Monster*, and hitting bottom with something called *Jesse James Meets Frankenstein's Daughter*(!).

At this writing there has been a surge of new interest in the classic with an excellent television version presented by Sam Hall and Dan Curtis starring Bo Svenson as the Giant (not Monster—he's very tall, but very personable) and Robert Foxworth as Victor.

Yet another version of the classic was written for NBC by Christopher Isherwood and Don Bachardy; it presented Michael Sarrazin as the Monster (beautiful when first created, lumpy and oozy later), and Leonard Whiting as Frankenstein (possibly the only actor ever to have played both this role and Romeo). James Mason plays the evil Dr. Polidori (Lord Byron's "Polly-Dolly"?). This particular Giant (Monster) harks back to the cultured original of Mary Shelley. The caliber of the writers and their affection for the project make this new version ("Frankenstein: The True Story") one of the best of what appears to be an endless chain of "Frankensteins."

As of 1975 there are in production a European *Frankenstein* and a black *Frankenstein* (probably because of the success of *Blacula*); already on view are Paul Morrissey's X-rated *Andy Warhol's Frankenstein*, Mel Brooks's hilarious put-on, *Young Frankenstein*, and a London stage musical called *The Rocky Horror Show*. Reviews of the last state that the "M*a*rster" (Dr. Frank N. Furter—Transvestite) is a cross between late Greer Garson and early Steve Reeves. The Monster wears net stockings and has hairy armpits. He wears glittering sequined briefs and likes to pose. When a young lady looks at him and says, "I don't like a man with too many muscles," the "M*a*rster" replies petulantly, "Well—I didn't make him for you!"

The Monster as a drag queen wouldn't have gone over well with Boris. He would undoubtedly have muttered, "How common!" Apparently, New Yorkers have agreed with him—*Rocky* didn't last long on Broadway.

Strangely, considering that *Frankenstein* comes under the category of "Horror," no one having anything to do with it, including its creator, has anything but affection for the character of the Monster. At the end of her preface to *Frankenstein*, Mary Shelley writes, "And now, once again, I bid my hideous progeny go forth and prosper. I have an affection for it, for it was the offspring of happy days when death and grief were but words which found no true echo in my heart."

From Mary Shelley to Boris Karloff, the word "affection" remained attached to the Monster. Boris always said, "God bless the old boy—without him I would have been nowhere."

OPPOSITE: *Boris with Dorothy and Silver. His first trip back to England.*

Frankenstein was such a smashing success that Boris was in demand in every studio in Hollywood. He thumped and bumped his way through numerous films, tampering with the secrets of the universe, lurking in door-ways, and sneering lines, some good, some ludicrous, but all delivered with the inherent dignity that, combined with his own delightful sense of non-sense, resulted in legitimate performances instead of burlesque.

In 1932 Boris made nine films; he went to Columbia for *Behind the Mask*, to First National for *Alias the Doctor*, and to Caddo–Howard Hughes for *Scarface*, then returned to Universal (oddly, he was not starred on his return), playing himself in a guest appearance in *The Cohens and Kellys in Hollywood*. Then on to Paramount for *The Miracle Man* (not playing the logical role for him, the one originated by Lon Chaney in the silent version); back to Universal for *Night World* and *The Old Dark House*, again directed by Whale, and with Boris given his first star billing; then to Metro-Goldwyn-Mayer for *The Mask of Fu Manchu*, co-starring Myrna Loy as his daughter (equally sinister). Charles Starrett, who also starred with Boris in *The Mask of Fu Manchu*, says: "Boris was a subtle, good-humored man—an actor's actor—a most adaptable man—he could think himself into any part. Never blew a line—except once—in *Mask*. I, the hero, was lying face down strapped to a table; he as Fu Manchu was about to do me in by injecting a hypodermic needle into the back of my neck—we couldn't get it right—it never looked like the real thing—so the director, I think it was Charles Brabin, suddenly yelled, 'I've got it!' He sent to the commissary for four especially baked potatoes—he tucked one of them into the collar of my shirt and said to Boris, 'Go ahead—jab it in—you can't hurt him—it will only go into the potato.' We started the scene, Boris plunged the needle into (allegedly) my neck—the potato exploded with a great pop, got all over Boris and all over me. The two of us couldn't stop laughing—we went through three more takes, using up the rest of the potatoes with the same results until we were hysterical. Finally the director said—'You two just go home—you're no use—we'll shoot it in the morning.'

"I worked with Boris also on the foundation of the Screen Actors Guild—he was magnificent—a fighter. I'll never forget before we worked to-gether in *Fu Manchu*, the summer we had a terrible drought—Boris was

Boris presenting a proud Jack Pierce with an award for his makeup work for The Mummy *(1932).*

making *Frankenstein*. I lived above him in Coldwater Canyon. One evening, I was driving home when I suddenly nearly drove my car into the ditch—there in the beautiful garden was the Monster itself, tenderly watering the roses—Boris was such a dedicated gardener, he was afraid he'd lose the roses to the heat, so had rushed home without taking off his makeup to catch them at sundown—the best time for watering . . . it was quite a sight."

After *Fu Manchu* Boris finally returned to Universal for *The Mummy*, for which he was billed simply as "Karloff," and in which he suffered through weeks of torturous makeup equal to the agony of the Monster's. Some year!

As Boris's fame spread, so did criticism of the subject matter of his films. His reaction was always defensive but logical. After all, a man who had survived a career in which he had once played Dr. Maniac in *The Brainsnatcher*, written by L. Du Garde Peach, had to be grateful for reaching the top of the field. He did not find horror for its own sake acceptable; he disliked the word, preferring the term "terror." "The shock must come from a good story line," he said, "not shock for the sake of shocking. Even 'Jack and the Beanstalk' is shocking," he used to say. "Many children's fairy tales are far more frightening than *Frankenstein*—as for Grimms', I'd never let a child of mine read them until she was old enough to analyze that they are dedicated to terrorizing the child."

On the other hand, as Boris sped from one plot involvement to another, the story lines all began to run together, and once in answer to an enquiry concerning the plot of his current film, he was "quoted" as saying, "Oh, I can't remember—all I know is I end up in a mass of fungus." Probably apocryphal—he regarded all scripts, no matter how nonsensical, respectfully.

In 1933 the leaping from studio to studio was broken up by a leap across the ocean—and it was a hair-raising leap. Boris was hired to perform in *The Ghoul* for Gaumont-British. For Britain and for Boris it was an important first. The film was Britain's first "horror" film, and the trip was Boris's first return to his homeland in almost twenty-five years.

With no warning, Boris and Dorothy were notified that they must leave immediately for London and that they would be gone for three months. Before there was a chance to be excited, pack, or think, the Karloffs were thrown into a nightmare. The ship on which they had to sail from New York for England, in order to make the film's schedule, was leaving in *two* days. Dorothy remembers that "Universal called at 9 a.m. on Thursday to say we were to catch a plane at 4:30 that afternoon. Neither of us had flown before, neither of us had passports, neither of us had any money." And the studio had no money to give them and no way to get it: It was the height of the Depression, only days before Roosevelt's first inaugural; the banks had been closed. So some imaginative executive went through all the pay telephones in the studio, removed the contents, and presented them to Boris in a paper bag. Dorothy and Boris arrived at the airport, twelve dollars between them— the entire output of the pay telephones. The studio representative said, "Don't worry, we'll wire ahead for money."

(Strangely, paper bags continued to figure in Boris's relationship with Universal. I recently spoke with Edward Muhl, for years head vice-president in charge of production at the studio. I received the usual answers: Boris— kind, cooperative, no trouble, etc. Then he said, "One odd thing I've never forgotten. Somewhere in the middle thirties, I can't remember exactly when, we wanted him for a picture. He agreed to do it but only if I would come to the set personally and give him a paper sack containing $2,500 in cash and no record go through the front office. I did it, but I've often wondered about it. Does seem odd, doesn't it?"

It certainly does. What was behind *that* closed door?)

When Boris and Dorothy saw the vehicle in which they—neophytes in the air—were to cross the country, they were terrified. It was a Ford tri-motor plane with four metal bucket seats. In this unlikely carrier they hopped across the country pursued by thunderstorms, lightning flashing around the wings, landing in various cities for refueling and to pick up the promised studio money. They refueled but there was no money—the banks were closed all the way across the country. Dorothy says: "We actually did get to New York at 12 noon on Saturday—and with a police escort raced to the S.S. *Paris*." At the dock the passengers had already boarded and the gangplank was up. The Karloffs were shoved into a small boat which churned its way through great rolling swells to the liner. The gangplank was lowered again, and she and Boris (sporting two days' growth of beard—"we were certainly two tired and disreputable-looking people," recalls Dorothy) staggered up. They then saw what appeared to be the entire passenger list staring over the rails at the commotion, wondering who had made such a spectacular arrival. As they clambered on board, three faces became identifiable in the crowd. Someone said, "My God—it's the Karloffs!" Dorothy said, "My God—it's the Gleasons!" They fell into the arms of James and Lucille Gleason and their son Russell, whom they had known in Hollywood only casually, but who were to become their closest life-long friends. (Russell and I were married years later, but at the time we had just met.)

The trip to England was hilarious—the Karloffs having no money,

Academy of Motion Picture Arts and Sciences annual awards dinner at the Cocoanut Grove in the Ambassador Hotel. Clockwise from Boris: Mary Brian, Russell Gleason, Ginger Rogers, Lew Ayres, Janet Gaynor, unidentified, Lucille Gleason, James Gleason, Dorothy Karloff.

not even the original twelve dollars from the telephone booths. "So we signed for everything," Dorothy says, "and arrived in England with a spectacular bar bill." They were met by another speeding boat, sirens screaming, carrying representatives of Gaumont-British—and money but no passports. Dorothy gives the conclusion of this part of the story: "Boris was able to get a re-entry permit [to the United States] while we were in London, but the record of my birth had been burned in a fire in the courthouse in Charlotte, Michigan. My mother eventually had to have a photostat made of the family Bible and to get two of her friends who knew her when I was born to go before a notary and swear I'd been born. The joke of the whole situation was that Boris—a non-native American—could return at will, but I was left stranded in England unable to get home until eventually all papers arrived. Only then was I issued a passport and allowed to come back—two weeks later."

Boris was overwhelmed by his return to his homeland, and when they arrived at the Dorchester in London he said, "I have to go out now and just walk, just walk—I have to walk all over London." So he and Dorothy walked and walked through the night. Knowing Boris, and knowing his passion (and that is the only word for it) for his own country, and knowing how he reacted to something that stirred him, I'm sure he kept repeating, "Damn—damn—damn!" The expletive was always used as a demonstration of enthusiasm for something good, not bad.

The Karloffs moved out of the hotel and took a house (complete with huge pipe organ) with the Gleasons. Dorothy and Lucille and Russell sight-saw in the daytime while Jimmy and Boris were working in their respective films.

Boris, not having kept in touch at all with his brothers for twenty-five years, felt a sense of shyness about their first visit. So one day during his lunch hour he decided to just "pop in" on his brother Sir John Pratt, then in charge of the British Foreign Office.

At the Foreign Office, Sir John's secretary suggested he go in, with no announcement, to surprise him. Boris opened the door, walked in, Sir John looked up from his work, and said, "Oh, Billy—how amusing!"

Later, there was a press party to which the other surviving Pratt

The four surviving Pratt brothers, reunited after Boris's twenty-five-year absence, together at a press party in London in 1933. Boris is at right.

brothers were invited. Boris had never overcome his awareness of family disapproval at his leaving a dignified and respectable future in the diplomatic corps for a life of barnstorming around, scaring people to death. So when a photographer requested a family picture, Boris said, "No-no-please, they wouldn't like it." But to the contrary, they loved it. Boris said, "I would never have believed it—they shoved each other about to get as close to me as possible for the picture."

Later, at the party, observing the attention of the press, the autograph seekers, the general carrying-on, Sir John (whom Boris always referred to as "My brother, the Sir") took Boris aside and hurrumphed, "Tell me, Billy, how much do you get paid for this sort of thing you do?" Boris told him, and he reared back, then put his hand on Boris's shoulder and lowered his voice. "Billy," he said, "save every farthing . . . this can never last!"

OVERLEAF: *Boris (center) and just some of his roles. Clockwise from top:* The Invisible Ray *(1936),* The Old Dark House *(1932),* Night Key *(1937),* The Mummy *(1932),* Frankenstein *(1931),* The Invisible Ray *again (though this makeup was not used),* The Mummy *again,* The Raven *(1935),* The Raven *again,* The Old Dark House *again (this makeup not used), and* Bride of Frankenstein *(1935).*

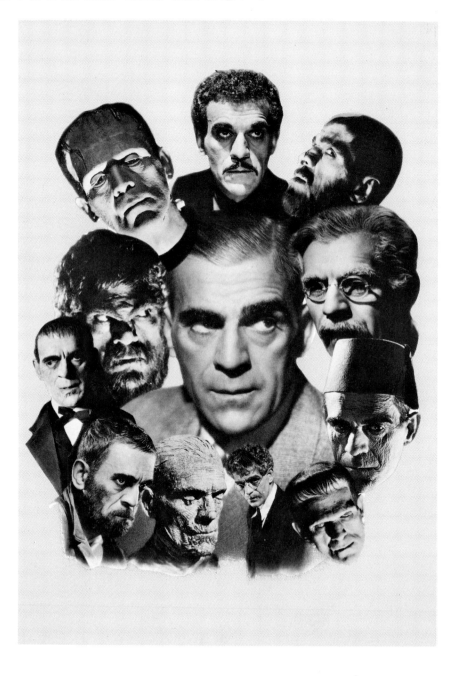

This," however, despite Sir John's lack of faith, *did* last and has gone on and on and on.

And despite his aversion to the word "horror," I think Boris would be "horrified" today to see the films he had made in good faith, even those with ludicrous content, being presented on television shows called "Bedtime for Boris," "Creature Feature," "The Wide Wide Scream," and "Screamorama" —one of which has an added attraction of a "Scream Contest," judging to be based on "Blood Curdlingness and Volume." The opening of a horror film is referred to as a "Screamiere," which brings us to the subject of the horror cult *per se*, if you are ready. Actually, it brings us to the subject whether you are ready or not, because Boris is one of its idols. The Frankenstein Monster and Count Dracula remain today first in the heart of the Horror Fan. According to the newspapers, Bela Lugosi's heirs have won a judgment against Universal Pictures using his image in merchandising. If true, the Karloff heirs haven't been so lucky. Boris's Monster is everywhere in every form, sometimes quite unattractive.

In the past the press has made many references to a deep-seated "rivalry" between Boris and Lugosi. Not true. Boris actually was fond of him although they seldom saw each other socially. Besides, in later years, Lugosi was a very ill man and Boris had a great deal of sympathy for him. In Robert C. Roman's excellent article on Boris in *Films in Review*, August-September 1964, the interviewer quotes Boris:

> "Poor old Bela," Karloff said nostalgically. "It was a strange thing. He was really a shy, sensitive, talented man who had a fine career on the classical stage in Europe. But he made one fatal mistake. He never took the trouble to learn our language. Consequently, he was very suspicious on the set, suspicious of tricks, fearful of what he regarded as scene stealing. Later, when he realized I didn't go in for such nonsense, we became friends. He had real problems with his speech, and difficulty interpreting lines. I remember he once asked a director what a line of dialogue meant. He spent a great deal of his time with the Hungarian colony in Los Angeles, and this isolated him."

I personally remember Boris's attitude toward Lugosi. In the late 1930's the Karloffs, Jimmy and Lucille Gleason, Russell, and I were riding in the Santa Claus Sleigh down Hollywood Boulevard, which becomes "Santa Claus Lane" during the holiday season. Every night the sleigh carries so-called celebrities who wave to the populace as Santa "Ho-ho-ho's" through a scratchy microphone. The night we rode, Santa was very, very drunk and commenting loudly on people in the profession, neglecting at times to switch off his microphone. Suddenly a voice from the crowd cried, "Boris! Boris! Down here!" It was Bela Lugosi loyally applauding his "compatriot." Boris waved back and shouted, "Bela! How are you, old boy?"

"Boo!" hiccupped Santa.

As we passed, Boris said quietly, "Poor Bela." He always called him "Poor Bela."

Boris himself used to refer to "the ancient art of raising gooseflesh"—but he took the subject seriously. In his preface to *Tales of Terror*, an anthology issued by World Publishing in 1943, he wrote:

> The essential element of true horror as opposed to so-called horror is *fear*. Fear of the unknown and of the unknowable. Are you afraid of the dark? You know perfectly well that you are, and you may as well admit it. You come by it honestly. Imagine the sensations of that ancestor of ours who was the first to fall from his treetop, stumbling around in the abysmal gloom of those primeval jungles peopled by heaven knows what, all waiting to pop out at him from every shadow. And when, or if, he managed to scramble back up his tree to safety, his oft-told tales of the nameless terrors he had suffered finally became a bore to his family. Then was when he really "went to town," and for the sake of his good name he began inventing all the ghosts and demons he might have seen but never did, and it is these which delight and terrify us today. Nor did he have to go too far afield to give his imagination full rein. He merely looked at what Joseph Conrad calls *The Shadow-Line . . . stars, sun,*

Lugosi and Karloff hefting steins. Obviously a publicity shot—they never looked at each other like this.

sea, light, darkness, space, great waters; the formidable Work of the Seven Days, into which mankind seems to have blundered unbidden. Or else destroyed. There, in all its implications, is one of the best descriptions of pure terror that has ever come my way. And maybe it's true. Ever since man began to think, he seems to have had a foreboding fear of a predecessor, or of a successor, stronger than himself in this new world; and, sensing his presence but being ignorant of the nature of this enemy, he created a whole race of occult beings, born of terror.

In the introduction to another anthology, *And the Darkness Falls*, also World Publishing, in 1946: "The French have a saying about the hour between dog and wolf when the mind is disposed to marvels. But alas, no matter how propitious the hour nor how well disposed the mind, we are most of us still too blind to see the authentic marvels that come our way in real life."

The televised old films now sport, along with their new names, odd characters who dart in and out as the films progress, making comments, and generally deriding the pictures. These characters have become celebrities in their own right and appear at celebrations of the Count Dracula Society and at the "Sci-Fi Cons" (Science Fiction Conventions). In the interests of research, I have attended these gatherings, and I hope I can in some way objectively report what goes on. Report, not explain.

So: It seems that a great many people of all ages are totally dedicated to the pursuit and collection of HORROR. This dedication may take the form of collections of awful objects from trick stores—wiggly rubber things, or miniature Draculas and Frankenstein Monster creations. The Monster figure I saw was rather well-made, and for a moment I considered buying one for Boris's grandsons, that is, until I pressed a lever, it emitted a low growl, lurched toward me, its pants fell off, its penis erected, a red light lit up on the tip of it, and a siren went off. It was only five ninety-five but I decided against it. Thank God, Boris never saw it.

In the huckster stands at the Conventions (with a capital C) these objects are sold along with "antique" comix (spelled *comix*—nothing is spelled the way anything is spelled and most words are run together); Fanzines (obviously an elision of "fan magazine"—this is the last effort at explanation); books—H. P. Lovecraft to Tolkien; advertisements for subscriptions to periodicals—*The Monster Times* ("EEK and Ye Shall Find") and *Granfalloon* (which won second prize in the Best Fanzine Contest). "*Granfalloon*," the ad states, "is a Genzine." This statement is followed by "Comments From Readers: 'I agree to become a subscriber in the next Disclave—if you sign me up in the sauna.' . . . 'The entire issue is enough to send a fan into a foetal stance.' . . . 'Your zine is the best.' " Then there is a Conzine called *Creepy*, a *Blackenstein* comix (I don't know the singular). And let's not forget The Hobbit—an outlet store for "mainline and underground comix," which features "Aries Conditioning," "Adult Fantasy," and many more delights. The Daily Newzing of the Thirtieth World Science Fiction Convention, incidentally, is called *Wabbit Twacks!!* (two exclamation points).

Wabbit Twacks!! carries ads for The Mythopoeic Society ". . . a unique balance between serious discussion and a variety of colorful costumed events, which publishes a monthly bulletin called *Mythprint*. There is also an ad for *Janus Psynergy* and *The Boris Karloff Tales of Mystery*, a comix with Boris on the cover addressing the reader. Then an ad for "Authentic Tribbles." A tribble seems to be a pebble, or rock, depending on its size, entirely covered with hair, or fur, or *something*—it's hard to tell.* They come in all sizes, "Small, Medium, or Immense," and in two colors, "Soft Russet or Shaggy Gray." There is also "a limited supply of 'mutated' tribbles in 'odd colors and shapes.' " (Horror Fans are very big on mutation.)

The huckster stalls also have specialized "people eaters"—rats, tarantulas, and giant toads, with hands coming out of their mouths—I really don't want to talk about it.

The "Con" gatherings are many, and they are usually named after the city they're in: the "Torcon" (Toronto), the "Chambancon" (Champaign-Urbana, Illinois), the "Ozarkcon" (you guess). There are also "Period Cons." A "Medieval Con" was advertised: "Sir Amarc of Catatonia, Knight of the Uncertain Lance—Wants YOU!" On occasion, the "Con" is based on a holiday—there was an "Eastercon" combining the best of both worlds.

The "Sci-Con" I attended in Los Angeles attracted milling throngs

---

* Fans of "Star Trek" won't have this difficulty; tribbles originated in a 1967 episode of the program.

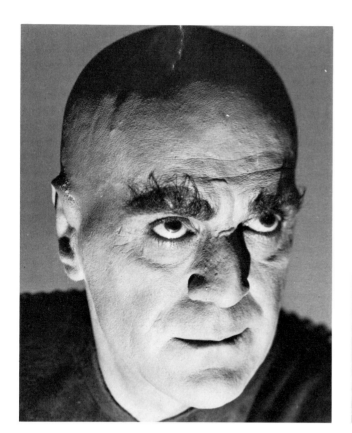 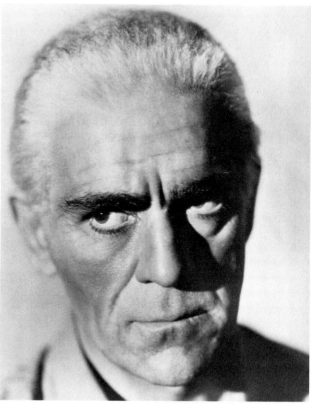

LEFT: Tower of London *(1939)*. RIGHT: The Invisible Menace *(1938)*.

of Spacemen, Batmen, Blobs, Draculas, Frankenstein Monsters, Hunchbacks, Werewolves, etc. It was also attended by science fiction writers of the quality of Ray Bradbury, Robert Bloch, and Richard Matheson. Seminars were conducted by varieties of specialists in the field. One, Forrest J. Ackerman, may be the world's greatest authority on horror. It is in fact his life. His business card reads: "Science Fiction, Filmonsters, Esperanto." I don't understand about the last. Mr. Ackerman, along with his business activities, has unquestionably the greatest personal collection of horror memorabilia extant. He is sometimes known as "Mr. Monster." His "Ackermansion" in Los Angeles is jammed to the turrets with giant figures of King Kong, "life masks" of Frankenstein's Creature and of Dracula, monster posters, dried manta rays, ray guns, pictures of alien landscapes and of exotic women in fetish outfits, rubber monsters holding stuffed alligators in their teeth. The castle is sometimes referred to as "Grizzlyland."

LEFT: The Mask of Fu Manchu *(1932)*. RIGHT: The Ghoul *(1933)*.

Mr. Ackerman edits *Famous Monsters of Filmland*, a periodical dedicated to same. He was a devoted fan of Boris's through his life, and when Boris died, Ackerman's Fanzine printed a page of letters from fans (this page is entitled "Fang Mail"), a personal letter of condolence to Mrs. Karloff, and a note to readers from the editor stating that he had received so many letters of condolence to him, personally, in his loss, that "tears ran down my mailbox." (Mr. Ackerman, by the way, plans to be cryogenically frozen upon his death, his body preserved in liquid nitrogen until some future scientist brings him back to become curator of his own collection "from here to eternity" —and it had better be intact.)

I missed a few displays at the "Con," but I did make some interesting contacts, one through Bongo Wolf, who has helped tremendously in compiling the filmography of this book. He introduced me to Don Blythe, who runs a horror museum called the Ram Occult Center upstairs on Hollywood

Boulevard. Blythe also conducts night-time spiritual meetings (by invitation only) entitled "The Ineffable Essence of Nothing."

Mr. Blythe used to be in partnership in vaudeville with a man called Tony Karloff, who swears he is Boris's disowned son. I went to call on Mr. Blythe and found him extremely pleasant and cooperative. He showed me some pictures of Tony Karloff in the act they shared, with his partner in the Monster makeup, and another without makeup. No resemblance. I said I doubted—and I still doubt—any relationship. As Blythe and I talked, I faced a case containing the skeleton of the "real Count Dracula." (Those of us in the know refer to him as "Vlad Dracule, the Impaler." You probably didn't even know that the *real* Dracule did people in with stakes, not teeth.) Mr. Blythe's skeleton wears a cape and has *very* long fangs. It's kind of nice. The rest of the items are not—particularly the ones in bottles.

With Mr. Blythe, via the "Con," I became apprised of "The She Creature," happy in being the only drag monster at the fair, and I rode up in an elevator with one of the future prize winners. The door of the elevator was just closing when someone yelled, "Hold it!" One of us stopped the doors, and a man pushed through, gasping, "Stand back—all of you! I've got ten gallons of hot peanut butter in this box!" He did have. We all stood back.

I mulled this about in my head as I went on to other exhibits until the public address system announced the costume party. I pushed into the International Ballroom with the rest of the humanoids, and the contest for the best costume started: Monsters and Moonchildren, Star Treks and Sinisters, they all paraded by; then suddenly, to a giant wave of applause, something rushed out onto the stage, growling, snarling, and waving a plumber's helper. The announcer bellowed, "And now by popular acclaim, the Grand Prize for 'The Most Repulsive,' nursed in the womb of Uranus, goes to—'The Turd From Outer Space!' " It was my friend from the elevator, completely covered in his hot peanut butter. The citation was justly deserved.

One does not know whence cometh the True Believer, what walk of life, what background extraordinarily catholic (small c—all those CROSSES!). For instance, Bongo Wolf, my helpful filmographer, who dedicates his life to his collection, lives with his parents in a handsome, highly respectable house in a handsome, highly respectable, and highly expensive section of Beverly Hills. He spends most of his time amassing his collection, searching through bookstores, and going to horror movies. On occasional evenings (probably at the full of the moon) he slips into his werewolf teeth (fine quality—his father is a dentist) and goes out on the town because he enjoys "scaring the hell out of the Jesus freaks." In other words, he brings on a sense of "horripilation" (it's a *real* word, meaning: ". . . a bristling of the hair of the head or body [as from disease, terror, or chilliness]: goose-flesh").

The international general acceptance of horror as a way of life (and of business) has led even Pan American Airways into the field. In the spring of 1973 they had a charter flight called "In Search of Dracula" from Budapest to Transylvania, an eighteen-day guided trip through black forests and blacker castles including the Dracula and Frankenstein originals, "with lectures along the way." I tried to get Sara Jane Karloff to go with me but she wouldn't. She was scared. And I wasn't about to go alone.

OVERLEAF: *Boris appearing on the "Lights Out" radio show.*

13 / HAND IN HAND
ACROSS THE RIVER STYX

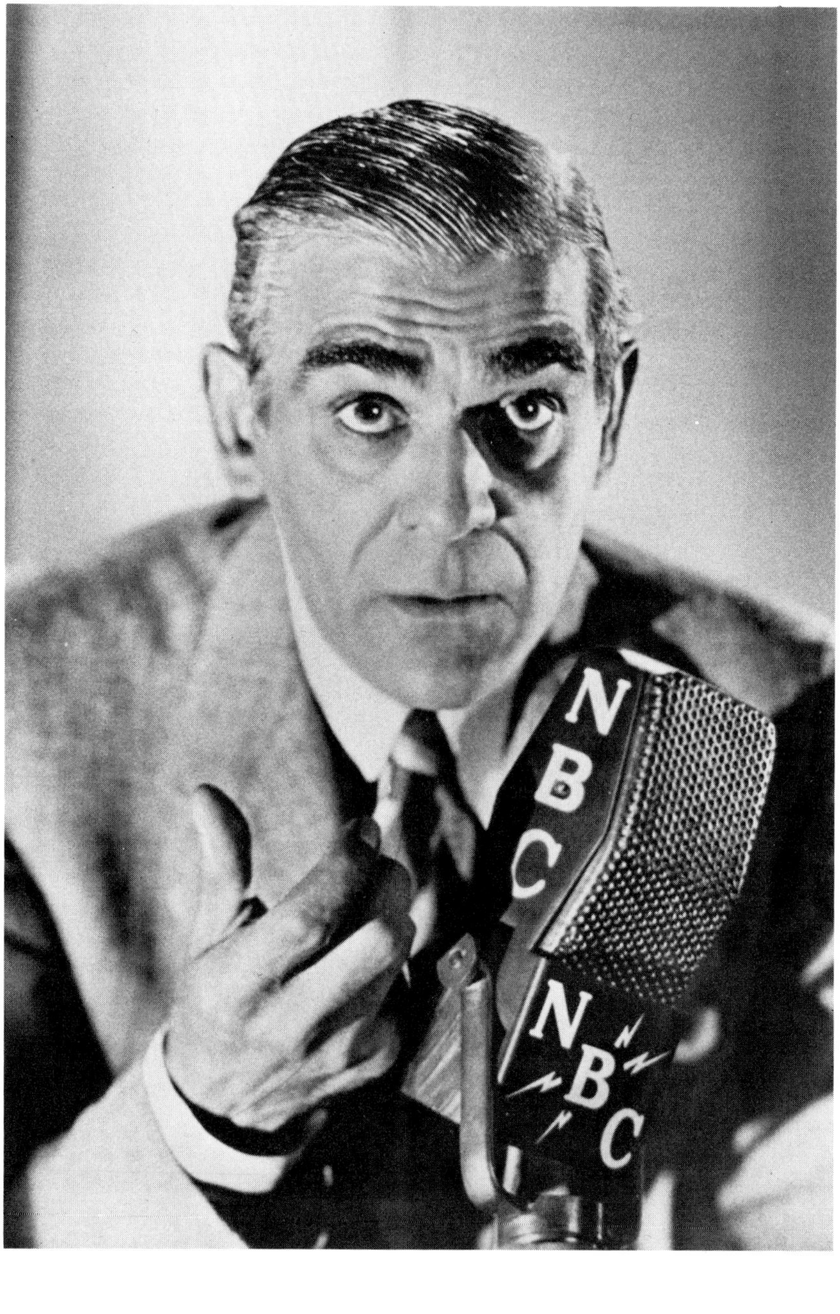

I have no recollection of what Boris was doing professionally or otherwise when I first met him. But I remember exactly what *I* was doing because I was having such a good time doing it. The year was 1933, and I had just left a private girls' boarding school in the middle of my last year, because suddenly there was no money. I was totally unequipped to make a living at anything, but I was a good athlete and Warner Brothers was about to start shooting Busby Berkeley's famous "By a Waterfall" number for *Footlight Parade*, starring Ruby Keeler, James Cagney, and Dick Powell. To my surprise, I was hired to swim in it.

Busby Berkeley was a certifiable genius. No one had ever done before with people or with cameras what he did, and no one has since. The "Waterfall" number has become a film classic, which when shown today in art houses brings cheers from audiences. It still gives me goose bumps.

On screen, the number starts with a close-up of Ruby Keeler (tulle and picture hat) and Dick Powell (black and white sport shoes) sitting under a tree singing, "There's a haunting melodeeeee-ee, Mother Nature brings to meeeee-ee. . . ." As they slip into "By a waterfall, I'm calling you-oo-oo-oo . . . ," there is an echo of "oo-oo-oo-oo. . . ." They register: "Hark! What is that?" The camera pulls back—way, way back and up, up, up, to a waterfall extending to the ceiling of the sound stage. Twenty thousand gallons of hydraulically drawn water pour down the falls over cement slides, and standing about on the rocks in the falls are numerous wood nymphs, crying "Oo-oo-oo-oo. . . ."

For weeks, we, the swimmers, had been sliding, diving, swimming to music, and gravely endangering life and limb. Now, the camera pulls in and down to Ruby and Dick. He has dropped off to sleep; she smiles and lets an apple blossom fall into the water. ZIP! The camera pulls back, as the petal trembles on the water. POP! Up from the water in the place of the petal, RUBY! In a rhinestone bathing cap, drippingly gasping in perfect key, "By a waterfall, I'm calling you-oo-oo-oo"—echo: "Oo-oo-oo-oo." ZIP! Up with the camera again; the entire stage a Ziegfeldesque rhinestone-studded pool surrounded by ten-foot diving boards (also rhinestone studded); we, the divers in rhinestone-studded suits (or rather, three carefully placed rhinestone patches), diving from the ten-foot boards into three-and-a-half feet of water (because the circle of girls into which we dived had to be able to stand on the floor of the pool with their shoulders above the water to form the patterns of the design).

All of this was shot from under the water as well as from above, and I clearly remember the close-up of Ruby trying to smile into the camera with the smile of rigor mortis as she passed the camera window (Ruby couldn't swim at all and was terrified of the water). The music crescendos, swimmers are photographed from the top of the sound stage as they form incredible geometric patterns: circles, stars, flowers; divers dive in and break the patterns (and nearly break their necks); fountains shoot water high above the pool. In the process, noses and, almost, backs were broken, faces were scraped to the bone. (Rhinestones are like cheese graters. I had the whole rear end of my suit stripped off; girls were taken to emergency hospitals; we worked frequently from seven in the morning to three-thirty the next and had to return at eleven once again.) On the screen at the end of the number, the camera returns to Ruby and Dick under the tree. He rubs his eyes, looks up, smiles; it turns out he's dreamed the whole thing. What a letdown!

Despite the fact that there was no Screen Actors Guild at the time and that we were being paid seven dollars and fifty cents a day, with no overtime for those three-thirty mornings, I never had a better time and never had better friends. Two of the friends were Marjorie and Gertrude Keeler, Ruby's sisters. They couldn't swim, either, but they could stand in the water and kick.

One day they said they were going to the Brown Derby to join some boys for lunch and why didn't I come too? The "boys" turned out to be Lew Ayres, William Bakewell, Ben Alexander, and Russell Gleason, the four friends from *All Quiet on the Western Front*. They had become inseparable friends off the *Front* as well as on; in fact, they ran in a pack. I started seeing Russell steadily and through him met and became close to the Karloffs.

My burgeoning career involved getting out of the water, onto horseback, falling off horseback into deep underwater shots (alone this time, not with a hundred other girls), doubling for stars in dangerous scenes, wrestling with Great Danes, and finally venturing out onto the ice in the chorus of a Sonja Henie film called *Thin Ice* (1937). I was always so anxious for work that I

The "By a Waterfall" number from Footlight Parade. The author is circled.
(The swimmers and divers were on top for action shots; the "Berkeley
Girls" replaced them for close-ups, as here.)

In the late 1930's, Boris appeared on many radio shows—here it's the "Shell Chateau." From left to right: Maxine Lewis, Victor Young, and Margaret Brayton. In the back row: George Jessel, Boris, and Al Jolson.

had never learned to say "No" when asked if I could do something—anything. I said "Yes" and learned. Nearly broke my neck, but learned.

For the Gleasons and Boris, the play being the thing, the impression must have been that I was working in pictures in search of an acting career. Actually I was working in pictures because my mother, my stepfather, and even my father (formerly a successful producer) needed my seven dollars and fifty cents *per diem*. So, on the portentous day that Boris said to me, "How would you like to play Grazia opposite me in *Death Takes a Holi-*

day?" I never hesitated, just said, "I'd love to." The fact that my entire acting career had consisted of playing a grandfather in a boarding school play and smiling underwater didn't deter me for a minute.

This production of the Alberto Casella–Walter Ferris classic was to be presented on radio on "The Camel Caravan." Boris would pick me up and take me to rehearsals, work with me over the script, put his arm around me, and draw me closer to the microphone if I backed away. It went surprisingly well. After a few rehearsals, Boris would drop me at the Gleasons, and say, "She's good—she's very, very good." And I felt wonderful.

Death Takes a Holiday was a Broadway success in 1929, with Philip Merivale playing Death, and Rose Hobart playing Grazia. It was a motion picture success in 1934, with Fredric March as Death and Evelyn Venable as Grazia. The play evolves around a beautiful young princess of eighteen years, described in the cast of characters as "charming and gentle, but oddly remote," who falls in love with Death. Death is taking a three-day holiday (no one dies, flowers keep their petals, no leaf falls) disguised as a mortal, Prince Sirki. In the last act, even when she knows his true identity, Grazia chooses to cling to him, despite the fact that his handsome face has now become a death's head. She has always seen him like that, it seems. She takes his hand, saying, "You seem beautiful to me." Death, referred to as the "Shadow," cries triumphantly, "Then there *is* a love which casts out fear, and I have found it!" (Bells peal, leaves begin to fall.) "And love is greater than illusion, and as strong as death!"

Almost every line of the play ends with an exclamation point and Bathos abounds. The whole cast had managed well. We were well prepared. I wasn't nervous.

The director said, "Okay. This is the last rehearsal before we go on the air tomorrow. There'll be several million people listening. Make it good!" Slowly the phrase sank into my consciousness and into the pit of my stomach. I made it through my first scene. Then we reached the love scene:

SHADOW [BORIS]: Here we are!

GRAZIA: Your Very Serene Highness. (*She makes a curtsy* [I was good at that but this was radio.])

SHADOW: Oh, please! Titles are too formal for me.

GRAZIA (*simply*): How shall I call you then?

SHADOW: Well, my name is Vasili Stephen Nicholas Sirki Alexander Alexandro-
vitch.

GRAZIA (*smiling*): But I couldn't call you that.

SHADOW: I have one name no one has ever used . . . Boris.

GRAZIA: But I shouldn't dare.

SHADOW: Not if I asked it? Try.

GRAZIA (*very low*): Boris.

Very low. It didn't come out at all. As I said the name "Boris," the
terrible reality of what the hell I was doing struck me. This wasn't Prince
Sirki, this was *Boris.* Suddenly I looked down. The theater was partly filled
with staring faces. Boris read the cue again. He had put his arm around my
shoulder. He pressed it lightly. I just stood there. I opened my mouth and
nothing came out. He read the cue again, and pressed my shoulder a little
harder. My throat was totally closed. One of Grazia's stage directions was:
"*Grazia is hysterical with fear, she is convulsed with terror. Her eyes are
wide and staring.*" Grazia had nothing on Cynthia. I began to hear the muf-
fled whispers, the word "replace" came through, and I remember to this day
the look on the faces, the whispers, the back-turnings, Boris saying, "It's just a
touch of laryngitis . . . she'll be fine . . . ," and my croaking, "No, I won't.
Not ever." People ran to telephones, people took Boris aside, and finally he
said, "Come on, love, I'll take you home." My replacement arrived as we
walked out the door. They had already started to cue her with her lines as we
left.

The "home" to which Boris referred was not mine, but the Gleasons',
where they were waiting to proudly congratulate the new member of the
actors' colony. In the car I started to sob. Boris said, "It's not your fault,
dear . . . it's the trouble with today. Today you make a mistake and a million
people catch you. In my day we had a chance to be bad in front of a few.
There's no place for practice today. You'll be fine, you'll see."

I was choking with sobs. "But I let you down. That's what I really
care about . . . I let you down! You went out on a limb for me and I let you
down. . . ."

"No you didn't. All that will be all right. There are always standby actresses dying for a chance. This just wasn't the right corner or the right time for you."

By now I was sobbing so hard my nose was running, and I saw, with horror, through the mist of tears, that it was running down the sleeve of Boris's coat. He said, "Here. Have another handkerchief. I haven't seen anything like this since the Johnstown Flood." He handed me his handkerchief and I sobbed, "Now I have to face all those people . . . what am I going to tell them?"

"You won't have to tell them anything, darling. They'll know by looking at your face. It looks pretty terrible, by the way."

I pushed my hair back off my sticky face and sniffled, "Who wants to be an actress anyway? I never said I wanted to be an actress."

"Cynie, darling," he said, "that may very well be true. Some people just don't have the fire in the belly for it . . . you may be one of them. It's not the greatest thing on earth. But if you *do* have the fire in the belly for it, it's the only way of life. Give me back my handkerchief."

I tell this story because it so reveals Boris's feeling toward acting—and Boris's generosity toward a friend: first, the impulse to give; next, the constant day-to-day helping; the total support in crisis, never criticizing or blaming; then, when the friend finally had managed an accomplishment, his total appreciation and approbation. "Full marks," he would say, "full marks, old girl" (or "old boy," as the case might be)—and it was like being knighted.

OVERLEAF: *Boris ready for action in his Hollywood Cricket Club gear.*

Boris's passion for sports, like his passion for acting, never left him. If there was a rugby game anywhere, he was in the stands; every nonworking day he was on the tennis court and he played well; he was a member of the Hollywood Field Hockey team; but first and foremost, he was a mad cricketer. When that magnificent old man C. Aubrey Smith (later, Sir Aubrey Smith) organized the Hollywood Cricket Club in 1932, Boris was one of its most eager charter members. The Club was a facet of a very solid, very distinguished British Colony in Hollywood and, since in all such outposts of civilization it was necessary to remain a tight, homogeneous group, so it was at this period in the development of motion pictures. The Colony accepted the natives socially—after all, they were coworkers in The Profession—but an Englishman is an Englishman, nonetheless. Sir Aubrey flew the Union Jack over his lawn, Boris had the New Year piped in (real bagpipers), people toasted the King. Through the Karloffs, the Gleasons saw a great deal of members of The Colony. Jimmy slipped into heavy tweeds and even bought a set of variously colored monocles for different occasions, but it wasn't quite the same thing, you know.

The Cricket Club boasted a roster which, on a marquee, would have filled any theater in the land. Ronald Colman, Clive Brook, Basil Rathbone, Nigel Bruce, R. C. Sherriff (in town for the filming of *Journey's End*), H. B. Warner, Noel Madison, Claude King, and later the younger boys, Frankie Lawton, Errol Flynn, Cary Grant, and David Niven, as well as distinguished gentlemen in fields other than the theater. Pretty ladies like Merle Oberon and Vivien Leigh watched their countrymen (and stray Americans) from the sidelines. It was all very exciting, particularly if one understood the game. I didn't.

Then one afternoon the Karloffs invited a party of friends to a match. I was seated next to Nigel Bruce, who was not playing that afternoon. I tried to pay attention, but my mind wandered. A group of us were going to the opening night of the Ballets Russes de Monte Carlo that evening. Mrs. Bruce was included in the group. Mr. Bruce was not. I slipped into idle conversation with Mr. Bruce. One does not converse during a cricket game. Particularly with Mr. Bruce. And *never* idly.

"Mr. Bruce," I said (I hadn't learned to call him "Willie" yet), "how is it you are not going to the ballet tonight?"

He never took his eyes off the batsman, puffed out his mustache, and answered, "Because, my dear, frankly, I don't care to see buggers leap!"

Later that evening, I told Boris "Willie's" line and he roared. Then I had to confess I didn't know the meaning of the word "bugger." He tried to explain, then looked at me and said, "It's an old English word—meaning—well—it's an old English word and right around the corner in my study there's an old English dictionary. Why don't you have a look?" I went in and had a look. The dictionary definition was: "A term of affection used by sailors."

Boris's keenness for cricket never waned and when he returned to England to live, he spent as much time as possible watching the game. One day, after his return home from the United States, he was in the oval at the Middlesex Cricket Club, sitting among its members. He looked out across the green, turned to a friend, and said, "This is like dying and going to heaven."

About himself and the game, Boris always said, "I was a frightful duffer, but I tried very hard."

About Boris, his teammates said, "He had a good innings." Which, in cricketing terms, in case you don't know, is as good as you can get.

Boris may have been a duffer at cricket, but he was anything but at the other interest even closer to his heart, the welfare of his fellow actors. 1933 was the height of the producers' exploitation of the craftsmen—writers, directors, actors, extras, even swimmers. That year the producers demanded that all actors take a fifty percent cut because of "The Depression." The producers were virtually paying for "protection" by the International Association of Theatrical Stage Employees. The IATSE, today a powerful union, was a totally different organization then. It was controlled by gangster leadership, locally by two men named George Bioff and Willie Brown. The names "Bioff and Brown" became synonymous with infamy. Because of their strong-arm tactics and threats of reprisals, the producers dealt with them. After an investigation, the FBI found that the producers were not only dealing with them, but paying them off to the tune of hundreds of thousands of dollars.

For more than thirty years, the IATSE and the craft unions had been

The British contingent was well represented at the Hollywood Cricket Club in the 1930's. C. Aubrey Smith dead center (as always); Boris is third from right in the second row.

involved in jurisdictional wars each followed by compromise agreements which resulted in little more than periods of armed peace. Actors Equity had conducted and lost a strike in 1929 because it had respected contracts and instructed the stars who were members under contract to studios to abide by their contracts—but Equity couldn't pull them off their jobs. This put the burden of the strike on free-lance players, who fought a lengthy, costly fight and lost. The outcome was an almost total disenchantment on the part of actors for unions.

In 1933 the Academy of Motion Picture Arts and Sciences was a company union dominated by the studios, with major stars as officers. Through the Academy, the studios granted occasional small concessions to the actors, but they were few and far between. That same year, also, the screen writers revived and reorganized their moribund organization. This gave impetus to a few actors who began to talk secretly of trying to organize.

Meanwhile—back at the Cricket Club: May 1933, the Hollywood

Cricket Club Annual Dance to promote funds for the following season. The usual group was in attendance. Boris was running things. As he cast his eye over the gathering, he noticed Kenneth Thomson, a fellow actor and friend, and remembered wondering what he was doing there, being neither British nor a cricket fancier. Many years later, Boris wrote in the *Screen Actors Guild Bulletin*:

> Anyhow, as the evening advanced and I was circumnavigating the floor in my customary slow and stately manner, Ken dropped anchor alongside me and muttered in my ear the magic words, "Would you be interested in an autonomous organization for film actors with an affiliation with Actors Equity?" Hastily scrambling off my unfortunate partner's foot, I practically yelled, "How . . . when . . . where?" At which he hissed, "Next Thursday, 8:00 p.m., my house," and practically vanished in a puff of smoke.
>
> Well, I went, I listened, and I was conquered. Dear Ralph Morgan was presiding over a crowded meeting of perhaps half a dozen people. Ken Thomson, of course, and his wife, Alden, James and Lucille Gleason, Noel Madison, Claude King, and perhaps one or two others.
>
> Anyhow, from then on it was a regular weekly event with one or two new recruits coming in . . . rather a thin trickle, but still a trickle. Amongst that trickle were Sir Aubrey Smith, Ivan Simpson, Murray Kinnell, all members of the Cricket Club. Among others who joined the group before the actual formation of the Guild were Leon Ames, Bradley Page, Charles Starrett, Lyle Talbot, and Alan Mowbray, whose personal check paid for the Guild's legal incorporation. [Laurence Bielenson, the lawyer who wrote the original charter for both the Screen Actors Guild and the Screen Writers Guild, says it was Jimmy Gleason's check.]
>
> From time to time various well-known luminaries in the film world came to listen and admire but not to enlist. . . . The general idea was to set the skeleton of an organization for film actors with a constitution and the machinery for making it work, get what recruits we could, but in the meantime sit back and hold the fort and wait for the producers to make the inevitable booboo that would enable us to interest the stars, without whose support we knew the Guild could not hope to function successfully.
>
> Well, the months ticked away and our growth was hardly phenomenal

and sometimes our spirits flagged a bit but never our firm belief that the producers would do the job for us by putting the cat among the pigeons and getting everybody into an uproar. Well, sure as fate they did just that, although for the life of me I can't remember what it was at this distance. [It was another attempt to reduce actors' salaries under the National Recovery Administration Code.] The producers chose the moment when our evening quota of visiting nobility and gentry consisted of Groucho Marx and the late Charlie Butterworth. They, of course, knew what the row was about and we told them what we had been up to. Proudly we dangled our skeleton before them and trotted out the proud roster of our members . . . all fifty or sixty of them. That did it. They sent telegrams to every important star in the business and they all convened at Frank Morgan's house the following Sunday and the Guild was off to the races at last. . . .

What days—what fun—what excitement—what glorious results and what leaders: Ralph Morgan, Bob Montgomery, George Murphy, Jim Cagney, Ken Thomson.

If one may be permitted to paraphrase Wordsworth—"They were the Happy Warriors, that every man in arms would wish to be."

I carry today in my heart the picture of Sir Aubrey Smith in impeccable snowy flannels, swooping about on the dance floor at the Hollywood Cricket Club, pausing, stage whispering through bristling white mustache to a fellow dancer . . . "My house tonight—not a word—park on another street—come in the back door. . . ." One, two, three, dip—and away.

The Guild continued to gather strength through the middle thirties, the central core of actors meeting at Boris's, the Gleasons', James Cagney's, Robert Montgomery's houses, and finally in Guild offices. John Dales, for years the Executive Secretary of the Guild, says, "Boris was marvelous in these meetings. He was firm, courageous, at a time when it was actually dangerous. . . ."

One does feel tremendous admiration for a group of actors whose careers were at stake—not just the greats, like the Cagneys or the Montgomerys, but the free-lances and small-part players whose actual livelihood was on the firing line. At a time when sticking your neck out might get your head lopped off, necks got "outer" all the time.

When I spoke to Robert Montgomery about Boris, he said, "When I was President of the Guild, Boris was on the board—he was a wise, astute member. Despite his gentleness, he was firm—immovable on issues he believed in, and endlessly helpful in very trying times."

Jack Dales also spoke to me of Boris: "Boris," he said, "was a philosophical anarchist. Simply couldn't tolerate injustice. He was fed up with the all-encompassing power of producers combined against the actor. He was funny in meetings—he couldn't stand the members who were always on their feet. When they went on too long, Boris would cut in and say, 'We know the situation—let's *solve* it, not *state* it.' I remember one meeting when Ralph Morgan was in a state of fury over some new atrocity the producers had pulled. He was terribly emotional anyway and he was sputtering . . . 'This is outrageous! It is disgraceful! It's, it's—*un-American*!' Boris just said quietly, 'It's also un-British, Ralph, but what's far more important—it's *unfair*.'

"The meetings would get a little sidetracked on occasion. I remember one . . . maybe I shouldn't tell you this?" I assured him whatever it was, I was up to it. "Well, in one meeting, somehow the conversation got around to the sexual prowess and durability of Arabs. 'God,' Boris said, 'I'd hate to follow Turhan Bey.' "

The "Happy Warriors" worked on, gaining strength, gaining members. In 1936 Boris was instrumental in bringing British Equity into the fold. Fights continued; threats were made; but slowly the Guild became a functioning, cohesive labor organization, and, more and more, the smaller people who previously had nowhere to turn—had. I know, because I was working in a skiing picture at MGM, called, if I remember correctly, *Paradise for Three*, starring Robert Young and Mary Astor. I was doubling for Miss Astor. An Olympic ski champion was doubling for Bob. We were working on an artificial mountain that rose to the height of the sound stage. The two of us (representing Astor and Young) were supposed to start skiing down the mountain side by side. I was supposed to slip, he try to catch me, the two of us roll to the bottom of the mountain, landing in each other's arms; then the camera returns to close-up on the real Astor-Young who are meeting for the first time. This, in films, is called "meeting cute."

It wasn't so cute. The powdered gypsum, representing snow, stuck to our skis. They tried graphite on them, which left black marks on the gypsum. Then they went away, returned with sheets of plate glass on which they sprayed glue, and sprinkled bleached cornflakes over the glue. This was all about eight hours after we had checked in for work.

I was standing looking down at the plate glass when Robert Young, the Star, arrived on the set. He looked up at me and asked, "*What* are you doing there? You can't ski on *snow!*" (Bob had been the star of *I Met Him in Paris*, the Sun Valley picture where I had learned the little I knew, which was *very* little—and he knew it.) I said, "Shhh. . . ." "Your secret will die with me," he said, "or maybe with *you*. . . . How is this whole stunt going to work?" The Olympic skier said, 'We ski onto the glass, which naturally will make us slip and fall, and if we aren't decapitated, we roll to the bottom." Bob said, "That is outrageous—you can't do anything of the kind—you'll be cut to ribbons." The director was off the set. Bob called the assistant director, who shrugged as they talked. The Olympic skier moaned, "Isn't there *anybody* you can go to at a time like this?"

Flash! There *was!* There was damned well a Screen Actors Guild! I took off my skis, went to the telephone, and called Boris. He let out a puff of rage and said, "Just sit tight. Do as you're told but try not to break your neck or cut your throat while you wait. A Guild representative will be there in an hour."

In exactly an hour, the representative arrived, accompanied by a fuming producer. The producer glared at me. "Are you the little troublemaker?" he snarled. I answered that I wasn't trying to make trouble, I was just scared. Besides, I felt that if we were doing stunt work we should be paid stunt fees. The producer stormed, "This is not stunt work! Look at your check. It says right on it you are an 'active extra.'" The Guild representative very quietly said, "Well, you'll admit this is pretty active. Besides, these are professional skiers [little did he know] and therefore should be paid more, and conditions should be less dangerous . . . with all that plate glass they could be killed." "Sure they could," said the producer, "and they could drown in their own goddamned bathtubs and I wish they had—what do you want me to do?" "Pay them for what they are doing—a dangerous stunt." The producer turned to the assistant director. "Okay their goddamned checks for stunt fee." He turned to the Guild representative. "Now you get off my goddamned set!" He turned again to the assistant director and pointed to me. "And list this one in casting as a goddamned troublemaker!"

The director watched him go, then said, "Okay, kids—let's shoot it. We'll try not to kill you." The Olympic skier and I climbed to the top of the mountain, put on our skis, prayed, and started down the mountain. The skis hit the plate glass, which cracked with a scream. The rest of it broke, followed us down as we rolled to the bottom, and landed on top of us in a flurry of cornflakes. We sat up, reacted to "meeting cute." The director yelled, "Cut—perfect!" and we started feeling ourselves to see if we were still there. Bob said, "Now that's *your* kind of skiing!"

We were congratulated by all, then picked up our checks for fifteen dollars—double pay! The Olympic skier said, "I don't think I like this business." I said, "I love it!" and went to call Boris and tell him of our triumph.

"The bastards," he said. Strong word for him, but a friend had been hurt.

"But fifteen whole dollars, Boris!"

"For breaking your neck? Next time don't say you'll do it until you find what they want you to do—and then double the price . . . there'll be a law for these things in a little while, but until we have it don't be stupid."

The Guild continued gaining strength and members until 1937, when the membership voted a major strike. At the last minute the producers met Guild demands, and it was, and is, a major force; today, the *only* force.

Ronald Reagan was President of the Guild after World War II, and when he was Governor of California he wrote me a long, glowing (naturally) letter about his association with Boris. An excerpt:

Boris was one of the warmest, kindest, most gentle human beings I have ever met, and at all times a perfect gentleman. He was modest and unassuming and, yet, in his quiet way, contributed so much in our deliberations. He had great, good common sense plus a sense of fairness typical of his great integrity. Nancy [now the governor's wife] was on the Board in those days and both of us held him in such great affection that love is the only word that fits. I left out one other descriptive word. When the stories would lead into banter and joking, he also had a most delightful sense of humor. I can only say that many a time I would find myself looking at him and wondering how this kindly man fell into the type-casting of monsters and villains. He was the complete opposite of the parts he played.

Boris remained on the Guild board through 1950, quietly (always quietly) fighting and slogging away, and in 1951, in a ceremony in New York,

Presentation of the Screen Actors Guild Honorary Life Membership card.
Seated, left to right: Lee Bowman, Warner Anderson, Boris (in tears,
naturally), and Walter Abel.

was presented with a gold Honorary Life Membership card, which naturally made him cry.

In later years, the sentimental union man demonstrated that his devotion to SAG was based on the desire to right terrible wrongs, not to promote the labor movement *per se*; in 1965, when he was seventy-seven years old, Boris gave an interview in a London paper to an interviewer who referred to him as "the great old man of the creepies." Boris stated:

The British actor is dreadfully treated. Far from being paid too much money, as popular opinion has it, he is not paid anything like enough— and I include film actors in that.

Apart from money, conditions of employment are often bad—sometimes terrible. Our trade union, Equity, ought to act far more strongly.

Of course, the whole salary structure in this country is ridiculously low. How can you talk of a high standard of living when managements of all kinds are so mean to their employees?

No other country would stand for it—look at the money paid in America.

But the awful thing that has been accomplished by trade unions is this —you can't be given the sack. However rotten a man is at the job, he seems safe. The union protects him.

One false move by the management and there's an unofficial strike. What nonsense. The words contradict each other. An unofficial strike is an illegal move and should be punished.

Boris ended the interview and he returned to work with, "Must hurry back to the set or they'll sack me." Then he turned, peevish. "But they can't, you see. They should be able to, but they can't."

Overleaf: *Sara Jane's first photograph. Disposition maintained.*

BORIS & SARA JANE

15 / HAPPY BIRTHDAY,

In 1936 Boris starred or co-starred in five films. In one of them, *Charlie Chan at the Opera*, his co-star was Nedda Harrigan, who speaks of him glowingly (what else?):

"He was a joy—every moment of the shooting was fun—so much so that we occasionally broke up—we had this great scene together—we were both opera stars—he played Mephistopheles—we had two genuine Italian opera stars dubbing the aria we were mouthing—Boris could never master the Italian so he bellowed away—'SAN FRANCISCO! SACRAMENTO! SANTA BARBARA!' Mephistopheles was a perfect part for him—he was full of the devil himself—what gaiety—what zest—he knew he could break me up so he did—constantly—I made two films with him and seem to remember howling with laughter through both of them. The second film was *Devil's Island* in 1939—he played a convict, formerly a famous surgeon, who saves my child after a head injury when our carriage went over a cliff—it almost did, incidentally, with us in it. Any work with Boris was a joy. I loved him." (*Charlie Chan at the Opera*, by the way, was further distinguished by a score by Oscar Levant.)

In 1939, as well as making four other films, Boris made *Tower of London* at Universal, playing Mord, the Tower's cold-hearted executioner. It was the second of many films with Basil Rathbone, and the first of many with Vincent Price. Vincent and Boris became immediate and lasting friends. I pursued Vincent for over a year for his memories of Boris. He gets around, that one—lecture tours, films abroad, and so forth, and so on. I finally snagged him by threatening to kill him if he didn't write something. The letter:

Belatedly and passionately my tribute to one of the few (very select) of my Hollywood life I'd even care to mention. Boris came into it early on— my second or third film, Tower of London, *and he and Basil Rathbone introduced me to a kind of joyousness of picture-making I too seldom encountered in the hundred films that came later. I identified with him immediately, as somehow I knew the villain was to be my role in movies, too. The mumble school of acting had been imported and the people who used English well were on their way out. Boris was a formidable star at that time—Franken-*

stein, The Mummy *were behind him, and behind me as a moviegoer at Yale, but he went out of his way to make me feel welcome in a business I knew I was going to like.*

*Over the years we met at parties and always enjoyed each other, but as always with actors it was on the set where friendships were amalgamated. You know the films we did, but I think two stand out in my mind—*The Raven *and* Comedy of Terrors.

The combo of Lorre, Boris, Rathbone, and self was very funny and we loved working together and inventing the things everyone thought were written for us. It was fast company and always fun. *I remember a writer was sent by* Playboy *to do a facetious article on "Camp Horror" who came for a day and stayed almost the whole shooting, he was so impressed with the seriousness of our approach to the script and our joy at working together. . . .*

His gratitude is [another] point of admiration—he never down-graded Horror flicks and always thanked God for Frankenstein's Monster.

Once Boris heard I was doing Captain Hook in Peter Pan *and sent me a message to be sure and wear knee pads, as getting* out *of Daddy Darling's Dog House was a strain to say the least. It made a quick change more difficult, but, after forgetting the warning in rehearsal, I saw what he meant and the knee pads were worn!*

We all have a problem with these movies—the suspicion that we are the victims of type-casting. Boris and I discussed this at length, coming to the obvious conclusion that so are John Wayne, Paul Newman, etc., etc.; you're only free of that taint when you begin. One interviewer said to me when I summed up success in the acting world with one word, "survival," that Boris had told him the same thing. I think we all know this—the privilege to be able to continue in one's career to whatever end is all-important and separates the men from the boys; and the desire to survive is what inspires the humanity in an actor—the wit—the possibilities that actor betrays that he is, after all, a human being.

Boris could be defined as a larger than life character—all successful actors are—the nature of the parts he was called upon to play has extended that to larger than death, too, for he is, by another definition of a more mistakenly accepted Art form, Surrealistic, beyond realism, and that, the fantastic, the imaginative, the real-unreal, are what make his work, the legend of himself go on and on. Think how few there are whose pictures are never out of style, or far from the demand of the public to be allowed to escape into pure entertainment.

> *Hope this keeps!*
>
> *Love,*
> *Vincent*

In the late thirties, in a spirit of ominous gloom, Boris stomped through a great many varied radio shows: from playing vis-à-vis Mae West, who portrayed Eve in an Adam and Eve sequence (which brought cries from religious groups as sacrilege), to verbal bouts with Charlie McCarthy. In one appearance on the "Lights Out" series, written by Arch Oboler, Boris co-starred with Mercedes McCambridge, who received excellent reviews as "the gal playing the part of the Evil Voice."*

On November 23, 1938, on his fifty-first birthday, Sara Jane was born to Boris and Dorothy. Sara was so like him it was ridiculous. The same incredible black pansy velvet eyes looking deep into your soul even when you knew she was too little to focus.

The other day, Sara and I looked at some home movies of her christening. Russell and I, who had been married the year before, were two of her godparents (godless parents, I fear, is the more accurate term). There were shots in the movie of everyone holding the baby (who was wearing a tiny white orchid to match her mother's). The one of me is particularly funny. I was hugely pregnant and having a hard time holding her over the mound. It must have been my son Michael's first picture. (The second is one of him, lying in a bassinet, with Sara Jane looking down at him over the edge. She looks as if she were going to bite him.)

Sara Jane and I also looked through an old guest book of this period that Dorothy had given her. We were amazed at how few screen names there were.

---

* Interesting, in that more than thirty-five years later, with a long list of fine performances and an Academy Award in between, she again received excellent reviews for the voice of the Devil Himself in *The Exorcist.*

I was trying to recall what had happened when, but it was too hard. I know that about this time I met Dorothy and Howard Lindsay; Anna Erskine and Russel Crouse (Anna is Russel's widow; at the time she was Russel and Howard's secretary); Ann and Dan Golenpaul, for whom Boris was about to do several guest appearances on their great "Information, Please!" radio show.

"Information, Please!" was one of the professional activities from which Boris derived the most enjoyment. It was the forerunner of all quiz shows, and it was literate, tasteful—and funny. The regular panel consisted of John Kieran, Franklin P. Adams, and Oscar Levant, the quiz master was Clifton Fadiman. These brilliant gentlemen provided a show with never a dull moment. The program, for Boris, represented the first public demonstration of his intellectuality. This was no Monster—this was an erudite gentleman with a sophisticated sense of humor.

Through the Golenpauls I met many more fascinating and delightful people, including Evelyn Helmore, a close friend of the Karloffs. Evie, divorced from actor Tom Helmore, had been working with Maurice Evans in the theater, and at this time—the middle forties—was employed in the story department at the Selznick Studio.

One day, after my return to Hollywood from living in New York, I received a call from Evie. She said there was an opening for readers in her office. I was deeply grateful; she knew I needed work badly. With my usual propensity for leaping at employment, qualified or not, I raced over for my assignment. It was *The Secret Life of Salvador Dali*.

While Evie, her best friend Jane Stone, and I were working on the lot, Boris walked by the window in a Greek army uniform. He must have been filming *Isle of the Dead*, because his hair was tightly curled, and I believe that film was only one of two in which he wore it that way (the other was *The Invisible Ray*). The film was an RKO picture, but they were probably doing location shots on the Selznick back lot. As he walked by, Evie leaned out the window and said, "Aha—I see they finally drafted you." Boris

Scenes from a Karloff home movie. Top: Boris and Sara Jane (complete with corsage) on her christening day. Middle: Boris with my son Michael. Author with Sara Jane. Bottom: Sara Jane and Boris in New York.

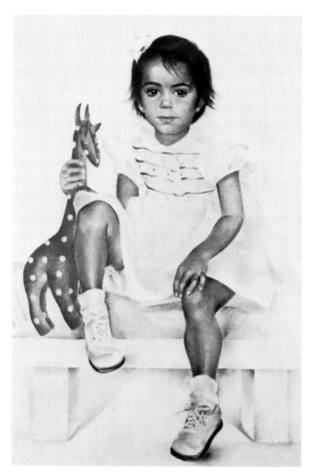 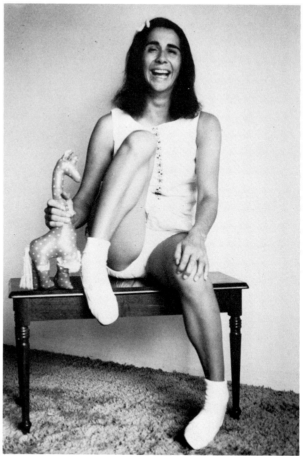

LEFT: *Sara Jane age five (Portrait by Isobelle Magor)*

RIGHT: *Sara Jane age thirty-five. (Photograph by Michael Lindsay)*

roared, came in for a visit, and was surprised to find me on hand, though he knew Jane and Evie worked there. It was explained that I was "an outside reader supposed to work at home" but, having no typewriter, had come in to borrow the one from the office.

That night he arrived at my home with a huge secondhand typewriter under his arm. "Might as well make it as easy on yourself as possible," he said. I expect he thought, having no "fire in my belly" for acting, this might point me toward something else, and, as always, he was there to help out.

Jane Stone, and her husband, Milburn Stone, the famous "Doc" in

"Gunsmoke," remained the Karloffs' close friends through the years, and they and the Ralph Edwardses are today Evie's closest. The Edwardses were the first people Evie took Boris to meet after their wedding, and years later, with combined skulduggery, Ralph and Evie managed to trick Boris into being the guest of honor on Ralph's "This Is Your Life."

While we were trying to put this book together—Evie as Boris's widow, I as Boris's friend—I asked her at what point everyone's position changed: she, the "friend of the family," to she, Boris's future wife. She says she doesn't remember. But Evie, like Boris, is a very private person and also closes a lot of doors. At any rate, the change in relations was not visible even to closest friends.

In trying to help me, Evie let me borrow her diaries of the period. They are no help because they are so impersonal. No "Dear Diary" notes. Just where and with whom she had been. They do include many visits to the hospital to visit Boris when he was there for a back operation, and many games of gin rummy with him.

Incidentally, Boris was outraged at the indignity of surgical preparations involving shaving. When the attendant approached him, Boris snorted, "You are going to *what*?" The attendant, pulling back the covers said, "I'm going to shave you." Boris looked down at the rude procedure. His doctor came in. Boris said, "You know something, this man ought to be on 'What's My Line?'"

Evie's diaries mention the many dinner guests who were entertained at the Karloffs', and there is the gradual emergence of the name of Edgar Rowe. Time passed and a pattern formed: Dorothy and Edgar, Boris and Evie. Eventually Dorothy and Boris were divorced; the pattern was cemented by marriages. Today, Dorothy and Edgar are happily married still. And Evie has the memory of the happiest years of her life—and of Boris's—to help her through missing him.

In 1945, at about the time the scheme of lives changed, my own life experienced tragedy. I was visiting in New York; so was Boris, and his enduring friendship to me was again demonstrated. My husband died under heartbreaking and public circumstances: "Fell or Jumped," the headlines read. My son and I were with the Golenpauls for Christmas. They and all my other friends were magnificent and one friend, Boris, particularly. He talked to the press. He comforted my little boy. He sat with me at the terrible funeral and drove with me through freezing weather to the bleak, frozen burial ground. He stood beside me staring at the Fellini-like scene. It was a military burial and at the incredibly ludicrous moment when the funeral director said, "There will be a two-hour delay—the firing squad is out to lunch," Boris stormed like an avenging angel at the frightened man, *"Get on with it! Now!"*

He got on with it—it was awful.

As we drove home, Boris took my hand and said, "Full marks, old girl—full marks." Somehow it made everything better.

At this time of changing life patterns, Boris was engaged in making some of his favorite films. Beginning in 1945 he did three pictures in a row for Val Lewton to fulfill a three-picture contract with RKO. Lewton, whom James Agee referred to as "the most sensitive movie intelligence in Hollywood," was a man of infinite taste and talent. He had an extremely low-budget unit at RKO for the production of horror films. With a passion for detail, Lewton meticulously followed his productions from conception to completion. For Boris, fresh from gory grunts and shock for shock's sake, Lewton was a savior, and the two worked in mutual admiration and pleasure.

The Lewton unit, with Robert Wise (director and film editor), Mark Robson (director), and Jacques Tourneur (director-producer-writer) among other talents, was a tight, hard-working group—almost a club—its sights set higher than the front office, which was uncooperative, wanting only tighter budgets and no "messages."

Lewton's production designs, and even some of his story lines, were based on paintings which had made deep impressions on him throughout his life: *Isle of the Dead*, inspired by a Böcklin painting he had seen in his childhood, with the battle scene sets suggested by Goya sketches; *Bedlam*, from Hogarth's *Rake's Progress*.

The Body Snatcher was Boris's first Lewton film—from the original Robert Louis Stevenson story, with screenplay by Philip MacDonald and Carlos Keith (Carlos Keith was Lewton's pseudonym—he worked on all screenplays, seldom taking credit), and directed by Robert Wise.

TOP: *Boris with Elsie the cow.*

BOTTOM: *Boris with Violet the pig*, au naturel *(divested of her sweater, hand-knit by author)*.

I went to see Bob to talk about Boris and he was no different from anyone else: regard, respect, admiration, affection. He hadn't known him, or even met him, before the film.

"It was strange—the first meeting," he said. "Boris came to the studio for a meeting with Val, Mark, and me. I had never seen him except on the screen—and this was before color film. When he first walked in the door I was startled by his coloring, the strange bluish cast—but when he turned those eyes on us and that velvet voice said, 'Good afternoon, gentlemen,' we were his, and never thought about anything else."

Isle of the Dead, taken from the Böcklin painting, amusingly has credits: original story (painting), Böcklin; screenplay, Ardel Wray and Josef Mischel. Miss Wray, an integral part of the Lewton unit, is credited with a statement about Boris in Joel E. Siegel's excellent book on Lewton. After very few days' shooting, Boris's back flared up and he was in agony. "Between shots, he was in a wheelchair but he made no complaints," she said. "He managed to be wryly humorous about it—not falsely, in that obnoxious 'see how brave I'm being way.' Everyone liked and respected him."

The pain in the back became so devastating that the company had to shut down on a production started in July, not to return until September, when Boris was out of the hospital.

Like *Isle of the Dead*, *Bedlam* gives original story credit to: painting, William Hogarth; screenplay, Mark Robson and Carlos Keith (Val Lewton); director, Mark Robson.

Bedlam was more an historical documentary than a "horror" film, but the history of Saint Mary of Bethlehem Hospital for the Insane, London, 1773, was so truly horrible, and Lewton and Robson's dedication to the truth so rigid, that the film is indeed terrifying. It was originally called *Chamber of Horrors*, then *A Tale of Bedlam*, and finally *Bedlam*, which was a contraction of Bethlehem, and which was the title of the original Hogarth picture.

Boris always spoke of Lewton as "the man who rescued me from the living dead and restored my soul."

Unfortunately, Val Lewton is no longer alive to answer questions about Boris. His wife, Ruth, is, and I called her at the suggestion of Robert Wise. By this time, I was almost hoping someone would say, "The man was a bastard." Ruth Lewton was charming. "Val adored him," she said. "I knew him only slightly, but what a lovely, lovely man."

OPPOSITE: Arsenic and Old Lace.

Boris continued to snort, snarl, stomp, and read seriously lines like, "Ha-ha! Thank you, Master, for letting me do the job—I've never killed in hot blood before!" And, "Man who flirt with dynamite may learn to fly with angels!" And he continued to give interviews. My favorite of all was one entitled "A Portrait of Boris Karloff—by Boris Karloff."* It was accompanied by a splendid drawing of a skeleton under which was written in Boris's hand, "Boris Karloff sketched in the nude." As follows:

Chief Phobia: Stage fright, somewhat relieved by inability to see the audience due to acute nearsightedness.

Fond Parental Desire: To place me in the British consular service in China along with my two brothers.

Favorite Reading Matter: Anything written by Joseph Conrad.

My Fortune: My face.

Supplementary Asset: My walk, which looks antediluvian but is just a special form of clumsiness.

Politest Role: The part of the unfrocked clergyman in *Five Star Final*.

Formula for Success: Stand on the right corner at the right moment.

Strangest Interlude: Driving a truck in Hollywood for eighteen months to keep off the extra list after once working up to the status of featured player.

Cosmic Suggestion: The complete abolition of all trade barriers to bring about at least a partial abolition of poverty.

Secret Ambition: To be an actor.

Most of Boris's interviews, nevertheless, involved questions about "typing." He always surprised reporters by answering he didn't mind at all because if the type happened to be popular, an actor was guaranteed employment. "A cobbler," he said, "should stick to his last. I'm happy to have a last."

At one point he was asked what he thought of the fact that Marilyn Monroe was about to co-star with Laurence Olivier in Terence Rattigan's

---

* The article was clipped from a newspaper by Evie Karloff—regrettably the name of the paper was cut off, and it can't be traced for proper credit.

The Sleeping Prince (released as *The Prince and the Showgirl*). Boris said, "I think the experience will be wonderful for both of them, particularly Larry, and I think Marilyn has great courage. Marilyn and I have something in common, you know—that extraordinary blonde I saw in *How to Marry a Millionaire* [—that performance] could become for her what *Frankenstein* was for me. That's why I admire her courage. The transition is painful, but she's young and she's wise to get out of that narrow type. Why, a woman of her natural endowments would be pinched in such a trap.

"Marilyn is probably grateful for the attention—not to mention the cash—her monster has won for her, just as I am. But can you imagine that girl living up to what she looks like?"

Along came the chance for his greatest piece of type-casting. Russel Crouse called Boris and invited him to lunch at the old Lucy's Restaurant in Hollywood. Howard Lindsay,* Russel Crouse, and Boris were long-time friends, so Boris went off happily for a social get-together. He was, therefore, completely taken aback when Russel said, "Boris, there's a play Howard and I want you to do in New York." Boris replied that he was flattered, but wouldn't consider it for a moment. "I am a provincial actor, Buck," he said (all Crouse's friends called him "Buck"), "and provincial actors no more than film actors belong on Broadway."

"But this is a very special kind of play," Crouse said.

"I don't care how special it is," Boris replied. "And being yours, I'm sure it is special—I just wouldn't consider doing a play unless there were at least three parts more important than mine. The responsibility of stardom on Broadway is too much for me."

"You're on," said Crouse. "There are exactly three parts more important than yours."

"Now, you interest me—tell me about the part."

"Suppose I tell you just one line you will have?"

"Fine. Can you sell me on one line?"

"I think so. You have just murdered a man, and when questioned

---

* No relation of mine except by deep affection: The Lindsay-Crouse family, however, were so close that the Crouses named their daughter Lindsay Ann Crouse, as in Lindsay and Crouse—get it? When I wired the two families of my marriage to Louis Lindsay, I added, "naming first daughter Crouse Ann." Although my daughter's name is Meg, Dorothy Stickney Lindsay still refers to her as "Crouse Ann."

about it, you answer, 'I killed him because he said I looked like Boris
Karloff.' "

Boris guffawed, and was so enchanted by the idea of making fun of
himself that he agreed to do the play. The rest, as they say, is theater history.
Arsenic and Old Lace ran for three-and-a-half years, made many millions of
dollars, and went on the road (is still on the road all over the world and has
piled up the world's record for attendance). Interestingly enough, two
motion picture companies refused to invest in the Broadway version because
they "couldn't see a play in it." Boris also was of little faith. So little, in fact,
that he initially refused to invest in the play. Howard and Russel held out a
$2,500 investment until the show opened, and then they asked him whether he
had changed his mind. He had. And they kidded him for his parsimony
throughout the run of the show. They also offered him a new contract:
twenty-five dollars a week and all the money tossed up on the stage.

When Boris went to New York for rehearsals in 1941 he was in
abject terror. His first reading for Lindsay and Crouse was disastrous. He
stammered. He stuttered. He sweated. Buck and Howard, as was their wont,
were kind and gentle and the performance improved; but Boris didn't think
so. He took to walking the streets at night. One night he walked from
Broadway to 57th Street over to Fifth Avenue all the way down to Green-
wich Village. "I made my decision," he said. "I was lousy. There were no
two ways about it. I was going to Buck and Howard and Windy [Bretaigne
Windust, the director] and say, 'Forgive me—tell me how much money I owe
you—I'm going home.' Then I turned and started uptown, and all I could
think of was how kind everybody had been—and I knew I had to do it."

He went to work, and whether from unaccustomed strain on his voice,
or pure nerves, lost his voice. The undaunted Windust calmly fixed him a
corncob pipe filled with cotton soaked in eucalyptus oil. Boris puffed away
between lines and the voice soon returned. He managed, however, while
sweating away at rehearsals, to lose fifty-six pounds.

Joseph Kesselring's insane frolic about two old ladies who go about
murdering people just because they are sorry for them, with the simple device

of a drop of arsenic in a glass of homemade elderberry wine, was a delight and a smash hit. Josephine Hull and Jean Adair as the aunts, flitting about eliminating folks, John Alexander, under the impression he was Teddy Roosevelt, in solar topee, lumbering up the stairs crying "Charge!" and Boris skulking in and out of doors and/or window boxes, held audiences in hysterics.

There was one moment better described by "Ollie" Carey, the widow of Harry Carey (remember *Trader Horn*?): "I remember in *Arsenic* when Boris held the audience for three minutes without speaking a word. He was going upstairs with his back turned to the audience—and there was not even a whisper or a sound—it was his magnetism and hypnotism that did it—such a fine actor—too bad that he isn't around any more to teach some of these pecker-necks that the movie producers are foisting on the public these days as stars."

After first-night rave reviews, Howard and Buck came in to Boris's dressing room to congratulate him and see if he had any complaints about anything. Boris was holding a fuzzy toy panda sent him for luck by his little daughter. Sara Jane said it looked like Boris (there *was* the same woolly quality about both of them). Boris just said, "What luck—what extraordinary luck! Think of it—a broken-down movie actor in a hit play!"

Boris's run in *Arsenic* was for over fourteen hundred performances in New York and six weeks on the road. The association was one of complete happiness for him with one great exception: Lindsay and Crouse gave his role (Jonathan) to Raymond Massey in the movie version. Boris was heartbroken. Most of the rest of the cast went to Hollywood, playing their original roles, and he was left bereft, to carry on alone—and angry. Anna Crouse remembers this: "There is one strange conflict in a story about Boris and the film of *Arsenic*. Howard and Russel always credited him with being a sweetheart and a gentleman in allowing Josephine and Jean to play the picture while he stayed in New York and kept the play going. 'What a saintly thing to do for two old ladies,' they said. I have heard rumors that he was bitter he did not make the picture and somehow blamed Howard and Russel. I know they went to their deaths believing that Boris offered to stay with the play."

Boris was not mad enough, apparently, to endanger his undying affection for Anna and Russel, and Howard Lindsay and Dorothy Stickney. When I asked Dorothy if she had anything particular to tell me of Boris, she said,

Boris, Russel Crouse, and Howard Lindsay hamming it up—preparing to toast the lucky backers of Arsenic.

"Just that I loved him. Who didn't? Of course, we had a great deal in common —he's the only other actor I know who played Minot, North Dakota."

Anna later wrote me:

During the first summer the play ran, Boris got even darker, and Howard and Russel told him he was going to have to purchase some white powder to look less healthy. He objected that it wasn't called for in his contract, so I was sent out to buy every form of powder on the market—foot, roach, baby, tooth, baking, gunpowder, Seidlitz powders, and powdered eggs. I remember wrapping it all in a Bergdorf Goodman dress box and delivering it to the Fulton Theater. They also paid him his two thousand dollar salary in nickels one week.

Before her marriage to Russel Crouse, Anna Erskine not only managed correspondence and varied business affairs for Lindsay and Crouse but also handled Boris's fan mail for three years. When the Crouses married, Boris wired Anna: "The best news we have had for years. When do we see you? Must make other arrangements for my mail. Refuse to contribute to Buck's support. Love, Boris."

In one special performance at West Point Academy, the *Arsenic* company set a record for itself and the Academy. It was the first Broadway play put on in the Academy's (then) 139-year history, and the audience of over three thousand cadets, officers, and friends was the largest to which the company had ever played. Said audience was also so appreciative with stompings, "Hurrahs!!" and general all-out enthusiasm, that after ten minutes of steady demonstration it had to be quieted by police. "I imagine they liked it," Boris said.

At about the same period—in the mid-forties—Boris took time for another special performance—playing Santa Claus in the Children's Wing at the Beekman Downtown Hospital. This audience also was so full of enthusiasm that additional aides had to be called in to quell it, because in their excitement to get to Boris the children knocked down the Christmas tree.

When Boris returned to Hollywood after three-plus years with *Arsenic* (on Broadway and on tour), he was in command of a salary three times what it had been when he left.

In 1945 Evie (still) Helmore came up to the Karloffs' house in Hollywood one day and said she had just heard from Maurice Evans, who was in charge of entertainment for the army in the Central Pacific. He had asked Evie to request a picture of Boris as Jonathan in *Arsenic*, as the section was about to do the play. "So I wrote him that I'd go him one better," Boris said later to the same alleged magazine reporter sent by Ralph Edwards. "If he could stand it, I would be pleased to come out and do it myself. So, out I went. It took a bit of arranging—not easy. I was not only the only actor, except for George Schaefer, who directed it—he played the Teddy Roosevelt part—he was good, too—but he and I were the only civilians outside of three local women. The others were all boys in uniform. I had the most wonderful time! We played every camp and air strip there was. I was gone almost four months. We were on Oahu, then up to Midway, to Canton, and to the Marshalls, and camped on Christmas Island. Then we went to Johnson's Island, my favorite. It's virtually just a landing strip, about a thousand miles from Hawaii. The island is only about three hundred yards long and a hundred yards wide. While we were there, I was wandering around one day at the far end—there isn't any *far* end, really—and I bumped into a young marine, just a kid who recognized me. He asked me what the hell I was doing there—a good question if you think about it—and I told him. He said, 'And are you playing here tonight?' I said, 'Yes.' He said, 'Well, I think I'll just take it in—you know, I haven't been downtown in two weeks.' Just marvelous. He was perfectly serious. I hope he heard some of the play. The little make-shift theater was cheek-by-jowl with the loading zone where they revved the planes up before taking them out on the runway—so always on your best lines, there'd be a blast of engines—talk about point killers. The whole trip was a wonderful experience. I wouldn't take anything for it."

George Schaefer, like anyone who ever worked with Boris, loved him. "I've never seen such enthusiasm," he said. "He was in and out of everything. The men were crazy about him. When he wasn't playing with them on stage he was visiting others in hospitals. He never complained—and we were pretty uncomfortable at times. Boris treated the whole thing like a picnic." (Schaefer, incidentally, later directed Boris in television versions of both *Arsenic and Old Lace* and *The Lark* and on the Broadway stage in *The Linden Tree*.)

When Boris returned from the Pacific, Evie had left Selznick and gone to New York to be Maurice Evans's production assistant on his modern-dress *Hamlet*. Boris and Dorothy's marriage had broken up, and he went to Nevada to get a divorce.

The last time Boris performed in *Arsenic* on the stage was long after he and Evie were married. It was 1957, and according to Arthur Kennedy, a friend and an actor Boris admired profoundly, "Boris read in the London *Times* that oil had been discovered in an area of Alaska where he had some holdings. Evie got busy, checked with Boris's agent regarding some job that would pay for a trip from London. The agent said the only thing possible was a stock company in Puerto Rico. Boris, being an old stock actor, was always up in a couple of plays, and he agreed to do *Arsenic* for them, then had the agent pick up a couple of TV shows in New York. From New York he called the president of the university in Anchorage, and offered to play *Arsenic*. The president was stunned, said this was an amateur performance— couldn't possibly pay Boris's salary. Boris said that could be worked out, and the Karloffs were off to the oil fields."

Boris's performance with the Anchorage Community College Workshop was, for Alaska, a cultural milestone. It was the first time a recognized star had gone to the Territory to perform in an Alaskan production. The Karloffs' reception was overwhelming. They loved the place and the people, and the feeling was reciprocated. When asked what could be done for them in gratitude, they replied there were some oil fields they wanted to see, and they needed a plane. Two small planes on skis were provided, and they took off for the fields, flew over frozen lakes, and landed at the drilling site. They were shown a well, and Evie said, "There really *is* oil, then? I want a bottle to take home." A small bottle of oil was provided, and they took off for the return to Anchorage. Evie said later, "I wanted to fly over an active volcano, so the pilot flew low over one to get a better view. Suddenly the cork popped out of the bottle of oil from the updraft from the volcano, and the oil spilt all over me. I took the remainder in the bottle back to New York, then to London with me, and said to Boris, 'Well—at least we have *some* oil.' Then we had to make a decision about whether to maintain the holdings—putting more money in, or what to do. Boris said, 'If it came in—it would be so much money that it would only be a burden—let's let it go.' So we let it go."

Apparently Boris was able to turn away from fortunes at will. According to Arthur Kennedy, he did the same thing on television. "It was 'The $64,000 Question,' in 1956," Kennedy said. "Before the scandal—Boris had chosen children's fairy tales as his subject—he was sensational—answered them all—went all the way to the $32,000 question. The announcer said, 'NOW! Will you try for the $64,000?' Boris threw them all by saying, 'No.' It seems he had consulted his tax lawyer and accountant and figured to the dime what it would have cost him if he had gone all the way and won."

To return to somewhere in the midst of later performances of *Arsenic*, one day I received a telephone call in Hollywood: "Cyn?" Unmistak-

able voice, and I hadn't seen Boris for over a year as I remember. It was 1946.

"I'm in Boulder City, Nevada." (What the hell was he doing in Boulder City, Nevada?) "I need a favor."

"Granted."

"I would be forever grateful if you would go down to the Miramar Hotel in Santa Monica and fill our room with flowers. I'm bringing my bride home and I'd hate to have Evie come into a room with no flowers when I carry her over the threshold."

Evie! Bride! I nearly dropped the telephone. I didn't even know Boris and Dorothy were divorced. I just sat there with the telephone in my hand.

"Are you there?"

"Yes," I answered. "I'm here, but you can understand that I'm a little stunned. When were you divorced?"

"Yesterday."

"And you were married today?"

"Right. No point in wasting time. Cyn?"

"Yes," I gasped.

"I'd appreciate it if you keep this our secret. The papers will get it, but I don't want anyone nosing around. I have been married four times before —they didn't matter really, mostly, but it would be nicer for Evie not to have it mentioned."

"Right."

He thanked me. "We'll see you very soon," he said.

I went to the hotel, fixed the flowers, put a bottle of champagne, a pot of caviar, and a Gideon Bible in the refrigerator, and left.

In talking of the wedding later with Sara Jane, I asked her what she remembered of it.

"Very little," she said. "There's nothing to remember. I was home from school sick. My mother came into my room and said, 'I have some good news and some bad—which do you want first?' I don't remember choosing. Then

Evie and Boris both looking glamorous as they emerge from a New York premiere.

she said, 'Your father and I are divorced. Your father married Evie this afternoon'—and she left."

Now, stick with me, because this is where it gets complicated. You will remember, Evie was formerly married to an actor-writer, Tom Helmore. You do *not* know that Tom, his present wife, writer Mary Drayton, and their daughter Kristin (called Kit) were among Evie and Boris's closest friends— still are among Evie's. Mary, a kind lady, realizing the problems of writing such a book as this, called me and said she had a few notes that might be helpful if I could use them. A portion of her letter:

Dear Cynie,

Herewith the little anecdotes about Boris, hope you'll find them helpful. Just in putting them down on paper I begin to see your problem . . . the aura or essence or whatever that thing is that he had in such abundance ain't all that easy to convey, is it? So, all I've done is just recount the incidents . . . which, I suppose, may give some hint of the man, for goodness knows none of them could have happened as they did with anyone else.

Tom and I had been married less than a year when a Metro contract brought us out here from N.Y. The red carpet started rolling out in Pasadena with the full limousine treatment, etc., plus the news that enough important strings had been pulled to get us into "a great hotel for two weeks." (In those days hotels would only keep you for a few days. . . .) When we asked what hotel we were told "the Miramar in Santa Monica. . . ." Tom and I looked at each other . . . that was where Evie and Boris, who had just been married, were staying. Naturally we'd known we'd be running into them sometimes if we were all to be living in California . . . but we hadn't expected it so soon.

When we got to our room we talked it over and decided that since no one had any rancor against anyone it would be silly not to behave in a normally friendly way, and both felt Evie and Boris would agree with that attitude. Still, we couldn't be sure and decided it would be less awkward to let them know we were there than to run into them in the lobby. So Tom called on the house phone and the conversation went something like this:

TOM: Evie? . . . Tom.

EVIE: Tom! We heard you were coming out. When did you get here?

TOM: Just now. Just checked into the hotel.

EVIE: Where are you staying?

TOM: Er . . . at the Miramar.

EVIE: The Miramar? You mean . . . ?

TOM: That's right. Only place Metro could get to keep us until we find a house.

EVIE: What's your room number?

TOM: 620.

EVIE: Ours is 622.

TOM: I know. I can hear you through the wall.

EVIE: Boris! It's Tom. He and Mary are here, and guess where they are! Right next door!

BORIS: Great! Ask them to have dinner with us. I know a good place near the hotel.

After that dinner we were firm and fast friends, saw each other frequently, and had great fun together. . . . While we were still at the Miramar we went together to the tennis matches one afternoon. After they were over the four of us were standing outside the Club with a lot of other people waiting for our cars to be brought around. As we chatted it happened that Boris and I were rather away from Evie and Tom, who were right at the curb. Suddenly Rex Harrison saw them and came over to them, saying, as they greeted each other . . .

REX: Well! The Helmores! Haven't seen you since London . . . that day in your flat in Grosvenor Gardens. What's been happening with you?

TOM: Quite a lot, actually. Evie is now Mrs. Boris Karloff.

REX (*Looking from one to another, frowning*): You don't say . . . I hadn't heard.

Evie was apparently so flustered that she became as confused as Rex. She pointed to Boris and me and said, "Yes, and Boris is married to Mary Drayton!"

REX (*Just looked from one to another of us and gasped*): "Really? . . . Well, it all sounds simply delightful!"

(His car arrived, and he got in and drove off.)

But Rex was right, it was all delightful. Throughout the years Tom and I saw Boris and Evie a great deal and no one ever had sweeter, kinder, more thoughtful or more fun friends. And our work seemed to throw us together whether in California or New York. If we had houses they were often in the same area, or we'd find ourselves at the Chateau Marmont at the same time. And then there were years when we both lived at the Dakota in New York.

The Dakota was a wonderful place to live and while we were there it seemed to be filled with theater people, most of whom were dear close friends whom we saw constantly, for cocktails, for poker, etc. Tom says we once went to five Christmas parties in our bedroom slippers . . . inaccurate but indicative of the coziness of the atmosphere. Kristin was five when we moved there so she was as delighted as Tom and I when the Karloffs took a charming apartment on the top floor shortly afterward. She had always adored Boris and Evie and felt a closeness already which just grew stronger living under the same roof.

The close relationship between Kit and the Karloffs continued as she grew older. They always were a large part of her life. . . .

As I read these incidents again I wonder if they'll be any use to you at all. I remember so many other things, his kindnesses, his patience, his wit, his bravery with all that pain . . . what a wonderful man. One often says it, but in his case it is certainly true that it was a privilege to know him.

Love,
Mary

Obviously, the Helmores knew more of the impending marriage than those of us friends who had been separated by miles for a long time, because Tom Helmore wrote Mrs. Lina Adamson, Evie's mother, a letter before Evie and Boris were married. It must be a one-of-a-kind letter from an ex-husband to his former mother-in-law:

Boris relaxed and happy (and unaware of double exposure of lady's leg in background.)

Dear Mrs. Adamson,

I expect you will have heard by now about Evelyn's forthcoming marriage to Boris and I realize it must be difficult for you to have any definite opinions about this, partly because you don't know the guy and partly because you probably feel that anything Evelyn may tell you about him would be slightly prejudiced!

Personally, I am so happy about it for her, that I cannot resist breaking a long silence to tell you so. To say that Boris is just about "the nicest person I have ever met" may sound trite and inadequate but it does truthfully sum up how I feel about him. In fact, when I first met him in Hollywood some five years ago the first thing that struck me was the utter incongruity that such a sensitive, kind, and altogether delightful person should be called upon to portray the roles that have made him famous. Thus do the moguls of Hollywood fool their worldwide audiences! [*The letter went on with personal greetings and news.*]

When, years later, I met Mrs. Adamson, it was obvious that she was a part of the Boris Admiration Society. After he and Evie returned to England, Mrs. Adamson lived next door to the Karloffs' London apartment, and frequently visited them in the cottage in Bramshott, so they were very close. She also spent six months in Hollywood with them during the early years of their marriage. This frail, beautiful lady talked to me of him:

"A sensitive, graceful man," she said. "So careful of others, so deeply considerate. I often think how dreadful for him to do those awful things—things I don't even like to *think* about! Of course, Boris always said they weren't really horrible—just fairy stories; and of course the children all loved him. I suppose they saw through all that stuff to *him*.

"He was keen—terribly keen, even when he was in the leg brace. He was keen on everything. It was hard to get around, but he got there. Even when he was so very ill at the last, he'd always say, 'I'm fine, just fine.'"

Wouldn't you think one could come up with something negative about the man from, at least, a mother-in-law?

OPPOSITE: *Patiently becoming a wolf.*

17 / "AS PATIENT AS A HORSE"

In 1947 Boris played in the screen version of James Thurber's *The Secret Life of Walter Mitty* starring Danny Kaye. And he gave that beautiful master of nonsense a run for his money in a vignette in which he played the head of a gang masquerading as a psychiatrist. Boris seldom had a crack at comedy and he loved this one. When I asked Danny if he had anything to say about Boris, I knew the answer I was going to get: "I didn't know him very well, he was lovely to work with, no trouble you know, a pro. . . ." Etc., etc., etc.

The same year, Boris co-starred with Lucille Ball in a foggy London overcoat film called *Lured*, in which his villainous meanderings were only a red herring dragged across the trail of the real killer.

Having survived that, he performed in a beaut called *Dick Tracy Meets Gruesome*, playing an ex-convict paralyzed by nerve gas who wakes in the mortuary, beleaguers the town, kills a number of people, imperils Mr. Tracy, and is finally done in by same.

Then he rose from Tracy-imposed death and landed in the middle of a gigantic Cecil B. De Mille epic called *Unconquered*, starring Gary Cooper, in which he played a Seneca Indian Chief called Guyasuta. The film cost four million dollars, had ninety-three speaking parts, and used more than four thousand extras. Nerves, at times, were bound to be frayed, and a man of Boris's temperament must have been a blessing to those in production. There was one wonderful moment in which Boris was in wardrobe being fitted into an Indian blanket, headdress (head shaved for this one; grew in good and fuzzy), and all the trimmings. His back was bad and he was wearing a brace, so the fitting was even more difficult than it would normally have been. He had been standing quietly for three hours while the costume was worked on by a wardrobe man who was a deaf-mute. The wardrobe man suddenly rose from his knees, where he had been pinning up Boris's blanket, and signaled in sign language to a man across the room. His friend smiled and nodded. Boris said, "What did he say?" The friend answered, "He said, 'This man is as patient as a horse.'"

Being used to type-casting, Boris was not surprised to find himself another Indian immediately following the De Mille film. This was in *Tap Roots* and Boris was a Choctaw. The tribes switched, but the part of Tishomingo, the medicine man, was not much progress from Guyasuta. By 1949

Al Hirschfeld cartoon of Una O'Connor and Boris in The Linden Tree.

the powers felt he had been disguised enough and threw him a number called *Abbott and Costello Meet the Killer, Boris Karloff*. Another red herring, but also another Indian—Eastern this time, the kind that wear turbans.

Despite business being good in films, Boris's first love remained the stage. He was not merely appreciative of fine performances by other actors, he was worshipful. Arthur Kennedy, Laurence Olivier, Alan Webb, and Alec

Boris and Maurice Evans on Arsenic *tour. Boris wrote Sara Jane: "Yes—*
I know the button on my shirt and the zipper on my pants show and I am
grinning so hard there is all the bridgework."

Guinness were his favorite actors. After leaving a performance of Alan Webb's he said, "I'm going back to California—I know nothing about acting." He left the theater crying after an Alec Guinness play, and once after watching Laurence Olivier he walked up the aisle shaking his head and saying, "And to think—he wore my boots." (Olivier had played at the Hollywood Cricket Club.)

So after all the spooking around, Boris was delighted to be called back again to his first love. In 1946 he had a brief run on the stage in Hollywood in Paul Osborn's *On Borrowed Time* (his favorite play, incidentally). In

1948 Maurice Evans was about to produce J. B. Priestley's *The Linden Tree* on Broadway, to be directed by George Schaefer, and both Evans and Schaefer wanted Boris to play the lead of the quiet, erudite professor of history who has one ruling passion: "Stick to the job." (True type-casting this time.) Boris said "Yes" with alacrity. Since their association in the Pacific, Evans, Schaefer, and Boris had wanted to be together again. The situation was ideal—but there was a hitch. J. B. Priestley, the author, told Evans, "Good Lord *no*! Not Karloff! Put that man's name on a marquee and people will think my play's about an axe murderer. I'll take your word for the fact he could play it, but I can't risk it." Boris cabled Priestley in London: "Dear Mr. Priestley. I am sorely disappointed that you do not wish me to do your play. It is a beautiful play, and I promise you I wouldn't have eaten the baby in the last act." Priestley was so amused he cabled Evans in New York: "Let him do it."

The play had been running for six months in London and all concerned were optimistic for the same in New York. It opened to rave reviews on March 2, 1948, and lasted for seven performances. For Boris, the play was a personal triumph, as witness:

Brooks Atkinson (*New York Times*): Give *The Linden Tree* credit for one achievement. It proves that Boris Karloff is an extraordinarily winning actor. He plays the venerable academician with attractive, humorsome conviction. He has warmth and magnetism and those beetling brows, which can scare you in his shiver-plays, can soothe you with wisdom when he is in a benevolent mood.

George Freedly (*Telegraph*): We all can be grateful—as were all the critics—for the fact that *The Linden Tree* brought us a new Boris Karloff. There is so much gentleness, so much perceptiveness in his portrayal that he really makes you feel he is an old university don. He projects perfectly in the theater and shows none of the inability to enlarge his character to full theater size that besets most of the people who have long acted in films. Mr. Karloff is a superb actor.

Howard Barnes (New York *Herald Tribune*): By the sheer sincerity of his performance he bolsters up one interlude after another which fall in no perceptible pattern. He works hard in a drama which he dominates for much of the three hours.

Boris tucked his reviews under his arm, returned home, but was called back in January 1949 to have a go at another play on Broadway. This was *The Shop at Sly Corner* by Edward Percy. It had run for two years in London, but closed after five days in New York, proving again that what the English like, the Americans do not necessarily also. Boris said, "It was the usual actor's trap—a jolly good part in a very bad play. I fell into the trap. No excuse, I should have known better."

OPPOSITE: *Alex Segal and Boris working on a script.*

The comment made by Evie's mother, Mrs. Adamson, about children seeing through to Boris was more true of him in real life than it was of what they saw on the screen. He displayed an incredible quality with them. I don't know of a child who ever met him who did not immediately succumb to the magic. He never talked down to them, he talked *to* them. It was effortless.

When he was in New York playing in *Arsenic*, he went to Marguerite and Howard Cullman's house in the country for the weekend. Their daughter was five years old and had never been to a motion picture, but Marguerite thought that one of the servants who had been titillated by Boris's presence might have brought up the bogeyman subject, and the child might be afraid. She went looking for her to explain that this was really a nice man and found the two of them in the bottom of the garden. The child was sitting in Boris's lap and he was reading her fairy tales. Later Marguerite said to her daughter, "Did you like Mr. Karloff?" "Oh, yes!" she said, "and it's not just because he's so beautiful!"

My children adored him, the Helmores' child adored him, and he returned their affection, particularly in the case of Kit Helmore. At one point Kit was in school in England, her parents in the United States. She was homesick and miserable. So her friend Boris wrote her parents:

Dear Tom and Mary,

Here comes the old man from the sea with his two cents worth, but I promise you it won't be long.

It all seems to boil down to this. She is too young for her to be so far away from you two with so large and expensive a body of water between you. Taking it for granted that Frithim was not the right school, and getting her into another school is not the answer. She would still be desperately homesick. Above all, she wants to be with you two, to have the family together or at least within reach of each other.

The letter goes on with recommendations for further schooling, and ends:

Advice from the sidelines is so damned easy and so tempting so please don't bloody my nose.

> *All our love*
> *as ever,*
> *Boris*

Even with long drawers on it's cold as hell at rugger but still. . . .

His line, "Above all, she wants to be with you two, to have the family together or at least within reach of each other," is tragic in view of the yearning his own child had to be in reach of him. I've wondered about it through the years. These two magnificent people who would have been so enriched knowing each other, never did. Boris and Evie were always on the wing—California to New York, to London, to Rome, to wherever the films or the plays took them. When they were in California, where Sara lived, visits were brief, unsatisfactory to both parties. He never really knew his grandchildren, Michael and David Cotten, another terrible loss—they are remarkable children. Michael has a publicity photo of Boris on his bulletin board. It is signed, "To Michael, from his grandfather, Boris Karloff."

Michael and David call Edgar Rowe, their mother's stepfather, "Granddad"; they called Boris and Evie "Opa" and "Oma"—names suggested by Boris on his return from a trip during which he had been charmed by the Dutch names for grandparents. He suggested them "to avoid confusion." When Sara told David that Boris had died, David said, "Oh, I hope Oma is not going to be lonely."

Recently, my son Michael and Sara were talking of Boris, and Michael reminisced about something funny Boris had done at some point. Sara said, "I didn't know about it. Of course, you knew him better than I did."

In talking of him with me, she said, "I remember him as a deep, warm, compassionate, truly kind human being, and I just didn't know him. I was an observer by infrequent invitation. When he was here, I'd take a three-and-a-half-hour trip to have a visit with him, and it wasn't really a visit. It wasn't his fault. He could have closed the door on me apart from legal support and the trust fund, but he didn't. He left it open a crack for me. I have so few personal memories . . . just that when I went to visit we always played gin

Publicity shots of Boris in costume. At left, as Mord in Tower of London, *he's with Baby Sandy (Sandra Henielle), and at right, as the Monster, he looms over baby Bela Lugosi, Jr. But no matter what the disguise, Boris never frightened children.*

rummy—and he always beat the pants off me. I do remember that when I was little he told me stories, and that his favorite was about Groundhog Day. Something about the little thing emerging from its hole, seeing its shadow, and scurrying back in always appealed to him. He died on Groundhog Day, you know.

"The saddest thing about our meetings was the acute sense of disappointment. I always hoped that *this* time we'd find each other. The meetings were so brief. I think *he* felt I did it out of duty. *I* was convinced that was the only reason he had seen me at all. And the meetings were over before he had a chance to say much more than, 'How are the boys?' "

When, at nineteen, Sara was wed—a marriage to which both her parents were strongly opposed—Boris wrote that he did not wish to be a part of a large, formal wedding and reception because he would be "an object of curiosity." But if she would have a small, private one he would certainly be there. However, if her heart was set on a large wedding, he would send her a check. Somehow another sad misunderstanding—Sara thought he didn't want to come at all. "I was hurt at the time," she said, "but I think he was right. He would have had to sneak into town, reporters would have come, and it would have changed the complexion of the wedding. Besides, I would have been hard put to decide on whose arm I should walk down the aisle—my father's or Edgar's. It was better in the long run." And another misunderstanding: Boris thought Sara preferred a large wedding to his presence.

Why was it that these two never found each other? Although Boris never completely closed the door on his daughter, leaving it open a chink (too narrow, sadly, to get through), he also left her to a life in which he did not participate. Did he feel that Edgar Rowe, whom he knew his daughter loved and for whom he had great respect, was doing the job so well he didn't want to interfere? Or were this father and daughter so basically, deeply shy that neither could reach out to the other? What a loss for both of them.

When Boris died, Sara first learned of his death from the television set and had to call the newspapers for details. Evie's cable never came through.

As he loved children, so did Boris love animals and spent the days when I first knew him trailed by a pack of them. If he visited a house, any animal about would land up either in his arms or leaning heavily on him. I always had a

sense that I should watch the goldfish bowl for fear the fish would end up in his lap.

He had friends who had a large, fierce German shepherd who would have nothing to do with anyone except his owners. Nobody dared approach the dog. But Boris spent every evening in the house with the beast's head heavy on his lap, Boris scratching away while chatting with them. Several months after Boris died, the friends heard the dog crying and went to see what was the matter. He was clawing at the back of the television set. Boris was on in an old movie, and the shepherd was trying to get to him once again.

In 1950 Boris returned to New York for a role that gave him an opportunity to play with and to as many children as he wanted. He signed to play Captain Hook and Mr. Darling to Jean Arthur's Peter Pan. But at the same time he was heavily engaged in television, the future of which he was one of the few important actors to appreciate. I remember well going to visit him on a set in New York, where the majority of live television was then being produced. He was in dinner clothes, looking magnificent; actresses were standing about in ball gowns; a couple of crystal chandeliers were strung from uprights—all very grand. Boris's enthusiasm was enchanting.

"These men, Cyn, are the future of the industry. These young directors are incredible. What they get on that little screen with very little to work with is nothing short of miraculous. Extraordinary. Full marks to them, I say, full marks."

"Mr. Karloff . . . ," the assistant director called.

"Coming," he answered. "Back in a moment, darling. This is a short scene." He leapt over a cable and loped toward the set. I was amused to see he was wearing black sneakers with his dinner clothes—the better to speed from one scene to another.

Later, in an interview, he answered a question regarding television: "Television has tremendous charm. It requires a continued sustained effort like a play; in that one half-hour you are absolutely on your own. Nobody can help you. There are eight million eavesdroppers but you are alone in the world for half an hour. As opposed to pictures, the clock is ticking and there's no stopping it. If your head falls off at five minutes to nine you have to screw it back on. It's a hideous kind of excitement, a terrific stimulus."

From the early days on, Boris enjoyed the medium that so many people mocked, and he was right about the directors—John Frankenheimer, George Schaefer, Alex Segal, Arthur Penn, George Roy Hill, Franklin Schaffner, Sidney Lumet, Robert Mulligan, Arthur Hiller, Norman Jewison, Ralph Nelson, all of whom received their training in those early days.

Frankenheimer directed Boris in a CBS "Playhouse 90" film produced by Martin Manulis in November 1956 called "Rendezvous in Black." Boris played a Good Guy for a change. In discussing with John their association during the filming, I hoped for some new point of view about Boris—fool that I was. "No trouble: kind, always ready—always gentle—totally cooperative." The people with whom he worked remained "fine friends," as he called them, through the years. His friendship with William Frye, who produced "Thriller," was life-long, and Bill and his friend and associate producer, James Wharton, are two of Evie's closest friends today.

Alex Segal—who is now head of the Department of Drama at the University of Southern California—directed Boris in the "Boris Karloff Presents" weekly anthology show. Naturally he loved him: "He had such respect—such total respect for the craft we shared and a love of art. Boris was willing to take chances—so many actors play it safe—in a way, they are saying, 'Do I have to know all you say I do?' These actors work toward mediocrity—make no demands on themselves—put themselves in a position of safety. He was always cheerful—he had the vision to see and recognize talent in others long before anyone else even sensed it.

"Our relationship started with this show—it was an MCA package—they were representing him as well as the show—David Susskind was his agent. This was no ordinary show—we did plays of all varieties—classic and otherwise.

"Boris always gave me unlimited credit for running things—it meant a great deal to me. I was young, inexperienced, he made the whole thing possible. Television was in its infancy—really none of us knew what we were doing, so when Boris gave out interviews expressing his appreciation for my

Jack Benny and Boris join Giselle MacKenzie and Margaret Truman Daniel at the piano during a rehearsal for a television show in the 1950's.

running things smoothly, it was marvelous for me. I remember one—he said, 'This man does everything—he's both a director and an engineer—as a matter of fact I think he sweeps up after we go home.'

"MCA insisted on crediting Boris as producer as well as star of the show, a situation that would have delighted another actor—more credit, more money—but not Boris. He called in Susskind and said, 'This is preposterous—I'm not producing this show—Alex is. Get rid of this title and put it where it belongs—with Alex.' MCA refused, and I heard no more about it until next payday—I was getting seventy-five dollars a week all the time. This week the check was one hundred twenty-five dollars. I went to the powers-that-be and said there had been a mistake. 'No mistake,' they told me. 'Boris was furious you weren't properly credited. You didn't get the credit he wanted you to, at least take the money. It comes out of his salary, incidentally.'

"This was at ABC. Our opening show was the opening of the studio. Boris was doing the radio version of the show at the same time . . . the same play. He said, 'I'm back in stock again—I love it—a new play every week—it keeps you on your toes—lucky for me I'm a quick study.'

"Along with a lot of equipment we had no knowledge of how to use, we had this huge new Huston Crane camera—we were dragging it around, making marks on the floor for placement—the whole crew, me—all of us yelling at each other: 'We'll pull the monster over here, drag it across here, then prop it here and swing it there—' Suddenly this voice said, 'Now, wait a minute—let's try to conduct this in a friendly atmosphere—' It was Boris—he thought we were referring to him."

During this same period of television, in the 1950's, Boris also worked with Max Wilk, who says: "I don't know how old he was at the time, but easily in his late sixties, wouldn't it be? Whatever his age, the man's energy and professionalism were absolutely astounding. If I remember the schedule correctly—George Axelrod and I wrote two original half-hour plays for him, the director was an as yet unknown character named Alex Segal—Boris had to rehearse three days in that vast barn that ABC had taken over (I believe it was an old riding stable originally). On the fourth day he went before the cameras and they blocked the show; on the fifth day they'd do camera rehearsals; and then that night, after a dress, they'd go on 'live.' No tape in those days! On the sixth day, Boris had the day off, and on the seventh he'd

Evie and Boris taping his Reader's Digest *radio show (which lasted twelve years).*

have a new half-hour script, starring himself, and the following day, he'd be in rehearsal all over again.

"You can imagine the treadmill we were on—each week writing forty pages of playable scenes for the star. But hell, he was out there doing it, every week. Not only working like a demon, but obviously enjoying the challenge. Never difficult. Always aware of the problems of a pair of novice writers who were far from skilled in the craft—what the hell, we were learning, so was everybody else in live TV. But Boris sailed serenely through the whole thing, working long hours and never getting into a flap about the technical messes, the inadequate sets (ABC was already Poverty Row), and the various rows that were induced—usually from the control booth. We loved him. We'd grown up worshipping this Frankenstein figure; he was a big star and here he was, cheerfully learning lines, helping us with rewrites, and treating two nervous writers like real pros. Both George and I were simultaneously subjected to nervous comics and prima-donna-type actresses. Everybody gave us some sort of hard time . . . not Boris. He was a pleasure. . . . In the words of my sons, 'Boris was a heavy talent and a heavy person.' "

To Boris's last days, when in acute pain, wearing a leg brace because of his old back injury and arthritic legs, breathing with great difficulty from emphysema, he remained in television. He loped about the plains of Spain playing an old man who thought he was Don Quixote in an "I Spy" episode, and arrived in a wheelchair on "The Name of the Game" set. According to director Lamont Johnson, Boris said, "Mr. Johnson, I can hardly get on my two feet—I can barely talk; other than that I am at your disposal. What are your desires?"

Vincent Price, in his letter to me, remarks on this period of Boris's life:

I suppose as I look back at my association with Boris, two things stick—his humor and his bravery. I knew his suffering, and even a little of his fear of stairs, tricks, etc., and almost at the end of his life had a really amazing experience of his bravery on a "Red Skelton Show." Boris, with braced legs, etc., was wheeled into the scene by a midget in Frankenstein makeup. In the audienced dress rehearsal he came off and asked if I had the same feeling he did that the humor of the scene was deadened by the audience sympathy for

A benefit show during World War II. Left to right, front row: Ed Wynn, Vincent Price, Clifton Webb, Danny Kaye, Boris, and Eddie Cantor. Back row: unidentified, Eve Arden, Sophie Tucker, Tallulah Bankhead, unidentified, and Gertrude Lawrence.

a man in a wheelchair. I had to admit that I did—whereupon Boris, with infinite courage, played the rest of the rehearsal on his feet and the show went well. Later Evie and I discussed this—she was naturally worried, but Boris's concern was for the show.

How could he do it? How, ill as he was, did he continue? Because Evie was at his side—always. She knew that work was his life and she made it possible for him to work and therefore to live. Sara has always said, "Evie has my undying gratitude. She not only added at least twenty years to my father's life, but she made them wonderfully happy years."

When questioned about retirement, Boris said, "You may *be* retired—you never *retire.*"

And Evie was responsible for his never quitting. She loved him, she nursed him, she helped him professionally. For twelve years they did the *Reader's Digest* radio show while on the road. Evie handled the tape recorder, Boris read the lines. She was at his side on the sets and drove him wherever they went by automobile. And, most importantly, she made him laugh. I have never seen two people who had as much in common or whose humor was so mutual as these two. When she brought him down to see me at the beach in Malibu the year before he died, she came in ahead of him and said, "I tried to get him to wait in the car, told him that you would come out, but he wouldn't." I went out to greet him and the shock was terrible. He was holding the railing to the four short steps down to the house and literally dragging himself along. The look of pain on the beautiful face, the heavy, torturous breathing, the expression in the eyes—*Can you think of anything as common as this happening to me?*—physically hurt me. He pulled the leg brace forward, shifted the cane to his other hand, embraced me, and said, "Here I am—a mess—but I'm here. The better for seeing you, old girl." I never saw him again.

OPPOSITE: *Boris as Captain Hook in* Peter Pan.

When Daphne du Maurier wrote a description of her father Gerald's performance as Captain Hook in the original *Peter Pan* in 1904, she might have been writing stage directions for Boris's performance of it in New York in 1950. It may have been that Boris remembered having seen at the age of sixteen du Maurier's performance and forty-six years later gave his the same quality, or perhaps he read Miss du Maurier's account of the way her father had played Hook and felt that was correct—I don't know. But the way she described it *is* the way Boris played it:

> When Hook first paced his quarter deck . . . children were carried screaming from the stalls, and even big boys of twelve were known to reach for their mothers' hands in the friendly shelter of the boxes. How he was hated, with his flourish, his poses, his dreaded diabolical smile!
>
> That ashen face, those blood-red lips, the long, dank, greasy curls; the sardonic laugh, the maniacal scream, the appalling courtesy of his gestures; and that above all most terrible of moments when he descended the stairs and with slow, most merciless cunning poured the poison into Peter's glass.
>
> There was no peace in those days until the monster was destroyed, and the fight upon the pirate ship was a fight to the death. Gerald *was* Hook; he was no dummy dressed from Simmons' in a Clarkson wig, ranting and roaring about the stage, a grotesque figure whom the modern child finds a little comic. He was a tragic and rather ghastly creation who knew no peace, and whose soul was in torment; a dark shadow; a sinister dream; a bogey of fear who lives perpetually in the grey recesses of every small boy's mind.
>
> Barrie knew; he was the phantom who came by night and stole his way into their murky dreams. He was the spirit of Stevenson and of Dumas; and he was father-but-for-the-grace-of-God; a lonely spirit that was terror and inspiration in one. . . .

Du Maurier is supposed to have played Hook with a great deal of humor. Boris romped through the part. In an interview at the time he said:

Boris and Jean Arthur in Peter Pan, *as seen by Frueh in a cartoon from*
The New Yorker.

In three ways I can claim to some originality in my portrait of a
celebrated stage character—apart from the singing. A long-time friend
of mine is actor John Williams, who was the child John Darling in one of
the first English *Peter Pan* productions, when Barrie rehearsed the play
himself. He recalls Barrie saying that the keynote of Hook must be his
elegance. I have that grim man carrying a lorgnette and fussing over his
lace cuffs, and yet not to neglect his evil side I have magnified the horror

Boris and children from the cast of Peter Pan.

of his hook by giving him two, a double prong, and shiny ones, not the dull black ones of yore.

I hope Gerald—and Barrie—are resting in their graves. If I have not haunted them hitherto as one of my film ghouls, undoubtedly I must be doing so now.

The 1950 production co-starring Jean Arthur with the added delight of music and lyrics by Leonard Bernstein was an immediate overwhelming success and had the longest run in the play's history. Reviews for the entire cast were uniformly enthusiastic, but for Miss Arthur and Boris they were superlative—

Brooks Atkinson (*New York Times*): This, Mr. Karloff's day of triumph. As the father of the Darling children and the pirate king, he is at the top of his bent. Although he is best known for the monsters he has played on stage and screen, Mr. Karloff is an actor of tenderness and humor, with an instinct for the exact inflection. His Captain Hook is a horrible cutthroat of the sea and Mr. Karloff does not shrink the villainies. But they are founded on an excellent actor's enjoyment of an excellent part, and a relish of Barrie's inscrutable humors. There is something of the grand manner in the latitude of his style and the roll of declamation; and there is withal an abundance of warmth and gentleness in his attitude toward the audience.

George Jean Nathan (New York *Journal American*): The casting of Boris Karloff, the screen monster, as the nefarious Captain Hook was a master stroke. His burlesque intensification of the villainy of the hook-handed pirate with its exaggerated film grimaces adds greatly to the humor of the character, which often has been played as if it were a Berlitz lesson in German gutturals combined with a Penzance demeanor.

Boris roared through two Bernstein songs, "Drink Blood!" and "The Plank" with excruciating villainy and a rather pleasant baritone. So pleasant, in fact, that one serious music critic referred to his "extensive operatic training." Boris said, "My vocal prowess has, in fact, been compared with some qualifications to that of Ezio Pinza. One critic wrote that my Hook was a character straight out of Gilbert and Sullivan. Who knows? Musical comedy may be just ahead."

It's a wonder he had breath to speak, let alone sing. He should have worn the sneakers left over from television instead of hip boots, because he had six changes of costume, three of makeup—*forty pounds* of makeup—and he had to climb up and down ladders wearing it all. "It's a man-killer for fair," he said at one point, "and right at Halloween—my busiest season!"

I wrote Jean Arthur enquiring if she had any anecdotes, and her answer ended: "I particularly remember Boris with the children in *Peter Pan*. They were always in his dressing room chatting away like mad." These were the young actors in the cast of *Peter Pan*. But the dressing room was always full of children—visitors—those who were permitted to come back and meet him. All of them wanted to wear the hook, but Boris didn't allow them to unless they said, "Yes" to his, "Did you clap for Tinker Bell?"

Miss Arthur (who was at the time teaching at Vassar) also enclosed a letter from Jane Bishop, a student of hers, which is ten pages long and encompasses and chronicles the effect Boris had on her life ("He is the love of my life"). The letter concludes:

I thank Heaven that Mr. Karloff lived in an era when films were concerned with the character of their monsters and villains, and so was able to make them noble and human; and that I missed seeing his films until I was old enough to appreciate them in a feudal and idealistic sense. He is, if I may use an old and worn expression (which I shouldn't), the guiding star of my existence; and whatever I can associate in some way with his presence, that thing is hallowed thereby.

Boris's rendition of Mr. Darling, the kindly, bumbling father of the children, was as gentle as his Hook was horrific. He always felt that Barrie's own original stage directions were the best clue to the interpretation of the character of Hook: "He is a public school man gone wrong." Mr. Darling, on the other hand, was close to Boris's own character. When he stood, hand on Nana's (the dog's) head, the true animal lover coming out, he *was* Boris, even though Nana was a man dressed as an animal.

During the run of the play, Boris brought Sara Jane in from California.

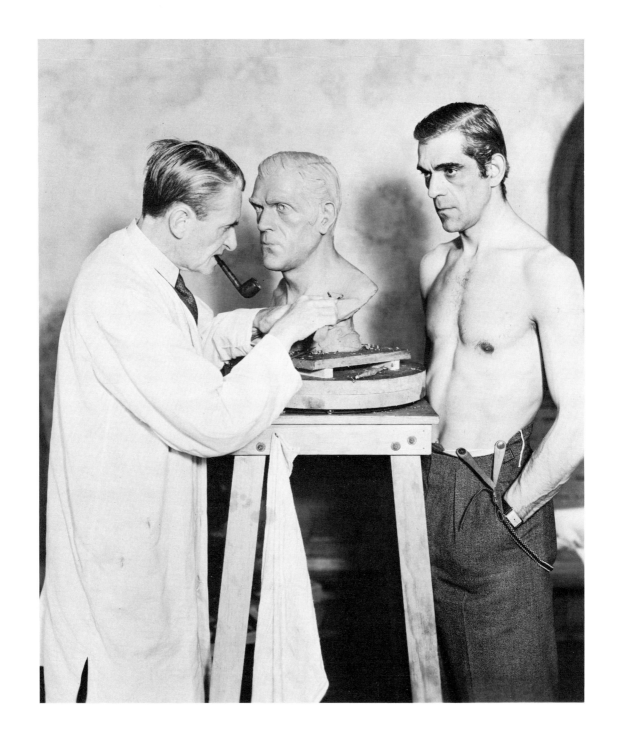

Ivan Simpson, actor and friend of Boris's, sculpting the (still missing) bust.

"I rather hoped, I guess," he said, "that she might catch fire—that the theater would get to her, but she was really more interested in the dog of one of the actors than she was in the play itself." Like me, "no fire in the belly for it," I suppose. (All of Barrie's rights to *Peter Pan*, incidentally, go to the Great Ormond Street Hospital for Sick Children in London, a fact that always delighted Boris.)

When Boris and Evie went to New York for *Peter Pan* they decided they probably would be in New York more than in Hollywood, so sold the house they had bought from Gregory Peck. It was a lovely place high on a hill above Beverly Hills. As they were packing to move, Evie came to Boris and said, "What shall we do with the bust?" (The bust was a bronze done by Ivan Simpson, a fellow actor and old friend of Boris's. It was very beautiful, and very Boris.) "I don't know. Just chuck it over the edge of the hill," he said. The Karloffs' maid, who had come in a moment before, begged for the bust so she "could always remember Mr. Karloff." Naturally—she loved him. So Bessie was given the bust.

Years later, when Evie was in Hollywood she went to see Bessie and talk about old times. Bessie was ill in bed. Evie sat beside her, looking around the neat room. On the bedside table was the bust—wearing glasses. Evie asked why. "Because," said Bessie, "that's the way I remember him." Evie later regretted having given up the bust and tried to find Bessie, even taking ads in the local paper, to no avail. I've often wondered if Bessie or her heirs might have my portrait along with the bust. I had given it to Boris somewhere along the line. The portrait of me was painted by a friend. It was life-size and horrendous. The friend felt I had an inner sorrow, which was true, but she painted it green. The last time I saw it, Boris had it sitting on the toilet in the guest bath.

OPPOSITE: *Boris and Julie Harris in* The Lark.

The Karloffs' peregrinations took them farther and farther afield, so, having given up the house, when they came to Hollywood for a film or television show, they usually stayed at the Chateau Marmont, one of the few remaining Old Hollywood edifices. The fact that it is still standing is a miracle in itself. Los Angeles (Hollywood *is* Los Angeles—there is no such place as Hollywood, really; like beauty, it exists only in the eye of the beholder) is noted for tearing down everything of quality and replacing it with cement blobs. The fact that the Chateau happens to be hideous is beside the point. It has housed and nurtured more famous actors than The Players and the Algonquin combined, up to and including Greta Garbo. The pinky-beige feudal towers rise above Sunset Strip, triumphing over the savings and loan compound built on the ground which once held the Garden of Allah, the Chateau's only rival as an actor's haven.

The lobby of the Chateau looks like an expensive funeral home, replete with Gothic colonnades, dark dark, stiff chairs, and a grand piano with some keys missing, standing under heavily curtained windows at one end. The windows formerly looked out on a twenty-foot-high plastic statue of a bikini-clad cow-girl waving a sombrero and advertising a Las Vegas hotel. She turned incessantly on her pedestal, and a few of the more racy thespians used to amuse themselves taking pot shots at her from their rooms with Daisy air pistols. Regrettably, the huge whirly-girly, like the Garden of Allah, is no more.

Actor Max Adrian, a fellow Marmont tenant and friend of the Karloffs, remembers that Boris entertained himself more quietly, but more beneficially, at least to the receptionist in the lobby. The lady had been there for more years than she cared to remember, and she and Boris were fast friends. Like the rest of the establishment, she insisted, "He was the nicest man in Hollywood." Each night when he returned from the studio, he would go up to his apartment, make a very dry, very stiff martini, tiptoe into the hall with it, ring for the elevator, place the martini carefully on the floor of the elevator, and wait for the door to close. The receptionist, ready on the ground floor, rang for the elevator, and her cocktail descended to her. There were a few occasions, of course, when the trip was intercepted by another tenant on another floor, who then had a pleasant surprise.

"This Is Your Life"—Boris embraces Sara Jane as Ralph Edwards (at left) and Evie look on (1957).

After a trip to England to film the "Colonel March of Scotland Yard" television series, the Karloffs went to Italy for three films, back to Hollywood for another, and then settled in New York because Boris had been signed to play opposite Julie Harris in *The Lark*.

Having decided to stay put for a bit (*The Lark* ran nine months), the

Boris (note the bowed legs) and Evie strolling while on location in Hawaii
for Voodoo Island.

Karloffs bought an apartment in the Dakota. This classic structure, No. 1, West 72nd Street, now happily a New York City designated landmark, so they can't tear it down, was built between 1880 and 1884. It was designed by Henry Janeway Hardenbergh, the architect also responsible for the old Waldorf-Astoria and the Plaza. When the Dakota was constructed, it was so far away from the center of the city that someone commented, "That must be Indian territory; you might as well have built it in the Dakotas"; hence its name, and hence the Indian head over the façade. The Dakota was built in grand style for privacy and comfort. The seclusion of its inhabitants has been interrupted in the course of its ninety-some years only by the filming of *Rosemary's Baby*, which was okay because everyone knows the building is haunted anyway. In fact, a newcomer tenant once said he was disappointed that he had never met Boris before his death because he admired him so. The doorman just commented, "That's all right—he'll be back."

The Karloffs' suite was in the former servants' quarters, way high up in the eaves, overlooking the verdigris roofs below. With her usual beautiful taste, Evie turned it into what felt like a sunlit English cottage. It must have been wonderful to come back to after an evening of a performance as exhausting as Boris's in *The Lark*.

Boris always referred to his role as Bishop Cauchon, the sinister prosecutor of Joan of Arc in her ordeal at Rouen in 1431, as the high point of his career. Lillian Hellman's adaptation of the Jean Anouilh play *L'Alouette* was a triumph for all concerned.

Julie Harris's glowing performance brought reviews that were almost hysterical in their enthusiasm. A *Time* cover story stated: "The girl has laid her life upon the stage like a candle upon an altar and the still strong flame of her talent shines through the nervous wattage of Broadway with a pure and steady light." Boris spoke of her performance: "That girl plays Joan with the hand of God."

Boris's own performance as Cauchon—a man torn between dedication to his beliefs and compassion for the girl—was played with passionate sincerity, quietness, and strength, the qualities sought by both M. Anouilh and Miss Hellman. She wrote Boris a note after the play, ending: "I am grateful to you for the fine honest work and the good friendship and I want that pleasure to continue. Love, Lillian."

Boris spoke of the character of Cauchon: "Cauchon, the priest, is based on Pétain. Anouilh wrote the play during the occupation of France and he meant it as a message of hope to Frenchmen. Both Cauchon and Joan suffer dreadfully, each in his own belief of what is best for France, and he with a tenderness for the girl and a deep desire to save her. It is a striking analogy."

Boris said that playing with Miss Harris was the most rewarding experience of his career. He always referred to her as "that girl," and he would shake his head in deep admiration and affection. The feeling was obviously mutual. She wrote him after the play:

Dearest Boris,

I have never been so happy acting with someone as I have been with you. I love you and am grateful for the unspoken help and encouragement you have given me.

They continued together on the television "Hallmark Hall of Fame" version of *The Lark*, with the same enthusiastic reviews—this time playing to an audience of over twenty-six million people, one hundred twenty-five times the number who saw the play.

After *The Lark*, Boris swung back into a stream of nonsensical spookeries involving constant travel. He and Evie island-hopped from Ischia and *Il Mostro dell' Isola* (*The Monster of the Island*) to Kauai, Hawaii, for *Voodoo Island* (some hop); back to Hollywood for *Frankenstein 1970*, a change for Boris because this time he played Dr. Frankenstein, not the Monster; to England for *The Haunted Strangler* and *Corridors of Blood*, in which he shared honors with Christopher Lee, who speaks of him (naturally) with admiration and affection and refers to him as an "unflappable" actor; and again to Hollywood for American International Pictures' glorious piece of tomfoolery called *The Raven*, which owes absolutely nothing to Edgar Allan Poe, including apologies. It (the raven) does, however, pick people's eyes out right and left. In it Boris lurched shoulder to shoulder with Vincent Price and Peter Lorre. Then, still in Hollywood and also for American International Pictures (henceforth referred to as AIP), *The Terror*; then to Italy for *I Tre Volti della Paura* (*Black Sabbath*); back to Holly-

Boris off Ischia on location for The Monster of the Island.

wood for two more AIPs—*The Comedy of Terrors*, which had a flying wedge of top horror interpreters consisting of Boris, Vincent Price, Peter Lorre, Basil Rathbone, plus (of all people) Joe E. Brown, charging through cemeteries, Gothic mansions, and mortuaries (background: thunder); and *Bikini Beach*, the forerunner of all the *Bikini* numbers. In this, Boris plays a guest shot and issues one word only. He watches the carryings-on of the teenaged beach-goers, shakes his head, says, "Monsters," and goes away. Then another AIP: *Die Monster Die!* (shot in England). And *another* AIP: *The Ghost in the Invisible Bikini*—a double whammy. Boris played a corpse, Hiram Stokeley, whose soul is unable to find peace but finally enters Heaven with the aid of the girl (the Ghost) in the I.B. The road to Heaven is not easy, being blocked by evil people such as Reginald Ripper (Basil Rathbone) and his daughter Sinistra, J. Sinister Hulk, Eric Von Zipper and his Rat Pack gang of motorcyclists, and last but hardly least, the Red Indian, Chief Chicken Feather. However, good prevails and the Ghost conquers all those standing in the way. Stokeley reaches Heaven and peace with the aid of the faithful butler, played (really) by Francis X. Bushman.

Leaving Heaven, Boris materialized (in voice only) for *The Daydreamer*, a combination of animation and live action film based on several Hans Christian Andersen stories, Boris playing the Rat in the "Thumbelina" sequence. Next, Boris became Dr. Vaugiroud, a political scientist with a *secret*, in a large spy film for MGM called *The Venetian Affair*, starring Robert Vaughn, which followed Vaughn's successful television series—"The Man from UNCLE."

Then Boris did another narration. This time of an Italian semidocumentary called *Mondo Balordo*, about which the less said the better; then, back went the Karloffs to England for *The Sorcerers*, following which to Spain for *El Coleccionista de Cadaveres* (American title: *Blind Man's Bluff*; British title: *Cauldron of Blood*); and then to Hollywood for what to me, at least, was the most important picture of his life. It is frequently mentioned as his last. It wasn't, he made several more. But *Targets* is his epitaph because in it he *is* Boris.

During the procession of horror films before and after *Targets*, the last of which were pure physical agony for him, Boris's fellow actors, in rapt admiration, continued to become life-long friends. I suddenly realize that this last is an often repeated phrase in this book—pure tautology. There is no such thing as anyone having been a friend of Boris's and not remaining forever so. And the word "life-long" in this case was not enduring, since there was little life left. But what there was, was full of dedicated devotion to his friends—and to his craft.

OPPOSITE: *Boris through the sniper's gunsight—the poster for* Targets.

Targets was not only a fitting swan song for Boris after years of unrewarding film vehicles, but it **was** also the auspicious debut of one of the screen's now important directors, Peter Bogdanovich. The film is remarkable in many ways, primarily because it is a good, intelligent, suspenseful picture which would hold its own in any competition with large-budget, large-company, large-money films. The fact that it was made for so little, and in such a short time, is miraculous.

The story of its production begins back in 1963. Roger Corman, who had produced and directed *The Raven* for AIP, found he had a few sets and a few days left over at the completion of the film. Boris shot some scenes in the sets, a story was woven about them, and Presto! *The Terror* was made, with at least one scene unforgettable, because Boris was flailing about with a young girl in a pool of water, with more water rushing into a dungeon through floodgates, and the force of the water was so great it flushed her "falsies" up and out of the bosom of her dress. The experience also led to Boris's final illness. Hours of immersion in cold water aggravated his already serious emphysema.

Now, at the end of *The Terror*, Corman was still owed two days of Boris's time, a commodity not to be wasted. Later, Corman went to Bogdanovich and said, "How would you like to become a director?" Peter answered that that was exactly what he wanted. Corman said, "Okay. We have two days of Karloff's time and that's all. That's twenty minutes on the screen. Now, we shot about twenty minutes of film we didn't use in *The Terror*. We can use that—it's forty minutes of Karloff. All you have to do is take a couple of other actors, write a story around them, and fill up the rest of the time, and we've got a picture."

Bogdanovich and his production designer (and wife at the time), Polly Platt, wrote an original story; from that Bogdanovich wrote a first draft screenplay in eleven days, the picture was shot in twenty-five days, and cost one hundred and thirty thousand dollars. When Peter took Evie Karloff and me to lunch to talk about Boris, he said, "A remarkable thing—two days before we shot the film [in 1967], Boris and I had never met. I had never directed a picture—just some second-unit stuff—and yet he demonstrated faith in me from the start. The first thing he said after reading the script was, 'I believe in this picture, but you can't do it in two days.' I said that regrettably nobody was coming up with more salary for him, so I'd have to. He simply answered, 'Take as long as you like.' He worked five days."

"He did it for Peter," Evie said.

"The film would have been impossible without him," Peter said.

The Bogdanovich-Platt story for *Targets* involves an aging horror star, Byron Orlok, who desperately wishes to retire and return to his native England, "because the world belongs to the young. Make way for them. Let them have it. I am an anachronism." Orlok cites the horrors of the headlines as "the real horrors."

The Bogdanovich script, with some form of sorcery, integrates the "real horror" story of a young sniper with an uncontrollable passion for killing, and the old star's wishing to leave the scene where such sickness exists. Miss Platt's set for the middle-class San Fernando home of the boy's parents is so (brilliantly) sterile and tasteless that it almost makes one wonder why more young people don't run out and kill. Tim O'Kelly plays the young man who has access to as many firearms as he needs, with the encouragement of his father. He assiduously shoots his wife, his mother, and an errand boy, places the women's bodies in their beds, closes their eyelids, and pulls covers over their heads. He then straightens the arm of the errand boy lying twisted on the floor, gets a towel, mops up some of the blood, places a paper towel over more of it, sets a clock upright, and, everything neat and tidy, sets out to kill some more. He is terrifying primarily because he looks and normally acts like "the boy next door."

Peter Bogdanovich as Sammy Michaels, the young writer who wants the old star to do just one more film, the one he has written for him, demonstrates a relaxed facility in front of, as well as behind, the camera, and he and Boris succeed in projecting to the audience the affection they held for each other. They have a couple of scenes which would not be out of place in a Marx Brothers epic, one of which Peter credits Boris for inventing: Sammy arrives in Orlok's hotel room, quite drunk, to try one more time to persuade him not to retire. Boris, as Orlok, is sitting, drink in hand, in front of the television set watching *The Criminal Code*. It is the famous scene in which Boris, as the convict, kills the stool-pigeon. (The film was used in *Targets* by courtesy of Columbia Pictures and Howard Hawks.) Sammy looks over

Peter Bogdanovich (lying across the bed) and Boris discussing the approach to the next scene, during the filming of Targets, *in 1967.*

Orlok's shoulder and says, "That was directed by Howard Hawks." The two stare at the televised film and the scene ends with them both drunk. Orlok won't let Sammy leave, so Sammy staggers into the bedroom and passes out on Orlok's bed. Orlok comes in, exclaims, "Hey, that's my bed." He sits on the edge of the bed, says, "Oh, Good Lord, I'm as drunk as he is," and passes out. Comes the dawn. Sammy wakes, sits up, holds his head, looks over at Orlok, does a wild "take," screams. Orlok jumps awake, sits up, says, "Have you gone mad?" Sammy says, "I had a nightmare—I open my eyes, the first thing I see is Byron Orlok." Orlok says, "Very funny. Very funny." There is a knock at the door, Orlok goes to answer, passes a mirror, looks at himself, does the identical "take," and screams.

There is another scene which is a particular delight, with a hip disk jockey, who Orlok obviously finds repulsive, interviewing him. The character carries on incessantly with hip-talk, ending, ". . . and that's no put-on. When I was a kid, Mr. O, I must have dug your flicks four zillion times! You blew my mind." Boris, as Orlok, just looks at him, then says very slowly, "Obviously."

Bogdanovich weaves the lives of the sniper, the star, and the young writer and his girl into a tight net in which to catch the climax—a scene of terror and carnage in a drive-in theater where the star is playing on the screen and is also making a farewell personal appearance in front of it. The sniper is up behind the screen, and the camera fixes through the sight of the gun as the sniper waits to pick off the innocent in their cars—sitting ducks for him.

The film ends when the sniper, after his blood bath, is pursued by Byron Orlok, impeccable in evening clothes, who corners him behind the screen and beats him to his knees with his cane. As the police arrive, the old star looks down at the cringing boy and says, "Is that what I was afraid of?" As a policeman takes him away, the boy whimpers, "I hardly ever missed, did I?"

Bogdanovich's integration of ideas and steady pursuit of the story—which is a frightening observation of the American way of life, and death—are successful because he explains nothing and shows everything. Laszlo Kovacs's photography and Polly Platt's art direction are equal to the quality of the direction. The filming, despite the speed at which it was done, the terrible hours, and the themes of freeway shooting and mass murder, must have been a rich experience and a labor of love for all concerned or it wouldn't have come out the way it did. Everyone, including Evie, who was with Boris throughout the filming, pitched in, helped, carried things about, and nurtured the project.

The day Evie, Peter, and I lunched, he said, "The only time I ever had trouble with Boris was when we had worked until three in the morning and he wanted to stay on and read his lines for the other actors—he wanted to help them in reacting in front of the camera. I made him go home and he was mad at me. One of the most extraordinary scenes I've ever witnessed before or since was the one in which Boris, as Byron Orlok, is wondering what to do to entertain the audience at his last appearance. 'I think I'll tell them a story,' he says, and he reads from an ancient fable about death [the one used by John O'Hara in *Appointment in Samarra*]. The speech is two pages long and I was going to break it up by panning around the room while he was speaking. Boris said, 'I want to do this without a script.' I asked him if he wanted cue cards instead. He said, 'No.' We rehearsed the mechanics of the scene—he was letter-perfect. I realized I was an idiot not to stay on him. The camera was at the end of a long table. I said to the cameraman, 'Stay on him. Start with a long shot, we'll sneak the table away as you dolly in.' It was electrifying. Boris did the whole two pages in one take! Then the entire crew burst into applause. Boris was pleased."

As the three of us rose to leave the table, Peter said, "I can't tell you the deference I felt for that man. He really *looked* at you! Think how lucky I was to have shared my first with him."

Evie said, "Think how lucky he was to have shared his last with you."*

* As I've mentioned, *Targets* was *not* Boris's last picture, but Evie has always referred to it as such because he loved the experience so and because he was not particularly proud of the others that followed.

OPPOSITE: *Close-up of Boris taken in Spain, where he was playing the Quixote role in an "I Spy" episode (1966). The illness and fatigue are evident.*

In a way, it is a pity *Targets*, a just tribute, was not actually Boris's last picture, but I expect it doesn't matter because so few people have ever seen the final ones. He went to England for *Curse of the Crimson Altar* (*The Crimson Cult* in the United States) with Christopher Lee as a warlock this time. Boris played in a wheelchair. At about this time (1968) an article appeared in *TV Guide* about horror films. Boris was mentioned, and the *Guide* received the following letter from his agent:

Your current issue of TV Guide *carries an article by Ron Smith entitled "My Favorite Monsters." In it, Mr. Smith bemoans the end of the cycle of horror movies and their enchanting other-worldly heroes. In summing up, he states that the old monsters are gone including many of the actors who portrayed them. He specifically mentions Boris Karloff as being "relatively inactive."*

On behalf of our friend and client who not long ago passed his 80th birthday, let me list a few of his most recent "inactivities."

During the year 1967, Mr. Karloff made a picture in Spain entitled Blind Man's Bluff, *a picture in London (* The Sorcerers*) under his long-standing contract with American International Pictures and a further picture here in the states at 20th Century-Fox [it was actually Paramount] entitled* Targets, *which is in current release. In January of 1968, he did another feature picture for AIP (* Reincarnation*), four pictures here in Los Angeles for Proveedora Filmica Azteca [also known as Azteca-Columbia], a Mexican production company, appeared on the "Red Skelton Show" in September, a "Name of the Game" at Universal City Studios, is currently taping the "Jonathan Winters Show," and will return to London soon to film another AIP picture tentatively entitled* The Dark. *In between these minor assignments, Mr. Karloff fills his idle time with such things as Class-A commercials for such upcoming corporations as Ronson, Ford Motor Company, A-1 Sauce, Sheaffer pens, Butternut Coffee, Volkswagen, etc., recordings for Reader's Digest, "How the Grinch Stole Christmas" for MGM, and a new holiday record to be produced by Capitol Records entitled "The Year Without a Santa Claus."*

We pray we may be fortunate enough to enjoy such "inactive" longev-

During the taping at MGM of "How the Grinch Stole Christmas," an animated full-length cartoon for television, based on the Dr. Seuss children's book, Boris was ill. The emphysema had him wheezing badly, and his back and legs were obviously painful.

A friend of Ted Geisel's (Ted Geisel is Dr. Seuss) was visiting on the set. The friend was a well-known cardiologist. He watched Boris for a while, then went to Ted. "That is a very sick man" he said. "I don't see how he will be able to last through this." Ted said, "It was an exhausting day—everything went wrong—at the end of the day we were all wilted—except Boris. As we dragged ourselves off, he left whistling."

Boris then signed with a Mexican company for four films, some of which, as far as anyone can find out, have never been shown anywhere but in Spanish-speaking countries.

To the very last he refused even to consider retirement. Crippled, stooped, unable to breathe without pain, he stumbled along, on time, letter-perfect, "unflappable." If questioned about retiring, he said, "I never will—I'm not really alive when I'm not working and have no part to look forward to. In fact, to know I would never work again would be something like a death sentence. I want only to die in harness."

Pablo Casals in his eighty-first year said, "The man who works and is never bored is never old. To retire from work is the beginning of death."

As he approached his own, Boris continued to make jokes about himself. "Apart from not being able to walk or talk, I am fighting fit. Managing to burst into tears at the right time gets everything done for me."

Then on the way home to England he caught a severe cold in Kennedy Airport in New York and was taken straight to the King Edward VII Hospital at Midhurst in Sussex. He was in the hospital for two months, suffering from a combination of arthritis, emphysema, and a heart condition. Evie was always there beside him. And they continued to do the *Reader's Digest* taping to the last. When it was difficult for him even to speak, he said to Evie, "God, I'm lucky—doing what I want—even now."

A theater billboard for Serenata Macabra, *one of his last Mexican films.*

Just before he died in harness—as he wished—he received a telephone call from his agent Arthur Kennard, who knew how ill he was. Kennard told him there was a "firm" offer from Federico Fellini, who wanted him for a film. Kennard added that he also had an idea for both a television and a radio program in New York for him.

Boris smiled, and said, "Think of the imagination and generosity it took to make that call." He gathered enough strength to write Kennard and thank him. "It really set me up," he said in his note.

· · ·

On February 2, 1969, he died. There was a very small private funeral, followed by cremation. He had stated he wanted to die privately, as he had lived, and his wishes were followed to the letter.

Newspapers all over the world carried headlines. The news media treated Boris's death with the dignity and importance accorded only to distinguished statesmen. The Council of the City of Los Angeles issued the statement: "In tribute to his memory all members stood in reverence as the Council adjourned its meeting February 4th, 1969."

On the same day, on the KNBC "Eleventh Hour News," Los Angeles, Piers Anderton on "Viewpoint" read:

Despite what I read, I know he isn't dead. The first time he died was in a flaming windmill on the Frankenstein estate. I was a subteener then, wondering what life was all about, and I can still see in my mind the picture, the moving picture, of his great hands groping for the inexplicable source of his life—the sun.

A year later, he returned out of the earth, unharmed by the flames, and this time he was rejected by a frizzy-haired, snub-nosed woman—the bride of Frankenstein. I had just entered my teens, and had just been rejected by the first of a series of snub-nosed girls . . . but I lived through it. *He* didn't . . . he died again in a pit of primeval ooze.

But he was resurrected in the third year, still looking for an explanation of his monstrous life. And all our lives were getting monstrous then, as the Thirties moved into the war years.

But he struggled on . . . a link with our innocent years.

If Boris Karloff is gone, my childhood . . . all of our childhoods . . . are gone.

And Evie was inundated by letters . . . from fans: "Millions you will never know grieve with you." . . . from friends, with loving words of his humility, his sense of fun and nonsense, his courage in the face of pain, his flawless manners, his scorn of the second-rate and shoddy, his affinity with nature (even including man) . . . from parents of children lucky enough to have known him . . . and from strangers and friends alike appreciations of Evie's devotion to him.

Evie, respecting Boris's request for no ceremony, has still clung to her desire for a memorial somewhere. She has been in constant touch with the authorities of St. Paul's Covent Garden, known as the "Actors' Church," regarding a commemorative plaque.

The decision was finally made, and the commemorative plaque is now in place. It quotes the famous lines from Andrew Marvell's Horatian ode "Upon Cromwell's Return from Ireland," in reference to Charles I. I am so glad because it is perfect:

> He Nothing Common Did or Mean
> Upon That Memorable Scene

In 1971, when a friend and I were in Ensenada, Mexico, we were fortunate enough to catch one of Boris's last films. It was called *Serenata Macabra*, and I have not found it listed in any filmography; it must be one of those loosely referred to as the "Mexican films." My Spanish is nonexistent and the film was not dubbed into English, but it must have been Boris's finest hour. I have never seen him look so magnificent. The evil baron of a giant feudal castle, he stormed about looking nine feet tall, wearing a superb full-length burgundy velvet Edwardian dressing gown (probably to cover the brace). The Spanish actor who dubbed his voice, even to the lisp, sounded so uncannily like him it was eerie.

The evil baron is given to playing the organ—a *"danse macabre"* which one knows foreshadows somebody's, or lots of bodies', death. In the final scene, he stalks to the organ, sits, raises his hands to concert height, crashes them onto the keys, and, to the organ accompaniment, the walls part and sheets of fire shoot out, pits open, flames shoot up, and as he plays madly away, every note brings on another burst of flame. The flames lick around him, finally encompassing him, and he perishes. For the last time.

I walked out into the hot Mexican sun depressed by the thought that this time there would be no resurrection and he would stalk no more. Then I thought: Hell! Two years after his death his image is charging around the screen of this Ensenada emporium; the audience was enthralled and exited chattering away, obviously having had a very good time at the show. Boris was here still—pleasuring the people, speaking in another tongue, and bringing a great deal of quality to the scrubby little town. My friend and I went to Ensenada's famous Hoosong's Bar, ordered two margaritas, clicked glasses, and said, "Boris—full marks." And I was comforted by the thought that somewhere, sometime, always, B. will go bump in the night.

OVERLEAF: *Boris—really Boris.*

OPPOSITE: *Boris's brother-in-law Arthur Donkin with the sexton at the parish church in Islington, where Boris lived for a time.*

A NOTE ON GENEALOGY

BORIS'S FAMILY TREE

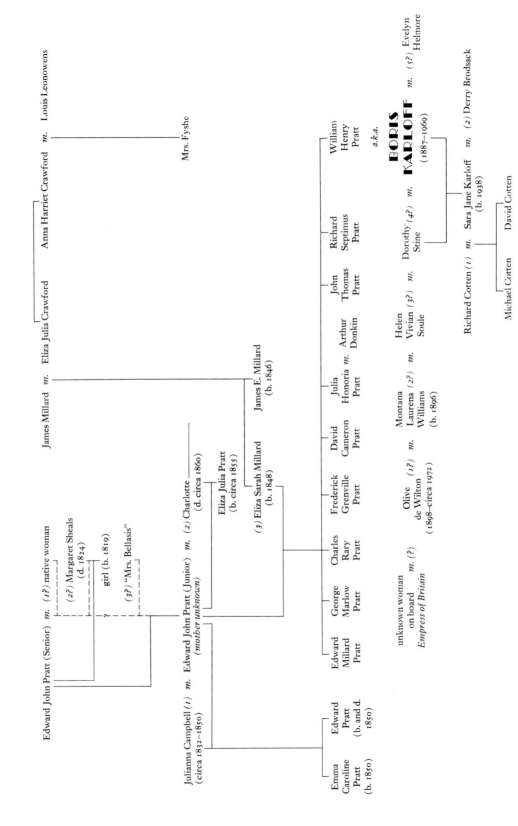

THE PRATTS

The mystery of Boris's beginnings is buried deep in the archives of Somerset House and in the India Offices, in 150 years of British and Indian maritime records. I traced his genealogy back on one side to 1806, to the birth of his maternal grandfather, James Millard, and on the other to 1815, when his paternal grandfather, Edward John Pratt, joined the Indian navy, known as "The Honourable East India Company's Marines," in Bengal, India.

In between these dates and Boris's birth in 1887 there is a density of detail which often serves only to confuse, because despite dates, places, baptism certificates, ship's logs, etc., it is still not always possible to say with complete certainty who exactly was who.

The great unsolved mystery is the question of which woman was actually the mother of Boris's father. It may have been a native woman, since in 1826 or thereabouts a native child was born—no record of to whom —and four years later was christened "Pratt." Many Europeans in India at that time had native "wives," and if the marriage had not been properly registered, the birth of children was usually not registered either. Or, perhaps Boris's father, Edward John, was born to his father, the senior Edward John and his first English wife, Margaret Sheals, who definitely was the mother of one girl child, born in 1819. But when Margaret Pratt died in 1824 at the age of 24, no mention was made in the Bombay newspaper death column of her having "died in childbirth," nor is there listed any birth registered in the name of Pratt in the next ten-year period of ecclesiastical records. Finally, there is a complicated and obscure family legend about a possible illicit relationship with a "Mrs. Bellasis," who did, indeed, adopt an "Edward John" in 1833—but we will never know.

In any case, by 1846 there appears an entry in the "Returns for Uncovenetted servants Civil Servants, European," which shows Edward John Pratt, aged 19 years, 7 months, and 14 days, as an uncovenanted civil servant drawing a salary of 50 rupees a month. If Edward John was indeed born in 1827 (and his age in these employment records might easily have been falsified) who could his mother have been? A second wife? Another native woman? The uncovenanted Civil Service often appointed men in India (not

LEFT: *Boris's father, Edward John Pratt.*

RIGHT: *Boris's mother, Eliza Sarah Millard Pratt.*

in London) who were of mixed blood. The job was a lowly one without pension, no university degree or training was required, and a man could leave or be sacked at any time. This Edward John was Boris's father.

In 1849 the same Edward John Pratt marries, for the first time, a Miss Julianna Campbell, aged 17, in Gargaum. Nine months later to the day, on January 12, 1850, a daughter is born. She is named Emma Caroline. In December 1850 Edward John and Julianna have a son, Edward, who dies the next day. Two weeks later Julianna Campbell Pratt dies. She is 19 years old.

In the Uncovenanted Civil Servants Returns for 1852, Edward John Pratt, listed as "single," is earning 116 rupees a month. By about 1854, he is married a second time—to a young lady named Charlotte. Neither their marriage nor her death was registered in the Bombay area. From the union of Edward John and Charlotte comes a daughter, Eliza Julia. From 1856 to 1858 Edward John Pratt is earning 400 rupees a month. We assume that Charlotte dies around 1860, because there is no further record of her.

On October 27, 1864, Edward John Pratt, listed as "widower," and now Assistant Commissioner of Customs, is married a third time—to Eliza Sarah Millard, spinster aged 16. Eliza Sarah Millard Pratt was Boris's mother.

THE MILLARDS

The family of Boris's mother, the Millards, can be traced back to 1806, when James Millard, Boris's grandfather, was born in Great Marlow, Buckinghamshire, England. At 19, James Millard enlists in London for unlimited army service in India, and in February 1826 embarks for India on the ship *Duchess of Atholl*. He arrives in India in June the same year. His description reads as follows: "Height—5 ft 7¼ inches; visage—fresh; complexion—swarthy; hair—brown; eyes—dark." Another entry gives: "Visage—long; eyes—gray." His occupation is listed as "Baker."

In 1845 James Millard marries Eliza Julia Crawford, sister of Anna Harriet Crawford, who later became governess to the children of the King of Siam.

In a letter from Charles Rary Pratt to Edward Millard Pratt (two of Boris's brothers) in 1948, Charles asks:

Can you supply any information about our Mother's Aunt Mrs. Leon Owens, who was the first English woman to live in Siam? Many years ago, Mrs. Leon Owens wrote a book called (I think) "A Governess in the Court of the King of Siam"* and two or three years ago, as you may remember, a certain

---

* It was not; it was called *The Romance of Siamese Harem Life*, published in 1837. The surname "Leon Owens" to which Charles refers was correctly spelled "Leonowens" and pronounced for no apparent reason "Leeowens."

Mrs. Landon, a connection of the family, published a book called Anna and the King of Siam, *which was afterwards turned into a film and she is seeking information which would help us fill gaps in the family tree.*

About a hundred years ago, there were two sisters named Crawford in Bombay—one married James Millard, our mother's father; and the other married Louis Leon Owens. Fifty years ago I met a Canadian lady who knew Mrs. Leon Owens' daughter who was married to a Canadian banker named Fyshe in Montreal. I wrote home to Mother about this, and she in reply told me that Mrs. Leon Owens had had much trouble and unhappiness and, after her husband died, had left Bombay and cut off all communications with her family. About ten years after this, our grandmother Mrs. Millard met a certain Captain Baldwin who had met her sister Anna Leon Owens in Siam— Mrs. Millard wrote to her sister and received a reply, evidently written under the influence of a strong emotion, and even went so far as to warn anyone who came to find her.

In 1899 I wrote to Mrs. Fyshe communicating the above information. I received a very friendly letter in reply, but got the impression that she did not want her mother's past unhappiness in Bombay raked up again.

At this point, the tangential danger to the writer is grave—why did Anna run off to Siam? What was the terrible unhappiness in Bombay? Why did she warn anyone against coming to find her? Just so she could wind up dancing with Yul Brynner? Never mind—this is not her story, except as she figures as Boris Karloff's great-aunt.

To return to our genealogy:

In 1846 James and Eliza Julia Millard have a son, James E. Millard. Two years later, in June 1848, a daughter, Eliza Sarah is born, and it is she

TOP: *The fort where Boris's grandfather James Millard was stationed is visible in the background of this nineteenth-century view of Bombay.*

BOTTOM: *Streets in Bombay looked much like this at the time Boris's grandfather resided there.*

who in 1864 marries Edward John Pratt. According to the records, six sons and one daughter were born to the Edward John Pratts before their return to England in about 1877. After five years Richard Septimus was born, and five years after that William Henry, a.k.a. Boris Karloff, on November 23, 1887. At the time of Boris's birth, Eliza Sarah was 39 and Edward John 60, assuming that he *was* 19 in 1846.

In 1888 Edward John leaves Eliza Sarah and goes to France, taking Richard Septimus with him. The journey is best described by Richard Septimus himself, in answer to an enquiry by Evie Karloff:

I think the last the family saw of him was when he left for France, incidentally kidnapping me, then aged about five. I don't suppose he had a special feeling for me and I expect he would have kidnapped Boris instead if Boris had been old enough. (Incidentally, when was Boris born?) I was rescued in Calais by an uncle, whose name I can't remember, snatching me from the Calais apartment when my father was out, blurring his track by driving by road to Dunkirk and crossing back to England by what must have been an exceedingly dirty cattle boat. It has stuck in my memory because I caught ringworm on the cattle boat and in due course was taken weeping to a barber to have my head shaved and the ringworm attended to!!

Of his father, Richard Septimus says in the same letter:

I don't think the old man was a very admirable character though I was too young to know anything of the details. I expect you know that he was legally separated from my mother and, I believe, steadily refused to pay her afterwards one penny of alimony!

Regardless of his treatment of his wife, Edward John did provide serious scholastic instruction for his children. He must have had tremendous driving ambition for his sons, to make up for his own lack of opportunity as a young man. He had made his living in a variety of professions, and his heart was set on the diplomatic corps for his sons. A number of them had very distinguished careers, and he provided all of them with at least a chance.

Edward Millard Pratt was Legal Remembrancer to the Governor of Bombay from 1918 to 1925. He was the author of Pratt's Indian Stamp Act.

George Marlow Pratt was on the stage for a short time, was a medical student at Guys Hospital in London in 1887, and later was with a paper firm, Elverstein & Co. While he was a medical student, George created a scandal known at the time as "The Shooting Affray," when he shot the husband of the lady next door, with whom he was enamored.

Charles Rary Pratt spent his adult life in Brazil, mainly employed by the French Cable Company.

Frederick Grenville Pratt became an Indian civil servant—Commissioner, Bombay Land Settlement Records.

David Cameron Pratt was with brother Charles in Brazil.

Boris's sister, Julia Honoria Pratt, married Arthur Donkin, Vicar of Semer, Suffolk.

John Thomas Pratt had perhaps the most distinguished career of the Pratt boys. He entered the British Foreign Office in 1898 and became Apprentice Interpreter in China. He was a barrister at law, Middle Temple, in 1905; British Assessor in the Mixed Court, Shanghai, 1909; Vice Consul in 1910; Consul in 1913; Acting Consul General at Tsinan in 1919; Acting Consul General at Nanking and Shanghai in 1925; Acting Counsellor, Diplomatic Service, 1929. In that year he was knighted for his services. Sir John also wrote several erudite books on China and served in the London Foreign Office before and during World War II.

Richard Septimus Pratt joined the British Consular Service and served in India and later in China.

William Henry Pratt migrated to Canada in 1909, where he changed his name to Boris Karloff. When, much later, people became interested, he stated that Karloff was his grandmother's name and that he had invented "Boris" because it seemed to go with Karloff. He added: "After all, one can't be an actor and be called 'Pratt'!" Possibly some member of the family had told Boris there was a Karloff in the Pratt background—he apparently believed it—but I could find no record of any Karloff in the entire Pratt-Millard genealogies.

The Dumb Girl of Portici (1916).

OPPOSITE—TOP: *His Majesty, the American* (1919); BOTTOM: *The Last of the Mohicans* (1920).

LEFT: *Without Benefit of Clergy* (1921); BELOW: *The Man from Downing Street* (1922).

LEFT: *Omar the Tentmaker* (1922);
BELOW: *The Gentleman from America*
(1923).

OPPOSITE—TOP: *Parisian Nights*
(1925); BOTTOM: *Forbidden Cargo*
(1925).

ABOVE: *The Phantom Buster* (1927).

OPPOSITE—TOP: *The Greater Glory* (1926—Boris lost in the crowd); BOTTOM: *The Nickel Hopper* (1926).

OPPOSITE—TOP: *Soft Cushions* (1927);
BOTTOM: *The Devil's Chaplain* (1929).

LEFT: *Two Sisters* (1929);
BELOW: *Mothers Cry* (1930).

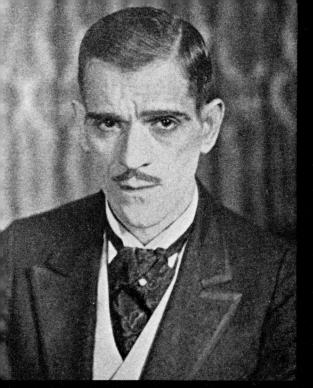

Above: *Cracked Nuts* (1931); right: *I Like Your Nerve* (1931).

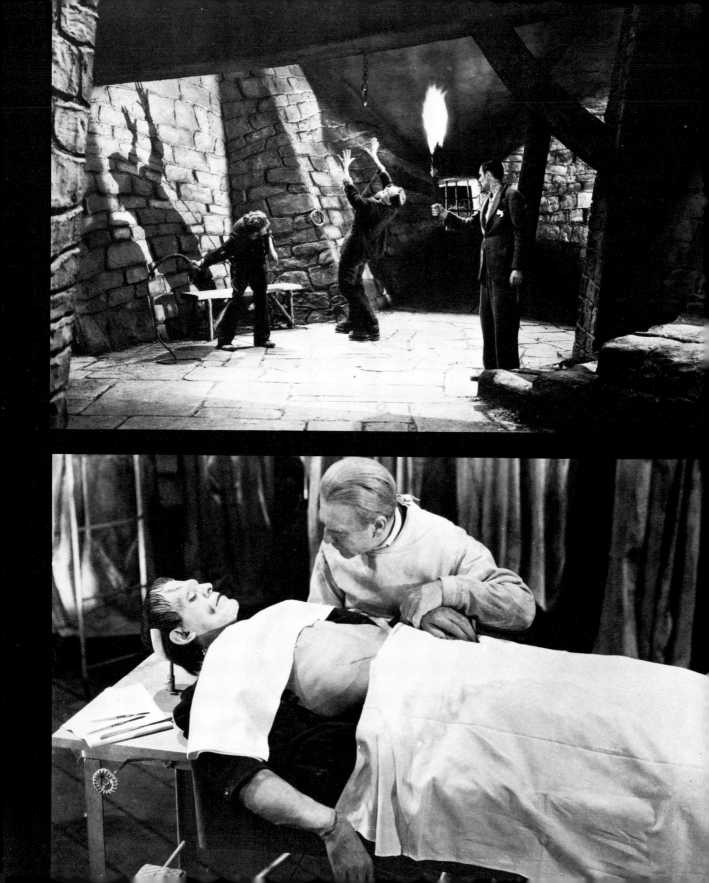

OPPOSITE: *Frankenstein* (1931).

ABOVE: *Behind the Mask* (1932);
RIGHT: *Scarface* (1932).

OPPOSITE—TOP: *The Miracle Man*
(1932); BOTTOM: *Night World* (1932)

LEFT: *The Old Dark House* (1932);
BOTTOM: *The Mummy* (1932).

OPPOSITE: *The Mask of Fu Manchu* (1932).

RIGHT: *The Ghoul* (1933); BOTTOM: *The Lost Patrol*
(1934).

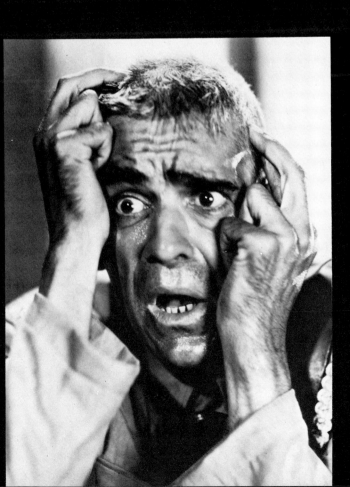

ABOVE: *The House of Rothschild* (1934); RIGHT: *The Black Cat* (1934).

LEFT: *Gift of Gab* (1934); BELOW: *The Bride of Frankenstein* (1935).

ABOVE: *The Raven* (1935); LEFT: *The Black Room* (1935).

OPPOSITE—TOP: *The Invisible Ray* (1936); BOTTOM: *The Walking Dead* (1936).

OPPOSITE—TOP: *The Man Who Lived Again* (1936); BOTTOM LEFT: *Charlie Chan at the Opera* (1936); BOTTOM RIGHT: *West of Shanghai* (1937).

ABOVE: *Night Key* (1937); LEFT: *The Invisible Menace* (1938).

LEFT: *Mr. Wong, Detective* (1938); BELOW: *Son of Frankenstein* (1939).

OPPOSITE—TOP: *The Mystery of Mr. Wong* (1939); BOTTOM: *The Man They Could Not Hang* (1939).

OPPOSITE: *Tower of London* (1939).

LEFT: *Devil's Island* (1940); BELOW: *The Man with Nine Lives* (1940).

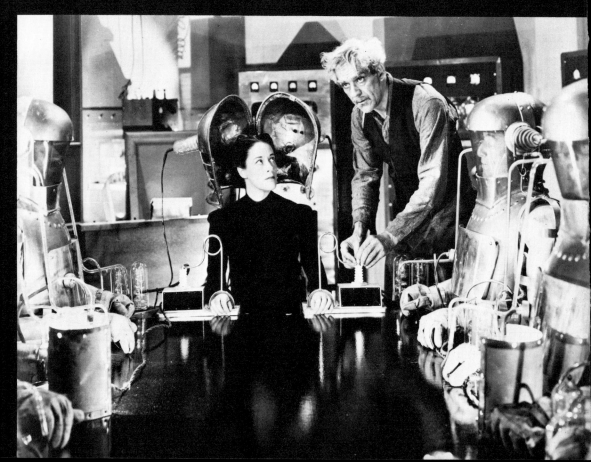

OPPOSITE—TOP: *The Boogie Man Will Get You* (1942); BOTTOM: *The Devil Commands* (1941).

ABOVE: *Before I Hang* (1940);
RIGHT: *Black Friday* (1940).

ABOVE: *The Climax* (1944)

OPPOSITE—TOP: *British Intelligence* (1940); BOTTOM: *The Fatal Hour* (1940).

ABOVE: *House of Frankenstein* (1944); RIGHT: *The Body Snatcher* (1945).

OPPOSITE—TOP AND BOTTOM: *Isle of the Dead* (1945).

ABOVE AND OPPOSITE—TOP: *Bedlam* (1946).

OPPOSITE—BOTTOM: *The Secret Life of Walter Mitty* (1947)

Opposite—top: *Unconquered* (1947);
bottom: *Tap Roots* (1948).

Above: *Abbott and Costello Meet the
Killer, Boris Karloff* (1949);
right: *The Strange Door* (1951).

Left: *The Hindu* (1953).

Right: *The Monster of the Island*
(1953).

LEFT: *Abbott and Costello Meet Dr. Jekyll and Mr. Hyde* (1953).

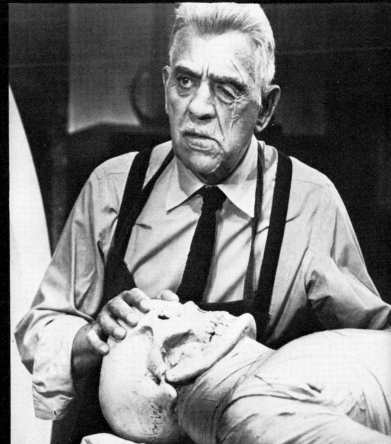

RIGHT: *Frankenstein 1970* (1958).

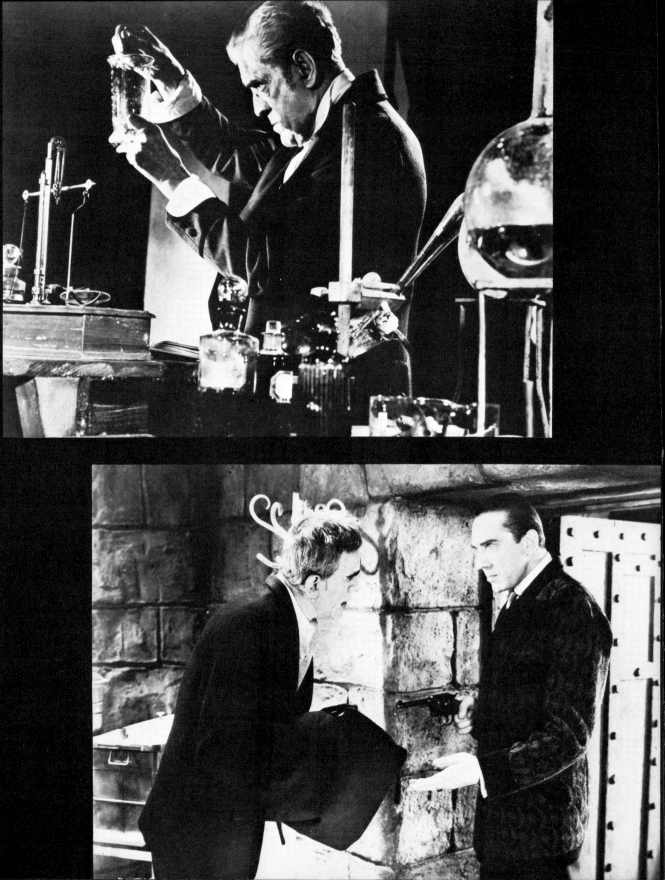

OPPOSITE—TOP: *Corridors of Blood*
(1963); BOTTOM: *The Raven* (1963).

RIGHT: *The Terror* (1963);
BELOW: *The Comedy of Terrors*
(1964).

ABOVE: *Die, Monster, Die!* (1965).

OPPOSITE—TOP: *The Venetian Affair* (1967); BOTTOM: *Targets* (1968).

House of Evil (1972).

FILMOGRAPHY

Years are the major release dates; U.S. titles are given first.

1916

THE DUMB GIRL OF PORTICI

Universal / *Silent*
Directed by Max Ratinoff (?)
Screenplay by Lois Weber
CAST: Anna Pavlova, Lois Wilson,
 R. Julian, Douglas Gerrard
Karloff as extra.

1919

THE MASKED RAIDER

Arrow / *Silent* / 15-part serial
Directed by Aubrey M. Kennedy
CAST: Harry Myers, Ruth Stonehouse,
 Paul Panzer
Karloff role unknown.

THE LIGHTNING RAIDER

Pathé / *Silent* / 15-part serial
Directed by George B. Seitz
Screenplay by Charles Goddard and
 John B. Clymer · From stories by
 May Yohe
CAST: Pearl White, Warner Oland,
 Henry G. Sell
Karloff role unknown.

HIS MAJESTY, THE AMERICAN

United Artists / *Silent*
Produced by Douglas Fairbanks
Directed by Joseph Henabery
Screenplay by Joseph Henabery and

"Elton Banks" · From a story by
 "Elton Banks"
CAST: Douglas Fairbanks, Marjorie Daw,
 Lillian Langton, Frank Campeau,
 Sam Southern, Jay Dwiggins
Karloff in bit part.

THE PRINCE AND BETTY

Pathé / *Silent*
Produced by Jesse D. Hampton
Directed by Robert Thornby
From a novel by P. G. Wodehouse
CAST: William Desmond, Mary Thurman,
 Anita Kay, George Swan, Walter
 Peng, Wilton Taylor, William Levaull,
 Frank Lanning
Karloff in bit part.

THE DEADLIER SEX

Pathé / *Silent*
Directed by Robert Thornby
Screenplay by Fred Myton
CAST: Blanche Sweet, Mahlon Hamilton,
 Winter Hall, Roy Laidlaw, Boris
 Karloff, Russell Simpson
Karloff as Jules Borney, a French-
 Canadian trapper.

THE COURAGE OF
MARGE O'DOONE

Vitagraph / *Silent*
Directed by David Smith
Screenplay by Robert North Bradbury ·
 From a novel by James Oliver Curwood

THE COURAGE OF MARGE O'DOONE (*continued*)

CAST: Pauline Starke, Niles Welch,
George Stanley, Jack Curtis, William
Dyer, Boris Karloff, Billie Bennett,
James O'Neill, Baree
Karloff as Tavish, a Canadian trapper.

1920

THE LAST OF THE MOHICANS

Associated Producers / *Silent*
Produced by Maurice Tourneur
Directed by Maurice Tourneur and
Clarence Brown
Screenplay by Robert Dillon · From
the novel by James Fenimore Cooper
CAST: Albert Roscoe, Barbara Bedford,
Lillian Hall, Wallace Beery, Henry
Woodward, Harry Lorraine, Theodore
Lorch, George Hackathorne, Nelson
McDowell, Sydney Deane, Jack
McDonald
Karloff as a Huron Indian.

1921

WITHOUT BENEFIT OF CLERGY

Pathé / *Silent*
Produced by Paul Brunton
Directed by James Young
Screenplay by Randolph C. Lewis · From
a short story by Rudyard Kipling
CAST: Virginia Brown Faire, Thomas
Holding, Evelyn Selbie, Otto Lederer,
Boris Karloff, Nigel De Brulier,
Herbert Prior, Ruth Sinclair, E. G.
Miller, Philippe De Lacey
Karloff as Ahmed Khan, villain.

THE HOPE DIAMOND MYSTERY (THE ROMANCE OF THE HOPE DIAMOND)

Kosmik Films / *Silent* / 15-part serial
Directed by Stuart Payton
Screenplay by Charles Goddard and
John B. Clymer · From a story by
May Yohe
CAST: Grace Darmond, William Marion,
Harry Carter, George Chesebro,
Boris Karloff, Carmen Phillips, May
Yohe, Frank Seka, Harry Archer,
Captain Clayton, Ethel Shannon,
William Buckley
Karloff as the villainous Priest of Kama-
Sita and as Dakar.

CHEATED HEARTS

Universal / *Silent*
Directed by Hobart Henley
Screenplay by Wallace Clifton · From
the novel *Barry Gordon* by William F.
Payson
Photographed by Virgil Miller
CAST: Herbert Rawlinson, Warner
Baxter, Marjorie Daw, Doris Pawn,
Winter Hall, Josef Swickard, Murdock
MacQuarrie, Boris Karloff, Anna Lehr,
Al MacQuarrie, Hector Sarno
Karloff as Nei Hamid, an Arab.

THE CAVE GIRL

An Inspiration Film Production / *Silent*
Directed by Joseph J. Franz
Screenplay by William Parker · From
the play by Guy Bolton and George
Middleton
Photographed by Victor Milner
Titles by Katherine Hilliker
CAST: Teddie Gerard, Charles Meredith,
Wilton Taylor, Eleanor Hancock,
Lillian Tucker, Frank Coleman, Boris
Karloff, Jake Abrahams, John Beck

Karloff as Baptiste, a villainous half-breed
  Indian guide.

1922

THE MAN FROM DOWNING STREET
(THE JADE ELEPHANTS)

Vitagraph / *Silent*
Directed by Edward José
Screenplay by Bradley J. Smollen · From
  a story by Clyde Westover, Lottie
  Horner and Florine Williams
Photographed by Ernest Smith
CAST: Earle Williams, Betty Ross Clarke,
  Boris Karloff, Charles Hill Mailes,
  Kathryn Adams, Herbert Prior, Henry
  Burrows, Eugenia Gilbert, James
  Butler, George Stanley
Karloff as master crook Dell Monckton
  and Indian "Maharajah Jehan Dharwar."

THE INFIDEL

A Preferred Pictures Production / *Silent*
Produced by B. P. Schulberg
Directed by James Young
Screenplay by James A. Young · From
  a story by Charles A. Logue
Photographed by Joseph Brotherton
CAST: Katherine MacDonald, Robert
  Ellis, Joseph Dowling, Boris Karloff,
  Melbourne McDowell, Oleta Otis,
  Charles Smiley, Loyola O'Connor,
  Barbara Tennant, Charles Force
Karloff as the Nabob, ruler of the South
  Sea isle of Menang.

THE ALTAR STAIRS

Universal / *Silent*
Directed by Lambert Hillyer

Screenplay by Doris Schroeder and
  George Hively · From a story by
  G. B. Lancaster
Photographed by Dwight Warren
CAST: Frank Mayo, Louise Lorraine,
  Lawrence Hughes, J. J. Lanoe,
  Harry De Vere, Hugh Thompson,
  Boris Karloff, Dagmar Godowsky,
  Nick de Ruiz
Karloff as Hugo.

OMAR THE TENTMAKER

First National / *Silent*
Produced by Richard Walton Tully
Directed by James Young
Screenplay by Richard Walton Tully ·
  From his play *Omar Khayam the
  Tentmaker*
Photographed by George Benoit
Art Director: Wilfred Buckland
CAST: Guy Bates Post, Virginia Brown
  Faire, Nigel De Brulier, Noah Beery,
  Rose Dione, Patsy Ruth Miller,
  Douglas Gerrard, Boris Karloff,
  Maurice B. Flynn, Edward M. Kimball,
  Walter Long, Evelyn Selbie, John
  Gribner, George Rigas, Will Jim
  Hutton, Gordon Mullen
Karloff as the Holy Imam Mowaffak,
  teacher and father of Shireen, Omar's
  love.

THE WOMAN CONQUERS

Preferred Pictures / *Silent*
Produced by B. P. Schulberg
Directed by Tom Forman
From a story by Violet Clark
Photographed by Joseph Brotherton
CAST: Katherine MacDonald, Bryant
  Washburn, Mitchell Lewis, June
  Elvidge, Clarissa Selwynne, Boris
  Karloff, Francis McDonald
Karloff as Raoul Maris, a French-
  Canadian trapper villain.

1923

THE GENTLEMAN FROM AMERICA

Universal / *Silent*
Produced by Carl Laemmle
Directed by Edward Sedgwick
Screenplay by George Hull · From a
    story by Raymond L. Schrock
Photographed by Virgil Miller
CAST: Hoot Gibson, Tom O'Brien,
    Louise Lorraine, Carmen Phillips,
    Frank Leigh, Jack Crane, Bob
    McKenzie, Albert Prisco, Rosa
    Rosanova
Karloff is shot by Gibson in one scene.

THE PRISONER

Universal / *Silent*
Directed by Jack Conway
Screenplay by Edward T. Lowe, Jr. ·
    From the novel *Castle Craneycrow* by
    George Barr McCutcheon
Photographed by Benjamin Reynolds
CAST: Herbert Rawlinson, Eileen Percy,
    George Cowl, June Elvidge, Lincoln
    Stedman, Gertrude Short, Bertram
    Grassby, Mario Carillo, Hayford
    Hobbs, Lillian Langdon, Bert Sprotte,
    Boris Karloff, Esther Ralston, P. J.
    Lockney, Milla Davenport, Fred
    Kelsey
Karloff as Prince Kapolski.

1924

RIDERS OF THE PLAINS

Arrow / *Silent* / 15-part serial
Directed by Jacques Jaccard
CAST: Jack Perrin, Marilyn Mills,
    Ruth Royce
Karloff role unknown.

THE HELLION

Sunset Pictures / *Silent*
Produced by Anthony J. Xydias
Direction and screenplay by Bruce
    Marshall (Mitchell?)
CAST: J. B. Warner, Marin Sais, William
    Lester, Alline Goodwin, Boris Karloff
Karloff as the outlaw.

DYNAMITE DAN

Sunset Pictures / *Silent*
Produced by Anthony J. Xydias
Direction and screenplay by Bruce
    Marshall (Mitchell?)
Photographed by Bert Longenecker
CAST: Kenneth McDonald, Diana Alden,
    Boris Karloff, Frank Rice, Harry
    Woods, Jack Waltemeyer, Jack
    Richardson, Eddie Harris, Carrie
    Daumery, Mrs. Harold Lockwood,
    Emily Gerdes
Karloff as Tony Garcia, villain.

1925

PERILS OF THE WIND

Universal / *Silent* / 15-part serial
Directed by Francis Ford
CAST: Joe Bonomo, Margaret Quimby,
    Jack Mower
Karloff role unknown.

PARISIAN NIGHTS

FBO / *Silent*
An R. C. Pictures Corporation Production
Directed by Alfred Santell
Screenplay by Fred Myton and C.
    Doty Hobart · From a story by
    Emil Forst
Photographed by Ernest Haller
Assistant Directors: Robert Florey and
    Roland Asher

CAST: Elaine Hammerstein, Gaston Glass,
    Lou Tellegan, William J. Kelly, Boris
    Karloff, Renée Adorée
Karloff as Pierre, a sadistic Parisian
    apache.

FORBIDDEN CARGO
(DANGEROUS CARGO)

FBO / *Silent*
An R. C. Pictures Corporation Production
Directed by Tom Buckingham
Screenplay and story by Frederick
    Kennedy Myton
Photographed by Silvano Balboni
CAST: Evelyn Brent, Robert Ellis,
    Boris Karloff
Karloff as Pietro Castillano, a villainous
    first mate on a ship.

THE PRAIRIE WIFE

MGM / *Silent*
Eastern Productions
Direction and screenplay by Hugo
    Ballin · From a story by Arthur
    Stringer
Photographed by James Diamond
Assistant Director: James Chapin
Titles by Katherine Hilliker and
    H. H. Caldwell
CAST: Dorothy Devore, Herbert
    Rawlinson, Gibson Gowland, Leslie
    Stuart, Frances Prim, Boris Karloff,
    Erich Von Ritzau, Rupert Franklin
Karloff as Diego, a Mexican half-breed.

LADY ROBIN HOOD

FBO / *Silent*
An R. C. Pictures Corporation Production
Directed by Ralph Ince
Screenplay by Fred Myton · From a
    story by Clifford Howard and
    Burke Jenkins
Photographed by Silvano Balboni
Assistant Director: Pandro S. Berman

CAST: Evelyn Brent, Robert Ellis, Boris
    Karloff, William Humphrey, Darcy
    Corrigan, Robert Cauterio
Karloff as Cabraza, a villain.

NEVER THE TWAIN SHALL
MEET

MGM / *Silent*
A Cosmopolitan Pictures Production
Produced by William Randolph Hearst
Directed by Maurice Tourneur
Screenplay by Eugene Mullin · From a
    novel by Peter B. Kyne
Photographed by Ira Morgan
Art Director: Joseph Urban
Edited by Donn Hayes
CAST: Anita Stewart, Bert Lytell, Huntly
    Gordon, Justine Johnstone, George
    Siegmann, Lionel Belmore, William
    Norris, Emily Fitzroy, Princess Marie
    de Bourbon, Florence Turner, James
    Wang, Ernest Butterworth, Ben Deeley,
    Roy Coulson, Thomas Ricketts
Karloff as a South Sea villain.

1926

THE GREATER GLORY

First National / *Silent*
Presented by Richard A. Rowland
Produced by June Mathis
Directed by Curt Rehfeld
Screenplay by June Mathis · From the
    novel *Viennese Medley* by Edith
    O'Shaughnessy
Photographed by John Boyle and
    Arthur Martinelli
Art Director: E. J. Shulter
Edited by George McGuire
CAST: Conway Tearle, Anna Q. Nilsson,
    May Allison, Ian Keith, Lucy Beaumont,
    Jean Hersholt, Nigel De Brulier,
    Bridgetta Clark, John Sainpolis,
    Marcia Manon, Edward Earle, Virginia
    Southern, Isabelle Keith, Kathleen

THE GREATER GLORY (*continued*)

Chambers, Hale Hamilton, Cora Macey, Carrie Daumery, Thur Fairfax, Boris Karloff, George Billings, Bess Flowers, Marcelle Corday, Manuel Acosta, Walter Shumley

Karloff as a scissors grinder.

HER HONOR, THE GOVERNOR
(THE SECOND MRS. FENWAY)

FBO / *Silent*
An R. C. Pictures Corporation Production
Produced by Joseph P. Kennedy
Directed by Chet Withey
Screenplay by Doris Anderson · From a story by Hyatt Daab and Weed Dickinson
Photographed by Andre Barlatier
CAST: Pauline Frederick, Carroll Nye, Thomas Santschi, Greta Von Rue, Stanton Heck, Boris Karloff, Jack Richardson, Kathleen Kirkham, Charles McHugh, William Worthington

Karloff as Snipe Collins, a crook.

THE BELLS

Chadwick Pictures / *Silent*
Produced by I. E. Chadwick
Direction and screenplay by James Young · From the play *Le Juif Polonais* by Emile Erckmann and Alexandre Chatrian
Photographed by William O'Connell
CAST: Lionel Barrymore, Gustav von Seyffertitz, Edward Phillips, Lola Todd, Boris Karloff, Fred Warren, Otto Lederer, Lorimer Johnston

Karloff as a Caligari-like mesmerist.

THE EAGLE OF THE SEA

Paramount / *Silent*
Produced by Adolph Zukor and Jesse L. Lasky

Associate Producer: B. P. Schulberg
Directed by Frank Lloyd
Screenplay by Julian Josephson · From the novel *Captain Sazarac* by Charles Tenney Jackson
Photographed by Norbert Brodine
CAST: Ricardo Cortez, Florence Vidor, Sam De Grasse, Boris Karloff, André Beranger, Mitchell Lewis, Guy Oliver, George Irving, Ervin Renard, James Marcus, Charles Anderson

Karloff as a pirate.

OLD IRONSIDES
(SONS OF THE SEA)

Paramount / *Silent*
Produced by Adolph Zukor and Jesse L. Lasky
Supervised by B. P. Schulberg
Directed by James Cruze
Screenplay by Dorothy Arzner, Walter Woods and Harry Carr
Adapted by Walter Woods and Harry Carr · From a novel by Laurence Stallings
Assistant Director: Harold Schwartz
Photographed by Alfred Gilks and Charles Boyle
Special Effects by Roy Pomeroy
Titles by Rupert Hughes
Process: Magascope
CAST: Charles Farrel, Esther Ralston, Wallace Beery, George Bancroft, Charles Hill Mailes, Johnnie Walker, Eddie Fetherston, George Godfrey, Guy Oliver, Fred Kohler, Nick De Ruiz, Mitchell Lewis, Edgar Washington Blue, Boris Karloff, Effie Ellsler, William Conklin, Duke Kahanamoku, Spec O'Donnell, Tetsu Komai, Jack Herrick, William Bakewell, Dick Alexander

Karloff as a Saracen pirate.

FLAMES

Associated Exhibitors / *Silent*
Produced and Directed by Lewis H.
   Moomaw
Screenplay and story by Alfred A. Cohn
Photographed by Herbert Brownell
   and King Gray
Edited by Frank Lawrence
CAST: Eugene O'Brien, Virginia Valli,
   Jean Hersholt, Bryant Washburn,
   George Nichols, Boris Karloff, Cissy
   Fitzgerald
Karloff as Blackie Blanchette, a railroad
   bandit.

THE GOLDEN WEB

Gotham / *Silent*
A Lumas Film Corporation Production
Presented by Sam Sax
Produced by Renaud Hoffman
Directed by Walter Lang
Screenplay by James Bell Smith · From
   a novel by E. Phillips Oppenheim
Photographed by Ray June
CAST: Lillian Rich, Huntly Gordon, Jay
   Hunt, Boris Karloff, Lawford Davidson,
   Nora Hayden, Syd Crossley, Joe
   Moore
Karloff as Dave Sinclair, a murder victim.

FLAMING FURY

FBO / *Silent*
An R. C. Pictures Corporation Production
Produced by Joseph P. Kennedy
Directed by James Hogan
Screenplay and story, "The Scourge of
   Fate," by Ewart Adamson
Photographed by Joe Walker
CAST: Ranger (the dog), Charles Delaney,
   Betty May, Boris Karloff, Eddie
   Chandler
Karloff as Gaspard, a French-Canadian
   half-breed villain.

THE MAN IN THE SADDLE

Universal / *Silent*
Directed by Clifford S. Smith
Screenplay and story by Charles A. Logue
CAST: Hoot Gibson, Virginia Brown
   Faire, Fay Wray
Karloff in bit part.

THE NICKEL HOPPER

Pathé-Hal Roach / 3-reeler / *Silent*
Produced by Hal Roach
Supervised by F. Richard Jones
Directed by Hal Yates
Titles by H. M. Walker
CAST: Mabel Normand, Theodore Von
   Eltz, Oliver Hardy, Boris Karloff
Karloff as a lecher.

VALENCIA (THE LOVE SONG)

MGM / *Silent*
Produced and Directed by Dmitri
   Buchowetzki
Screenplay by Alice D. G. Miller · From
   a story by Dmitri Buchowetzki and
   Alice D. G. Miller
Photographed by Percy Hilburn
Edited by Hugh Wynn
Art Director: Cedric Gibbons
Costumes by André-Ani
CAST: Mae Murray, Lloyd Hughes, Roy
   D'Arcy, Max Barwyn, Michael Vavitch,
   Michael Visaroff
Karloff in bit part.

1927

TARZAN AND THE GOLDEN LION

FBO / *Silent*
An R. C. Pictures Corporation Production
Produced by Joseph P. Kennedy
Directed by J. P. McGowan

TARZAN AND THE GOLDEN LION (*continued*)

Screenplay by William E. Wing · From
a novel by Edgar Rice Burroughs
Photographed by Joseph Walker
CAST: James Pierce, Dorothy Dunbar,
Edna Murphy, Frederic Peters, Harold
Goodwin, Liu Yu-Ching, D'Arcy
Corrigan, Boris Karloff, Robert Bolder,
Jad-Bal-Ja (the lion)
Karloff as Owaza, a Waziri Chief.

LET IT RAIN

Paramount / *Silent*
Produced by Douglas MacLean
Directed by Edward Francis Cline
Screenplay and story by Wade Boteler,
George J. Crone, and Earle Snell
Photographed by Jack MacKenzie
CAST: Douglas MacLean, Shirley Mason,
Wade Boteler, Frank Campeau, James
Bradbury, Jr., Lincoln Stedman, Lee
Shumway, Edwin Sturgis, Boris Karloff,
James Mason
Karloff as one of the crooks.

THE MEDDLIN' STRANGER

Pathé / *Silent*
Produced by Lester F..Scott, Jr.
Directed by Richard Thorpe
Screenplay and story by Christopher
B. Booth
Photographed by Ray Ries
CAST: Wally Wales, Nola Luxford,
James Marcus, Boris Karloff, Charles
K. French, Mabel Van Buren
Karloff as Al Meggs, a villain.

THE PRINCESS FROM HOBOKEN

Tiffany / *Silent*
Produced by John M. Stahl
Directed by Allan Dale
Screenplay and story by Sonya Levien
Photographed by Joseph Dubray and
Robert Martin

Art Director: Edwin B. Willis
Edited by James McKay
CAST: Edmund Burns, Blanche Mehaffey,
Ethel Clayton, Lou Tellegen, Babe
London, Will R. Walling, Charles
McHugh, Aggie Herring, Charles
Crockett, Robert Homans, Harry
Bailey, Sidney D'Albrook, Broderick
O'Farrell, Boris Karloff
Karloff as Pavel, a Frenchman.

THE PHANTOM BUSTER

Pathé / *Silent*
Produced by Lester F. Scott, Jr.
Directed by William Bertram
Screenplay by Betty Burbridge · From a
story by Walter J. Coburn
CAST: Buddy Roosevelt, Alma Rayford,
Charles Whitaker, Boris Karloff, John
Junior, Walter Maly, Lawrence
Underwood
Karloff as a Mexican border-smuggler.

SOFT CUSHIONS

Paramount / *Silent*
Produced by Douglas MacLean
Directed by Edward Francis Cline
Screenplay by Wade Boteler and
Frederic Chapin · From a story by
George Randolph Chester
Photographed by Jack MacKenzie
CAST: Douglas MacLean, Sue Carol,
Richard Carle, Russell Powell, Frank
Leigh, Wade Boteler, Nigel De
Brulier, Albert Prisco, Boris Karloff,
Albert Gran, Fred Kelsey, Noble
Johnson, Harry Jones
Karloff as a villainous Chief Conspirator.

TWO ARABIAN KNIGHTS

Caddo–Howard Hughes / *Silent*
Produced by Howard Hughes
Supervised by John W. Considine, Jr.
Directed by Lewis Milestone

Screenplay by James O'Donohue and
Wallace Smith · From a story by
Donald McGibney
Adapted by Wallace Smith and
Cyril Gardner
Photographed by Tony Gaudio and
Joseph August
Titles by George Manon, Jr.
Art Direction by William Cameron
Menzies
Technical Direction by Ned Mann
Assistant Direction: Nate Watt
CAST: William Boyd, Mary Astor, Louis
Wolheim, Michael Vavitch, Ian Keith,
De Witt Jennings, Michael Visaroff,
Boris Karloff
Karloff as the Purser.

THE LOVE MART

First National / *Silent*
Produced by Richard A. Rowland
Directed by George Fitzmaurice
Screenplay by Benjamin Glazer · From
the novel *The Code of Victor Jallot*
by Edward Childs Carpenter
Photographed by Lee Garmes
Titles by Edwin Justus Mayer
Edited by Stuart Heisler
Costumes by Max Ree
CAST: Billie Dove, Gilbert Roland, Noah
Beery, Raymond Turner, Armand Kaliz,
Emil Chautard, Boris Karloff, Mattie
Peters
Karloff as Fleming, a villain.

1928

VANISHING RIDER

Universal / *Silent* / 10-part serial
Directed by Ray Taylor
CAST: William Desmond, Ethlyne Clair,
Bud Osborne, Nelson McDowell
Karloff role unknown.

VULTURES OF THE SEA

Mascot / *Silent* / 10-part serial
Produced by Nat Levine
Directed by Richard Thorpe
CAST: Johnnie Walker, Shirley Mason,
Tom Santschi, Boris Karloff, John
Carpenter, George Magrill, Joe
Bennett, Arthur Dewey, Frank Hagey,
Joseph Mack, J. P. Lockney, Lafe
McKee
Karloff role unknown.

THE LITTLE WILD GIRL

Hercules-Trinity / *Silent*
Directed by Frank Mattison
Screenplay by Cecil Burtis Hill · From a
story by Putnam Hoover
Photographed by Jules Cronjager
Titles by Gordon Kalem
Edited by Minnie Steppler
CAST: Lila Lee, Cullen Landis, Frank
Merrill, Sheldon Lewis, Boris Karloff,
Jimmy Aubrey, Bud Shaw, Arthur D.
Hotaling, Cyclone
Karloff as Maurice Kent, a Canadian
Northwoodsman.

1929

BURNING THE WIND

Universal / *Silent*
Directed by Henry MacRae and
Herbert Blache
Screenplay by Raymond Schrock, George
Plympton, and George Morgan · From
the novel *A Daughter of the Dons* by
William MacLeod Raine
Photographed by Harry Neumann and
Ray Ramsey
Titles by Gardner Bradford
Edited by Maurice Pivar and Thomas
Malloy
CAST: Hoot Gibson, Virginia Brown

Faire, Cesare Gravina, Robert Homans, George Grandee, Boris Karloff, Pee Wee Holmes

Karloff as Pug Doran, a villain.

THE FATAL WARNING

Mascot / *Silent* / 10-part serial
Produced by Nat Levine
Directed by Richard Thorpe
CAST: Helen Costello, Ralph Graves, Tom Lingham, Phillips Smalley, Lloyd Whitlock, George Periolat, Boris Karloff, Syd Crossley, Martha Mattox, Symona Boniface

Karloff as Mullins, a villain.

THE DEVIL'S CHAPLAIN

Rayart-Richmont / *Silent*
Produced by Trem Carr
Directed by Duke Worne
Screenplay by Arthur Hoerl · From a novel by George Bronson Howard
Photographed by Hap Depew
Edited by J. S. Harrington
CAST: Virginia Brown Faire, Cornelius Keefe, Josef Swickard, Wheeler Oakland, George McIntosh, Boris Karloff, Leland Carr

Karloff as Boris, a villain.

THE PHANTOM OF THE NORTH

Biltmore Productions–All Star / *Silent*
Directed by Harry Webb
Screenplay by George Hull and Carl Krusada · From a story by Flora E. Douglas
Photographed by Arthur Reeves and William Thornley
CAST: Edith Roberts, Kathleen Key, Donald Keith, Joseph Swickard, Boris Karloff, Muro (the dog), Arab (the horse)

Karloff as Jules Gregg, a French-Canadian villain.

ANNE AGAINST THE WORLD

Rayout / *Silent*
Directed by Duke Worne
Screenplay by Arthur Hoerl · From a story by Victor Thorne
Photographed by Hap Depew
Edited by J. S. Harrington
CAST: Shirley Mason, Jack Mower, James Bradbury, Jr., Isabel Keith, Belle Stoddard, Henry Roguemore, Billy Franey, Tom Curran

Karloff in minor role.

TWO SISTERS

Rayart / *Silent*
Produced by Trem Carr
Directed by Scott Pembroke
Screenplay by Arthur Hoerl · From a novel by Virginia Terhune Vandewater
Photographed by Hap Depew
CAST: Viola Dana, Rex Lease, Claire Du Brey, Irving Bacon, Boris Karloff, Tom Lingham, Tom Curran, Adalyn Asbury

Karloff as Cecil, a crook.

BEHIND THAT CURTAIN

Fox
Produced by William Fox
Directed by Irving Cummings
Screenplay by Sonya Levien and Clarke Silvernail · From the novel *Behind That Curtain* by Earl Derr Biggers
Photographed by Conrad Wells, Dave Ragin, and Vincent Farrar
Titles by Wilbur Morse, Jr.
Edited by Alfred De Gaetano
Sound recording by George P. Costello
Assistant Director: Charles Woolstenhulme
CAST: Warner Baxter, Lois Moran, Gilbert Emery, Claude King, Philip Strange, Boris Karloff, Jamiel Hassen,

Peter Gawthorne, John Rogers,
Montague Shaw, Frank Finch-Smiles,
Mercedes de Velasco, E. L. Park
Karloff as a Soudanese Servant.

KING OF THE KONGO

Mascot / *Silent and Sound* / 10-part serial
Produced by Nat Levine
Directed by Richard Thorpe
CAST: Jacqueline Logan, Walter Miller,
Richard Tucker, Boris Karloff, Larry
Steers, Harry Todd, Richard Neil,
Lafe McKee, J. P. Leckray, William
Burt, Gordon Russell, Robert Frazer,
Ruth Davis
Karloff as Martin, the gang leader revealed
as Martin, the heroine's father.

THE UNHOLY NIGHT
(THE GREEN GHOST)

MGM
Directed by Lionel Barrymore
Screenplay by Edwin Justus Mayer · From
a story by Ben Hecht
Adapted by Dorothy Farnum
Photographed by Ira Morgan
Titles by Joe Farnham
Recording Engineers: Douglas Shearer
and Paul Neal
Art Direction by Cedric Gibbons
Gowns by Adrian
Edited by Grant Whytock
CAST: Ernest Torrance, Roland Young,
Dorothy Sebastian, Natalie Moorhead,
Claude Fleming, John Miljan,
Richard Tucker, John Loder, Philip
Strange, Polly Moran, Sojin, Boris
Karloff, Sidney Jarvis, Clarence
Geldert, John Roche, Lionel Belmore,
Gerald Barry, Richard Travers, George
Cooper
Karloff as Abdoul, a Hindu servant.

1930

THE BAD ONE

United Artists
Produced by Joseph M. Schenck
Supervised by John W. Considine, Jr.
Directed by George Fitzmaurice
Screenplay by Carey Wilson · From a
story by John Farrow
Dialogue by Howard Emmett Rogers
Photographed by Karl Struss
Art Direction by William Cameron
Menzies
Assistant Art Director: Park French
Recording Engineer: Frank Grenzbach
Assistant Director: Walter Mayo
Costumes by Alice O'Neill
Music by Hugo Riesenfeld
Edited by Donn Hayes
CAST: Dolores Del Rio, Edmund Lowe,
Don Alvarado, Blanche Frederici,
Adrienne D'Ambricourt, Ullrich Haupt,
Mitchell Lewis, Ralph Lewis, Charles
McNaughton, Yola D'Avril, John
Sainpolis, Henry Kolker, George
Fawcett, Victor Potel, Harry Stubbs,
Tom Dugan
Karloff as a prison guard.

THE SEA BAT

MGM
Directed by Wesley Ruggles
Screenplay by Bess Meredyth and John
Howard Lawson · From a story by
Dorothy Yost
Photographed by Ira Morgan
Titles by Philip J. Leddy
Art Direction by Cedric Gibbons
Sound by Douglas Shearer and
Karl E. Zint
Song "Lo-Lo" by Reggie Montgomery
and Al Ward
Edited by Harry Reynolds and
Jerry Thoms

THE SEA BAT (*continued*)

CAST: Raquel Torres, Charles Bickford, Nils Asther, George F. Marion, John Miljan, Boris Karloff, Gibson Gowland, Edmund Breese, Mathilda Comont, Mack Swain

Karloff as a Corsican, an evil half-breed.

THE UTAH KID

Tiffany
Directed by Richard Thorpe
Screenplay and story by Frank Howard Clark
Photographed by Arthur Reed
Sound by Carson J. Jowett
Edited by Billy Bolen
CAST: Rex Lease, Dorothy Sebastian, Tom Santschi, Mary Carr, Walter Miller, Lafe McKee, Boris Karloff, Bud Osborne

Karloff as Baxter, a bandit.

MOTHERS CRY

First National
Produced by Robert North
Directed by Hobart Henley
Screenplay by Lenore J. Coffee · From a novel by Helen Grace Carlisle
Photographed by Gilbert Warrenton
Edited by Frank Hare
CAST: Dorothy Peterson, Helen Chandler, David Manners, Sidney Blackmer, Edward Woods, Evalyn Knapp, Jean Bary, Pat O'Malley, Claire McDowell, Charles Hill Mailes, Reginald Pasch

Karloff as a murder victim.

1931

KING OF THE WILD

Mascot / 12-part serial
Produced by Nat Levine
Directed by Richard Thorpe and B. Reeves Eason

Screenplay and story by Wyndham Gittens and Ford Beebe
Photographed by Benjamin Kline and Edward Kull
Musical Direction by Lee Zahler
CAST: Walter Miller, Nora Lane, Dorothy Christy, Tom Santschi, Boris Karloff, Arthur McLaglen, Carroll Nye, Victor Potel, Martha Lalade, Mischa Auer

Karloff as Mustapha, a nefarious sheik.

THE CRIMINAL CODE

Columbia
Produced by Harry Cohn
Directed by Howard Hawks
Screenplay by Fred Niblo, Jr. and Seton I. Miller · From a play by Martin Flavin
Photographed by James Wong Howe
Sound by Glenn Rominger
Edited by Edward Curtis
CAST: Walter Huston, Phillips Holmes, Constance Cummings, Mary Doran, De Witt Jennings, John Sheehan, Boris Karloff, Otto Hoffman, Clark Marshall, Arthur Hoyt, Ethel Wales, Nicholas Soussanin, Paul Porcasi, James Guilfoyle, Lee Phelps, Hugh Walker, Jack Vance

Karloff as a prison trusty, Ned Galloway.

CRACKED NUTS

RKO
Produced by Douglas MacLean
Directed by Edward Francis Cline
Screenplay by Ralph Spence · From a story by Douglas MacLean and Al Boasberg · With dialogue by Ralph Spence and Al Boasberg
Photographed by Nick Musuraca
Sound by Hugh McDowell
CAST: Bert Wheeler, Robert Woolsey, Edna May Oliver, Dorothy Lee, Leni Stengel, Stanley Fields, Harvey Clark,

Boris Karloff, Ben Turpin, Frank
Thornton, Frank Lackteen, Wilfred
Lucas
Karloff as a revolutionary.

YOUNG DONOVAN'S KID
(DONOVAN'S KID)

RKO
Produced by Louis Sarecky
Directed by Fred Niblo
Screenplay by J. Walter Ruben · From
the novel *Big Brother* by Rex Beach
Photographed by Edward Cronjager
Sound by John Tribby
CAST: Richard Dix, Jackie Cooper,
Marion Shilling, Frank Sheridan, Boris
Karloff, Dick Rush, Fred Kelsey,
Richard Alexander, Harry Tenbrook,
Wilfred Lucas, Phil Sleeman, Charles
Sullivan, Jack Perry, Frank Beal
Karloff as Cokey Joe, a dope-pusher.

THE PUBLIC DEFENDER

RKO-Radio
Produced by Louis Sarecky
Directed by J. Walter Ruben
Screenplay by Bernard Schubert · From
the novel *The Splendid Crime* by
George Goodchild
Photographed by Edward Cronjager
Edited by Archie Marshek
CAST: Richard Dix, Shirley Grey, Edmund
Breese, Boris Karloff, Paul Hurst,
Purnell Pratt, Alan Roscoe, Ruth
Weston, Nella Walker, Frank Sheridan,
Carl Gerrard, William Halligan
Karloff as the Professor, an ex-forger.

SMART MONEY

Warner Brothers–First National
Directed by Alfred E. Green
Screenplay and dialogue by Kubec
Glasmon, John Bright, Lucien Hubbard
and Joseph Jackson

Photographed by Robert Kurle
Edited by Jack Killifer
CAST: Edward G. Robinson, Evalyn
Knapp, James Cagney, Noel Francis,
Morgan Wallace, Paul Porcasi, Maurice
Black, Margaret Livingston, Billy
House, Edwin Argus, Ralf Harolde,
Boris Karloff, Mae Madison, Walter
Percival, John Larkin, Polly Walters,
Clark Burroughs, Gladys Lloyd
Karloff as Sport Williams, a crooked
gambler.

I LIKE YOUR NERVE

Warner Brothers–First National
Directed by William McGann
Screenplay by Houston Branch · From a
story by Roland Pertwee · With
dialogue by Roland Pertwee and
Houston Branch
Photographed by Ernest Haller
Edited by Peter Fritsch
CAST: Douglas Fairbanks, Jr., Loretta
Young, Edmund Breon, Henry Kolker,
Claud Allister, Ivan Simpson, Paul
Porcasi, André Cheron, Boris Karloff,
Henry Bunston
Karloff as Luigi, a butler.

PARDON US

Roach–MGM / *French-language version*
Directed by James Parrott
Screenplay and dialogue by H. M. Waller
Photographed by Jack Stevens
Sound by Elmer Roguse
Edited by Richard Currier
CAST: Stan Laurel, Oliver Hardy, June
Marlow, Guido Trento, James
Finlayson, Walter Long, Wilfred Lucas,
Robert Kortman, Leo Willis, Charlie
Hall, Tiny Sandford, Harry Woods,
The Etude Ethiopian Chorus
Karloff as a menacing convict.

FIVE STAR FINAL

Warner Brothers–First National
Directed by Mervyn LeRoy
Screenplay by Byron Morgan · From a
  play by Louis Weitzenkorn · Adapted
  by Robert Lord
Photographed by Sol Polito
Edited by Frank Ware
CAST: Edward G. Robinson, Marian
  Marsh, H. B. Warner, Anthony
  Bushnell, George E. Stone, Frances
  Starr, Ona Munson, Boris Karloff,
  Robert Elliott, Aline MacMahon,
  Purnell Pratt, David Torrence, Oscar
  Apfel, Gladys Lloyd, Evelyn Walsh
  Hall, Harold Waldridge, Polly Walters
Karloff as Vernon Isopod, a villainous
  ex-preacher.

THE MAD GENIUS

Warner Brothers–First National
Directed by Michael Curtiz
Screenplay by J. Grubb Alexander and
  Harvey Thew · From the play *The
  Idol* by Martin Brown
Photographed by Barney McGill
Edited by Ralph Dawson
CAST: John Barrymore, Marian Marsh,
  Donald Cook, Charles Butterworth,
  Luis Alberni, Carmel Myers, André
  Luguet, Frankie Darro, Boris Karloff,
  Mae Madison
Karloff as a villainous father.

DIRIGIBLE

Columbia
Directed by Frank Capra
Screenplay by Jo Swerling and
  Dorothy Howell · With dialogue by
  Jo Swerling · From a story by Lt.
  Commander F. W. Wead
Photographed by Joe Wilbur and
  Elmer Dyer
Sound by E. L. Bernds
Edited by Maurice Wright

CAST: Jack Holt, Ralph Graves, Fay
  Wray, Hobart Bosworth, Roscoe
  Karns, Harold Goodwin, Clarence
  Muse, Emmett Corrigan, Al Roscoe,
  Selmer Jackson
Karloff in bit part as a member of an
  expedition that went down in the
  dirigible.

THE LAST PARADE

Columbia
Directed by Erle C. Kenton
Screenplay and dialogue by Dorothy
  Howell · From a story by Casey
  Robinson
Photographed by Terry Tetzlaff
Sound by Russell Malmgren
Edited by Gene Havelick
CAST: Jack Holt, Tom Moore, Constance
  Cummings, Gaylord Pendleton, Robert
  Ellis, Earl D. Dunn, Jess De Vorska,
  Ed Le Saint, Edmund Breese, Clarence
  Muse, Gino Corrado, Robert Graham
Karloff in bit part as a prison warder.

THE GUILTY GENERATION

Columbia
Produced by Harry Cohn
Directed by Roland V. Lee
Screenplay by Jack Cunningham · From
  a play by Jo Milward and J. Kirby
  Hawkes
Photographed by Byron Haskin
Edited by Otis Garrett
CAST: Leo Carrillo, Constance Cummings,
  Robert Young, Leslie Fenton, Boris
  Karloff, Jimmy Wilcox, Elliott Roth,
  Phil Tead, Frederick Howard, Eddie
  Boland, W. J. O'Brien, Ruth Warren
Karloff as Tony Ricca, a rival gangster.

GRAFT

Universal
Produced by Carl Laemmle, Jr.
Directed by Christy Cabanne

Screenplay and story by Barry Barringer
Photographed by Jerome Ash
Edited by Maurice Pivar
CAST: Regis Toomey, Sue Carol, Dorothy
  Revier, Boris Karloff, William
  Davidson, Richard Tucker, Willard
  Robertson, Harold Goodwin, George
  Irving, Carmelita Geraghty
Karloff as Joe Terry, a murderer.

THE YELLOW TICKET
(THE YELLOW PASSPORT)

Fox
Directed by Raoul Walsh
Screenplay by Jules Furthman · From a
  play by Michael Morton · With
  dialogue by Jules Furthman and Guy
  Bolton
Photographed by James Wong Howe
Sound by Donald Flick
Edited by Jack Murray
CAST: Elissa Landi, Lionel Barrymore,
  Laurence Olivier, Walter Byron, Sarah
  Padden, Arnold Korff, Mischa Auer,
  Rita LaRoy, Boris Karloff, Edwin
  Maxwell, Max Melesh
Karloff as a drunken aide to a Czarist
  official.

TONIGHT OR NEVER

United Artists
Produced by Samuel Goldwyn
Directed by Mervyn LeRoy
Screenplay by Ernest Vajda · From a
  play by Lili Hatvany · Adapted by
  Frederick Hatton and Fanny Hatton
Photographed by Gregg Toland
Musical Direction by Alfred Newman
Edited by Grant Whytock
CAST: Gloria Swanson, Melvyn Douglas,
  Ferdinand Gottschalk, Warburton
  Gamble, Alison Skipworth, Robert
  Grieg, Greta Meyer, Boris Karloff
Karloff as a waiter.

FRANKENSTEIN

Universal
Presented by Carl Laemmle
Produced by Carl Laemmle, Jr.
Directed by James Whale
Screenplay and dialogue by Garrett Fort
  and Francis Edwards Faragoh · From
  the novel by Mary W. Shelley and the
  play by Peggy Webling · Adapted by
  John L. Balderston · Scenario Editor:
  Richard Schayer · Additional Dialogue
  by Robert Florey
Photographed by Arthur Edeson
Special Effects by John P. Fulton
Make-up by Jack P. Pierce
Edited by Clarence Kolster
Supervising Editor: Maurice Pivar
Art Direction by Charles D. Hall
Sets by Herman Rosse
Electrical Properties by Kenneth
  Strickfaden
Technical Assistant: Dr. Cecil Reynolds
Recording Engineer: C. Roy Hunter
Musical Theme by David Broekman
CAST: Colin Clive, Mae Clarke, John
  Boles, Boris Karloff, Edward Van
  Sloan, Dwight Frye, Frederick Kerr,
  Lionel Belmore, Marilyn Harris,
  Michael Mark, Arletta Duncan,
  Francis Ford
Karloff as the Monster.

BUSINESS AND PLEASURE

Fox
Produced by Al Rockett
Directed by David Butler
Screenplay and dialogue by Gene Towne
  and William Conselman · From the
  novel *The Plutocrat* by Booth
  Tarkington and the play by Arthur
  Goodrich
Photographed by Ernest Palmer
CAST: Will Rogers, Jetta Goudal, Joel
  McCrea, Dorothy Peterson, Peggy Ross,

BUSINESS AND PLEASURE (*continued*)

Cyril Ring, Jed Prouty, Oscar Apfel, Vernon Dent, Boris Karloff
Karloff as the Sheik.

1932

BEHIND THE MASK

Columbia
Produced by Harry Cohn
Directed by John Francis Dillon
Screenplay and dialogue by Jo Swerling · Adapted from the story "In the Secret Service" by Jo Swerling
Photographed by Ted Tetzlaff
Continuity by Dorothy Howell
Sound by Glenn Rominger
Edited by Otis Garrett
CAST: Jack Holt, Constance Cummings, Boris Karloff, Claude King, Bertha Mann, Edward Van Sloan, Willard Robertson
Karloff as Jim Henderson, dope-pusher.

ALIAS THE DOCTOR

Warner Brothers–First National
Directed by Michael Curtiz
Screenplay by Houston Branch · From a play by Imre Foeldes · With dialogue by Charles Kenyon
Photographed by Barney McGill
Art Direction by Anton Grot
Technical Advisor: Dr. Henry Morton
Edited by William Holmes
CAST: Richard Barthelmess, Marian Marsh, Lucille La Verne, Norman Foster, Adrienne Dore, Oscar Apfel, John St. Polis, Wallis Clark, Claire Dodd, George Rosener, Boris Karloff, Nigel De Brulier, Reginald Barlow, Arnold Lucy, Harold Waldridge, Robert Farfan
Karloff as the Autopsy Surgeon.

SCARFACE

Caddo
Produced by Howard Hughes
Directed by Howard Hawks
Screenplay by Seton I. Miller, John Lee Mahin, and W. R. Burnett · From a screen story by Ben Hecht
Photographed by Lee Garmes and L. W. O'Connell
Musical Direction by Adolph Tandler, Gus Arnheim
Edited by Edward Curtiss
CAST: Paul Muni, Ann Dvorak, Karen Morley, Osgood Perkins, Boris Karloff, C. Henry Gordon, George Raft, Purnell Pratt, Vince Barnett, Inez Palange, Harvey Vegar, Edwin Maxwell, Tully Marshall, Henry Armetta, Bert Starkey
Karloff as Gaffney, a molester.

THE COHENS AND KELLYS IN HOLLYWOOD

Universal
Produced by Carl Laemmle, Jr.
Directed by John Francis Dillon
Screenplay and story by Howard J. Green · With dialogue by James Mulhouser
Photographed by Jerome Ash
Edited by Harry Webb
CAST: George Sidney, Charlie Murray, June Clyde, Norman Foster, Emma Dunn, Esther Howard, Eileen Percy, Edwin Maxwell, Dorothy Christy, Luis Alberni, John Roche, Robert Greig, Tom Mix, Lew Ayres, Sidney Fox, Boris Karloff, Genevieve Tobin, Harry Barris
Karloff as himself.

THE MIRACLE MAN

Paramount
Directed by Norman Z. McLeod

Screenplay by Waldemar Young · From a novel by Frank L. Packard and a play by George M. Cohan and Robert H. Davis · With dialogue by Waldemar Young and Samuel Hoffenstein
Photographed by David Abel
Art Direction by Hans Dreier
CAST: Sylvia Sidney, Chester Morris, Robert Coogan, John Wray, Ned Sparks, Hobart Bosworth, Lloyd Hughes, Virginia Bruce, Boris Karloff, Irving Pichel, Frank Darien, Florine McKinney
Karloff as Nikko, a con man.

NIGHT WORLD

Universal
Directed by Hobart Henley
Screenplay by Richard Schayer · From a story by P. J. Wolfson and Allen Rivkin
Photographed by Merritt Gerstad
Edited by Maurice Pivar
CAST: Lew Ayres, Mae Clark, Boris Karloff, Dorothy Revier, Russell Hopton, George Raft, Hedda Hopper, Dorothy Peterson, Clarence Muse, Bert Roach, Florence Lake, Huntly Gordon, Gene Morgan, Paisley Noon, Greta Granstedt, Louise Beavers, Sammy Blum, Harry Woods, Eddie Phillips, Tom Tamarez, Robert Emmett O'Connor, Geneva Mitchell
Karloff as Happy MacDonald, a nightclub owner.

THE OLD DARK HOUSE

Universal
Presented by Carl Laemmle
Produced by Carl Laemmle, Jr.
Directed by James Whale
Screenplay and adaptation by Benn W. Levy · From the novel *Benighted* by J. B. Priestley · With added dialogue by R. C. Sherriff

Photographed by Arthur Edeson
Recording Supervisor: C. Roy Hunter
Art Direction by Charles D. Hall
Makeup by Jack P. Pierce
Edited by Clarence Kolster
CAST: Boris Karloff, Melvyn Douglas, Charles Laughton, Gloria Stuart, Lillian Bond, Ernest Thesiger, Eva Moore, Raymond Massey, Brember Wills, John Dudgeon
Karloff as Morgan, the mute, scarred butler.

THE MUMMY

Universal
Presented by Carl Laemmle
Produced by Carl Laemmle, Jr.
Directed by Karl Freund
Screenplay by John L. Balderston · From a story by Nina Wilcox Putnam and Richard Schayer
Photographed by Charles Stumar
Special Effects by John P. Fulton
Art Direction by Willy Pogany
Makeup by Jack P. Pierce
Edited by Milton Carruth
CAST: Boris Karloff, Zita Johann, David Manners, Edward Van Sloan, Arthur Byron, Bramwell Fletcher, Noble Johnson, Leonard Mudie, Katheryn Byron, Eddie Kane, Tony Marlow, Arnold Gray, James Crane, Henry Victor
Karloff as Im-Ho-Tep, the high priest, and Ardath Bey, the mystic.

THE MASK OF FU MANCHU

MGM
Directed by Charles Brabin
Screenplay by Irene Kuhn, Edgar Allan Woolf, and John Willard · From a novel by Sax Rohmer
Photographed by Tony Gaudio
Art Direction by Cedric Gibbons
Costumes by Adrian

THE MASK OF FU MANCHU (*continued*)
Recording Direction by Douglas Shearer
Edited by Ben Lewis
CAST: Boris Karloff, Lewis Stone, Karen
  Morley, Myrna Loy, Charles Starrett,
  Jean Hersholt, Lawrence Grant, David
  Torrence, O. P. Heggie
Karloff as Fu Manchu.

1933

THE GHOUL

Gaumont-British
Produced by Michael Balcon
Directed by T. Hayes Hunter
Screenplay by Leonard Hines, Roland
  Pertwee and John Hastings Turner ·
  Adapted by Rupert Downing · From a
  novel by Frank King
Photographed by Gunther Krampf
Art Direction by Alfred Junge
Musical Direction by Louis Levy
Makeup by Heinrich Heitfeld
Recording Engineer: R. Birch
Edited by Ian Dalrymple
CAST: Boris Karloff, Cedric Hardwicke,
  Ernest Thesiger, Dorothy Hyson,
  Anthony Bushell, Harold Huth,
  Kathleen Harrison, D. A. Clarke-Smith,
  Ralph Richardson, Jack Raine
Karloff as Professor Morlant.

1934

THE LOST PATROL

RKO
Executive Producer: Merian C. Cooper
Produced by Cliff Reid
Directed by John Ford
Screenplay by Dudley Nichols · Adapted
  by Garret Fort · From the novel *Patrol*
  by Philip MacDonald

Photographed by Harold Wenstrom
Sound by Glen Portman
Music by Max Steiner
Art Direction by Van Nest Polglase
Edited by Paul Weatherwax
CAST: Victor McLaglen, Boris Karloff,
  Wallace Ford, Reginald Denny, J. M.
  Kerrigan, Billy Bevan, Alan Hale,
  Brandon Hurst, Douglas Walton,
  Sammy Stein, Howard Wilson, Neville
  Clark, Paul Hanson
Karloff as Sanders, a religious fanatic.

THE HOUSE OF ROTHSCHILD

Twentieth Century
Produced by Darryl F. Zanuck
Directed by Alfred Werker
Screenplay by Nunnally Johnson · From
  a play by George Humbert Westley
Photographed by Peverell Marley
Music by Alfred Newman
Edited by Alan McNeil
Technicolor
CAST: George Arliss, Boris Karloff,
  Loretta Young, Robert Young, C.
  Aubrey Smith, Arthur Byron, Helene
  Westley, Reginald Owen, Florence
  Arliss, Alan Mowbray, Noel Madison,
  Ivan Simpson, Holmes Herbert, Paul
  Harvey, Georges Renavent, Murray
  Kinnell, Oscar Apfel, Lumsden Hare,
  Leo McCabe, Gilbert Emery, Charles
  Evans, Desmond Roberts, Earl
  McDonald, Ethel Griffies, Lee Kohlmar,
  William Strauss, Matthew Betz, Leonard
  Mudie, Reginald Sheffield, Crauford
  Kent, Gerald Prince, George Offerman,
  Jr., Bobbie La Mauche
Karloff as Count Ledrantz.

SCREEN SNAPSHOTS, NO. 11

Columbia
CAST: Boris Karloff, Bela Lugosi,
  Genevieve Tobin, Pat O'Brien, James

Cagney, Maureen O'Sullivan, Eddie
Cantor
Karloff as himself.

THE BLACK CAT
(THE HOUSE OF DOOM,
THE VANISHING BODY)

Universal
Presented by Carl Laemmle
Produced by Carl Laemmle, Jr.
Directed by Edgar G. Ulmer
Screenplay by Peter Ruric · Screen story
   by Edgar G. Ulmer and Peter
   Ruric · Suggested by a story by Edgar
   Allan Poe
Photographed by John Mescall
Special Effects by John P. Fulton
Art Direction by Charles D. Hall
Makeup by Jack P. Pierce
Music Direction by Heinz Roemheld
Edited by Ray Curtis
CAST: Boris Karloff, Bela Lugosi, David
   Manners, Jacqueline Wells, Lucille
   Lund, Egon Brecher, Henry Armetta,
   Albert Conti, Anna Duncan, Herman
   Bing, André Cheron, Luis Alberni,
   Harry Cording, George Davis,
   Alphonse Martell, Tony Marlow,
   Paul Weigel, Albert Polet, Rodney
   Hildebrand
Karloff as Hjalmar Poelzig, an architect
and Satanist.

GIFT OF GAB

Universal
Produced by Carl Laemmle, Jr.
Directed by Karl Freund
Screenplay by Rian James · Adapted by
   Lou Breslow · From a story by Jerry
   Wald and Philip G. Epstein
Photographed by George Robinson and
   Harold Wenstrom
Edited by Raymond Curtis
CAST: Edmund Lowe, Gloria Stuart, Ruth
   Etting, Phil Baker, Ethel Waters, Alice

White, Alexander Woollcott, Victor
Moore, Hugh O'Connell, Helen Vinson,
Gene Austin, Tom Hanlon, Henry
Armetta, Andy Devine, Wini Shaw,
Marion Byron, Sterling Holloway,
Edwin Maxwell, Leighton Noble,
Maurice Block, Tammany Young,
James Flavin, Billy Barty, Florence
Enright, Dick Elliott, Warner
Richmond, Paul Lukas, Chester
Morris, Roger Pryor, The Downey
Sisters, Douglass Montgomery, Candy
and Coco, Douglas Fowley, Binnie
Barnes, June Knight, Boris Karloff,
Bela Lugosi, The Beale Street Boys,
Rian James Graham McNamee, The
Three Stooges, Gus Arnheim and His
Orchestra
Karloff as himself.

1935

THE BRIDE
OF FRANKENSTEIN

Universal
Produced by Carl Laemmle, Jr.
Directed by James Whale
Screenplay by Willam Hurlburt · Adapted
   by John L. Balderston and William
   Hurlbut · From the novel *Frankenstein*
   by Mary W. Shelley
Photographed by John Mescall
Special Effects by John P. Fulton
Special Properties by Kenneth
   Strickfaden
Art Direction by Charles D. Hall
Music by Franz Waxman
Musical Direction by Mischa Bakaleinikoff
Makeup by Jack P. Pierce
Edited by Ted Kent
CAST: Boris Karloff, Colin Clive, Valerie
   Hobson, Elsa Lanchester, O. P. Heggie,
   Una O'Connor, Ernest Thesiger,
   Gavin Gordon, Douglas Walton, E. E.

THE BRIDE OF FRANKENSTEIN (*continued*)

Clive, Lucian Prival, Dwight Frye, Reginald Barlow, Mary Gordon, Anne Darling, Gunnis Davis, Tempe Piggot, Ted Billings, Neil Fitzgerald, Walter Brennan, Lucio Villegas, Edwin Mordant, Grace Cunard, Helen Gibson, John Carradine, Monty Montague, Joan Woodbury, Norman Ainsley, Peter Shaw, Billy Barty, Kansas De Forest, Josephine McKim, Helen Parrish

Karloff as *The Monster*.

THE RAVEN

Universal
Presented by Carl Laemmle
Produced by David Diamond
Directed by Louis Friedlander (Lew Landers)
Screenplay by David Boehm · Suggested by the poem by Edgar Allan Poe and "The Pit and the Pendulum"
Photographed by Charles Stumar
Art Direction by Albert S. D'Agostino
Music by Gilbert Harland
Choreography by Theodore Kosloff
Dialogue Director: Florence Enright
Makeup by Jack P. Pierce
Edited by Alfred Akst
CAST: Boris Karloff, Bela Lugosi, Irene Ware, Lester Matthews, Samuel S. Hinds, Inez Courtney, Ian Wolfe, Spencer Charters, Maidel Turner, Arthur Hoyt

Karloff as Edmond Bateman, a fugitive criminal.

THE BLACK ROOM

Columbia
Produced by Robert North
Directed by Roy William Neill
Screenplay by Henry Myers and Arthur Strawn · From a story by Arthur Strawn

Photographed by Al Seigler
Art Direction by Stephen Goosson
Musical Direction by Louis Silvers
Costumes by Murray Mayer
Edited by Richard Cahoon
CAST: Boris Karloff, Marian Marsh, Robert Allen, Thurston Hall, Katherine De Mille, John Buckler, Henry Kolker, Colin Tapley, Torben Meyer, Egon Brecher, John Bleifer, Frederick Vogeding, Edward Van Sloan, Herbert Evans, Lois Lindsay, Alan Mowbray

Karloff as Baron Gregor de Berghman and as Anton de Berghman.

1936

THE INVISIBLE RAY

Universal
Presented by Carl Laemmle
Produced by Edmund Grainger
Directed by Lambert Hillyer
Screenplay by John Colton · From a story by Howard Higgin and Douglas Hodges
Photographed by George Robinson
Special Effects by John P. Fulton
Art Direction by Albert S. D'Agostino
Music by Franz Waxman
Makeup by Jack P. Pierce
Edited by Bernard Burton
CAST: Boris Karloff, Bela Lugosi, Frances Drake, Frank Lawton, Walter Kingsford, Beulah Bondi, Violet Kemble Cooper, Nydia Westman, George Renavent, Frank Reicher, Paul Weigel, Adele St. Maur, Lawrence Stewart, Etta McDaniel, Daniel Haines, Inez Seabury, Winter Hall, Lloyd Whitlock, Edwards Davis, Alphonse Martell, Daisy Bufford, Clarence Gordon

Karloff as Dr. Janos Rukh.

THE WALKING DEAD

Warner Brothers–First National
Directed by Michael Curtiz
Screenplay by Ewart Adamson, Peter
    Milne, Robert Andrews, and Lillie
    Hayward · From a story by Ewart
    Adamson and Joseph Fields
Photographed by Hal Mohr
Art Direction by Hugh Reticker
Dialogue Direction by Irving Rapper
Costumes by Cary Odell
Edited by Thomas Pratt
CAST: Boris Karloff, Ricardo Cortez,
    Edmund Gwenn, Marguerite Churchill,
    Warren Hull, Barton MacLane, Henry
    O'Neill, Joseph King, Paul Harvey,
    Robert Strange, Joseph Sawyer, Eddie
    Acuff, Ruth Robinson, Addison
    Richards, Kenneth Harland, Miki
    Morita, Adrian Rosley
Karloff as John Ellman.

THE MAN WHO LIVED AGAIN
(THE MAN WHO CHANGED
HIS MIND; DR. MANIAC; THE
BRAINSNATCHER)

Gainsborough
Produced by Michael Balcon
Directed by Robert Stevenson
Screenplay by L. DuGarde Peach and
    Sidney Gilliat · From a story by
    John L. Balderston
Photographed by Jack Cox
Art Direction by Alex Vetchinsky
Edited by R. E. Dearing
CAST: Boris Karloff, Anna Lee, John
    Loder, Frank Cellier, Donald Calthrop,
    Cecil Parker, Lyn Harding
Karloff as Dr. Laurience.

JUGGERNAUT
(THE DEMON DOCTOR)

J. H. Productions
Produced by Julius Hagen

Directed by Henry Edwards
Screenplay by Cyril Campion and H.
    Fowler Mear · Adaptation and dialogue
    by Heinrich Fraenkel · From a novel
    by Alice Campbell
Photographed by Sidney Blythe and
    William Luff
Art Direction by James Carter
Music by W. L. Trytel
Edited by Michael Chorlton
CAST: Boris Karloff, Arthur Margetson,
    Joan Wyndham, Mona Goya, Anthony
    Ireland, Morton Selten, Nina Boucicault,
    Gibb McLaughlin, J. H. Roberts,
    Victor Rietti
Karloff as Dr. Sartorius.

CHARLIE CHAN AT THE OPERA

Twentieth Century-Fox
Produced by John Stone
Directed by H. Bruce Humberstone
Screenplay by W. Scott Darling and
    Charles Belden · From a story by
    Bess Meredyth · Based on the characters
    from the novels by Earl Derr Biggers
Photographed by Lucien Androit
Opera Music *Carnival* by Oscar Levant ·
    Libretto by William Kernell
Musical Direction by Samuel Kaylin
Orchestrations by Charles Maxwell
Sound by George Leverette and Harry
    H. Leonard
Costumes by Hershell
Edited by Alex Troffoy
CAST: Warner Oland, Boris Karloff, Keye
    Luke, Charlotte Henry, Thomas Beck,
    Margaret Irving, Gregory Gaye, Nedda
    Harrigan, Frank Conroy, Guy Usher,
    William Demarest, Maurice Cass, Tom
    McGuire
Karloff as Gravelle.

·   ·   ·

1937

NIGHT KEY

Universal
Produced by Robert Presnell
Directed by Lloyd Corrigan
Screenplay by Tristram Tupper and
    John C. Moffitt · From a story by
    William Pierce
Photographed by George Robinson
Special Effects by John P. Fulton
Musical Direction by Lou Forbes
Edited by Otis Garrett
Makeup by Jack P. Pierce
CAST: Boris Karloff, Jean Rogers, Warren
    Hull, Hobart Cavanaugh, Samuel S.
    Hinds, Alan Baxter, David Oliver,
    Edwin Maxwell, Ward Bond
Karloff as Dave Mallory.

WEST OF SHANGHAI
(THE WAR LORD)

Warner Brothers–First National
Produced by Bryan Foy
Directed by John Farrow
Screenplay by Crane Wilbur · From the
    play *The Bad Man* by Porter Emerson
    Browne
Photographed by L. William O'Connell
Edited by Frank Dewar
CAST: Boris Karloff, Beverly Roberts,
    Ricardo Cortez, Gordon Oliver, Sheila
    Bromley, Vladimir Sokoloff, Gordon
    Hart, Richard Loo, Douglas Wood,
    Chester Gan, Luke Chan, Selmer
    Jackson, James B. Leong, Tetsu Komai,
    Eddie Lee, Maurice Lui, Mia Ichioaka
Karloff as General Wu Yen Fang.

1938

THE INVISIBLE MENACE
(WITHOUT WARNING)

Warner Brothers
Produced by Bryan Foy

Directed by John Farrow
Screenplay by Crane Wilbur · From a
    play by Ralph Spencer Zink
Dialogue Direction by Harry Seymour
Photographed by L. William O'Connell
Edited by Harold McLernon
CAST: Boris Karloff, Regis Toomey,
    Marie Wilson, Eddie Craven, Cy
    Kendall, Frank Faylen, Harland Tucker,
    John Ridgely, Anderson Lawlor,
    Eddie Acuff, Henry Kolker, Charles
    Trowbridge, William Haade, Phyllis
    Barry, Jack Mower, Jack Harron
Karloff as Jevries, a murder suspect.

MR. WONG, DETECTIVE

Monogram
Produced by Scott R. Dunlap
Associate Producer: William T. Lackey
Directed by William Nigh
Screenplay by Houston Branch · From
    the story by Hugh Wiley
Photographed by Harry Neumann
Musical Direction by Art Meyer
Edited by Russell Schoengarth
CAST: Boris Karloff, Grant Withers,
    Maxine Jennings, Evalyn Brent,
    Lucien Prival, John St. Polis, William
    Gould, Hooper Atchley, John
    Hamilton, Frank Bruno, Lee Tong Foo,
    George Lloyd, Wilbur Mack,
    Grace Wood
Karloff as James Lee Wong.

1939

SON OF FRANKENSTEIN

Universal
Produced and Directed by Rowland V.
    Lee
Screenplay by Willis Cooper · Suggested
    by the novel *Frankenstein* by Mary
    W. Shelley

Photographed by George Robinson
Special Effects by John P. Fulton
Sound Direction by Bernard B. Brown
Art Direction by Jack Otterson
Associate Art Director: Richard H. Riedel
Set Decoration by Russell Gausman
Makeup by Jack P. Pierce
Music by Frank Skinner
Musical Direction by Lionel Newman
Assistant Director: Fred Frank
Technician: William Hedgcock
Costumes by Vera West
Edited by Ted Kent
CAST: Basil Rathbone, Boris Karloff, Bela
  Lugosi, Lionel Atwill, Josephine
  Hutchinson, Donnie Dunagan, Emma
  Dunn, Edgar Norton, Perry Ivins,
  Lawrence Grant, Lionel Belmore,
  Michael Mark, Caroline Cook, Gustav
  Von Seyffertitz, Edward Cassidy
Karloff as the Monster.

THE MYSTERY OF MR. WONG

Monogram
Produced by Scott R. Dunlap
Associate Producer: William T. Lackey
Directed by William Nigh
Screenplay by W. Scott Darling · From
  a story by Hugh Wiley
Photographed by Harry Neumann
Edited by Russell Schoengarth
CAST: Boris Karloff, Grant Withers,
  Dorothy Tree, Craig Reynolds, Lotus
  Long, Morgan Wallace, Holmes
  Herbert, Ivan Lebedeff, Hooper
  Atchley, Bruce Wong, Lee Tong Foo,
  Chester Gan
Karloff as James Lee Wong.

MR. WONG IN CHINATOWN

Monogram
Produced by Scott R. Dunlap
Supervised by William T. Lackey
Directed by William Nigh
Screenplay by W. Scott Darling · From
  a story by Hugh Wiley
Photographed by Harry Neumann
Edited by Russell Schoengarth
CAST: Boris Karloff, Grant Withers,
  Marjorie Reynolds, Peter George Lynn,
  William Royle, Huntly Gordon, James
  Flavin, Lotus Long, Richard Loo,
  Bessie Loo, Lee Tong Foo, Little
  Angelo, Guy Usher
Karloff as James Lee Wong.

THE MAN
THEY COULD NOT HANG

Columbia
Produced by Wallace MacDonald
Directed by Nick Grinde
Screenplay by Karl Brown · From a
  story by Leslie T. White and George
  W. Sayre
Photographed by Benjamin Kline
Art Direction by Lionel Banks
Musical Direction by Morris W. Stoloff
Edited by William Lyon
CAST: Boris Karloff, Lorna Gray, Robert
  Wilcox, Roger Pryor, Don Beddoe, Ann
  Doran, Joseph De Stefani, Charles
  Trowbridge, Byron Foulger, Dick
  Curtis, James Craig, John Tyrrell
Karloff as Dr. Henryk Savaard.

TOWER OF LONDON

Universal
Produced and Directed by Rowland
  V. Lee
Screenplay and story by Robert N. Lee
Photographed by George Robinson
Art Direction by Jack Otterson
Associate Art Director: Richard H. Riedel
Set Decoration by Richard Gausman
Orchestrations by Frank Skinner
Musical Direction by Charles Previn
Makeup by Jack P. Pierce
Sound Direction by Bernard B. Brown

Technician: William Hedgcock
Costumes by Vera West
Edited by Edward Curtiss
CAST: Basil Rathbone, Boris Karloff, Barbara O'Neil, Ian Hunter, Vincent Price, Nan Grey, John Sutton, Leo G. Carroll, Miles Mander, Lionel Belmore, Rose Hobart, Ralph Forbes, Frances Robinson, Ernest Cossart, G. P. Huntley, John Rodion, Ronald Sinclair, Donnie Dunagan, John Herbert Bond
Karloff as Mord, the clubfooted executioner.

1940

DEVIL'S ISLAND

Warner Brothers–First National
Produced by Bryan Foy
Directed by William Clemens
Screenplay by Don Ryan and Kenneth Gamet · From a story by Anthony Coldeway and Raymond L. Schrock
Photographed by George Barnes
Art Direction by Max Parker
Technical Advisor: Louis Van Den Ecker
Edited by Frank Magee
CAST: Boris Karloff, Nedda Harrigan, James Stephenson, Adia Kuznetzoff, Rolla Gourvitch, Will Stanton, Edward Keane, Robert Warwick, Pedro de Cordoba, Tom Wilson, John Harmon, Richard Bond, Earl Gunn, Sidney Bracey, George Lloyd, Charles Hickman, Stuart Holmes, Leonard Mudie, Egon Brecher
Karloff as Dr. Charles Gaudet.

THE FATAL HOUR
(MR. WONG AT HEADQUARTERS)

Monogram
Produced by William T. Lackey
Directed by William Nigh
Screenplay by W. Scott Darling · Adapted by Joseph West · From a story by Hugh Wiley
Photographed by Harry Neumann
Edited by Russell Schoengarth
CAST: Boris Karloff, Grant Withers, Marjorie Reynolds, Charles Trowbridge, John Hamilton, Craig Reynolds, Jack Kennedy, Lita Chevret, Frank Puglia, I. Stanford Jolley, Jason Robards, Sr., Pauline Drake
Karloff as James Lee Wong.

BRITISH INTELLIGENCE
(ENEMY AGENT)

Warner Brothers–First National
Directed by Terry Morse
Screenplay by Lee Katz · From the play *Three Faces East* by Anthony Paul Kelly · Additional dialogue by John Langan
Photographed by Sidney Hickox
Music by Heinz Roemheld
Edited by Thomas Pratt
CAST: Boris Karloff, Margaret Lindsay, Maris Wrixon, Bruce Lester, Leonard Mudie, Holmes Herbert, Winifred Harris, Lester Matthews, John Graham Spacey, Austin Fairman, Clarence Derwent, Frederick Giermann, Louise Brien, Frederick Vogeding, Carlos de Valdez, Willy Kaufman, Frank Mayo, Stuart Holmes, Sidney Bracey, Jack Mower
Karloff as Franz Strendler.

BLACK FRIDAY

Universal
Produced by Burt Kelly
Directed by Arthur Lubin
Story and Screenplay by Curt Siodmak and Eric Taylor
Photographed by Elwood Bredell
Special Effects by John P. Fulton

Art Direction by Jack Otterson
Associate Art Director: Harold
  MacArthur
Set Decoration by Russell Gausman
Musical Direction by Hans J. Salter
Sound Direction by Bernard B. Brown
Makeup by Jack P. Pierce
Costumes by Vera West
Technician: Charles Carroll
CAST: Boris Karloff, Bela Lugosi, Stanley
  Ridges, Anne Nagel, Anne Gwynne,
  Virginia Brissac, Edmund MacDonald,
  Paul Fix, Murray Alper, Jack Mulhall,
  Joe King, John Kelly
Karloff as Dr. Ernest Sovac.

THE MAN WITH NINE LIVES
(BEHIND THE DOOR)

Columbia
Produced by Wallace MacDonald
Directed by Nick Grinde
Screenplay by Karl Brown · From a story
  by Harold Shumate
Photographed by Benjamin Kline
Art Direction by Lionel Banks
Musical Direction by Morris W. Stoloff
Edited by Al Clark
CAST: Boris Karloff, Roger Pryor, Jo Ann
  Sayers, Stanley Brown, John Dilson,
  Hal Taliaferro, Byron Foulger, Charles
  Trowbridge, Ernie Adams, Lee Willard,
  Ivan Miller, Bruce Bennett
Karloff as Dr. Leon Kravaal.

DOOMED TO DIE
(THE MYSTERY
OF WENTWORTH CASTLE)

Monogram
Produced by Paul Malvern
Directed by William Nigh
Screenplay by Michael Jacoby · From
  a story by Ralph Gilbert Bettinson
  and a story by Hugh Wiley
Photographed by Harry Neumann

Edited by Robert Golden
CAST: Boris Karloff, Grant Withers,
  Marjorie Reynolds, Melvin Lang, Guy
  Usher, Catherine Craig, William
  Stelling, Kenneth Harlan, Wilbur Mack,
  Henry Brandon
Karloff as James Lee Wong.

BEFORE I HANG

Columbia
Produced by Wallace MacDonald
Directed by Nick Grinde
Screenplay by Robert D. Andrews · From
  a story by Karl Brown and Robert D.
  Andrews
Photographed by Benjamin Kline
Art Direction by Lionel Banks
Musical Direction by Morris W. Stoloff
Edited by Charles Nelson
CAST: Boris Karloff, Evelyn Keyes, Bruce
  Bennett, Edward Van Sloan, Ben
  Taggart, Pedro de Cordoba, Wright
  Kramer, Barton Yarborough, Don
  Beddoe, Robert Fiske, Kenneth
  MacDonald, Frank Richards
Karloff as Dr. John Garth.

THE APE

Monogram
Produced by Scott R. Dunlap
Associate Producer: William T. Lackey
Directed by William Nigh
Screenplay by Curt Siodmak and Richard
  Carroll · From the play by Adam Hull
  Shirk
Photographed by Harry Neumann
Art Direction by E. R. Hickson
Musical Direction by Edward Kay
Assistant Director: Allen Wood
Production Manager: Karl Lind
Sound Engineer: C. L. Bigelow
Edited by Russell Schoengarth
CAST: Boris Karloff, Maris Wrixon,
  Gertrude Hoffman, Henry Hall, Gene

THE APE (*continued*)

O'Donnell, Dorothy Vaughan, Jack Kennedy, Jessie Arnold, Selmer Jackson, Philo McCullough, George Cleveland
Karloff as Dr. Bernard Adrian.

YOU'LL FIND OUT

RKO
Produced and Directed by David Butler
Screenplay by James V. Kern · From a story by David Butler and James V. Kern
Photographed by Frank Redman
Special Effects by Vernon L. Walker
Art Direction by Van Nest Polglase
Music and Lyrics by Jimmy McHugh and Johnny Mercer
Music Direction by Roy Webb
Edited by Irene Morra
Cast: Kay Kyser, Peter Lorre, Boris Karloff, Bela Lugosi, Helen Parrish, Dennis O'Keefe, Alma Kruger, Joseph Eggenton, Ginny Simms, Harry Babbitt, Sully Mason, Ish Kabibble
Karloff as Judge Mainwaring.

1941

THE DEVIL COMMANDS

Columbia
Produced by Wallace MacDonald
Directed by Edward Dmytryk
Screenplay by Robert D. Andrews and Milton Gunzberg · From the novel *The Edge of Running Water* by William Sloane
Photographed by Allen G. Siegler
Art Direction by Lionel Banks
Musical Direction by Morris W. Stoloff
Edited by Al Clark
Cast: Boris Karloff, Richard Fiske, Amanda Duff, Ann Revere, Ralph Penney, Dorothy Adams, Walter

Baldwin, Kenneth MacDonald, Shirley Warde
Karloff as Dr. Julian Blair.

INFORMATION PLEASE NO. 8

RKO
Movie adaptation of the radio panel game show.
Panelists: Clifton Fadiman, John Kieran, Franklin P. Adams, Boris Karloff
Karloff as guest panelist.

INFORMATION PLEASE NO. 12

RKO
Movie adaptation of the radio panel game show.
Panelists: Clifton Fadiman, John Kieran, Franklin P. Adams, Oscar Levant, Boris Karloff
Karloff as guest panelist.

1942

THE BOOGIE MAN WILL GET YOU

Columbia
Produced by Colbert Clark
Directed by Lew Landers
Screenplay by Edwin Blum · Adapted by Paul Gangelin · From a story by Hal Fimberg and Robert B. Hunt
Photographed by Henry Freulich
Art Direction by Lionel Banks
Associate Art Director: Robert Peterson
Set Decoration by George Montgomery
Musical Direction by Morris W. Stoloff
Sound Technician: C. Althouse
Edited by Richard Fantl
Cast: Boris Karloff, Peter Lorre, Maxie Rosenbloom, Larry Parks, Jeff Donnell, Maude Eburne, Don Beddoe, George McKay, Frank Puglia, Eddie Laughton, Frank Sully, James Morton
Karloff as Professor Nathaniel Billings.

1944

THE CLIMAX

Universal
Produced and Directed by George
  Waggner
Screenplay by Curt Siodmak and Lyn
  Starling · Adapted by Curt Siodmak ·
  From a play by Edward Locke
Photographed by Hal Mohr and W.
  Howard Greene
Technicolor Consultant: Natalie Kalmus
Special Effects by John P. Fulton
Art Direction by John B. Goodman and
  Howard Golitzen
Set Decoration by Russell A. Gausman
  and Ira S. Webb
Musical Score by Edward Ward
Musical Direction by Don George
Sound by William Fox and Bernard B.
  Brown
Makeup by Jack P. Pierce
Costumes by Vera West
Assistant Director: Seymour Friedman
Edited by Russell Schoengarth
Technicolor
CAST: Boris Karloff, Susanna Foster,
  Turhan Bey, Gale Sondergaard,
  Thomas Gomez, June Vincent, George
  Dolenz, Ludwig Stossel, Jane Farrar,
  Erno Verebes, Lotte Stein, Scotty
  Beckett, William Edmunds, Maxwell
  Hayes, Dorothy Lawrence
Karloff as Doctor Hohner.

HOUSE OF FRANKENSTEIN

Universal
Produced by Paul Malvern
Directed by Erle C. Kenton
Screenplay by Edward T. Lowe · From
  a story by Curt Siodmak
Photographed by George Robinson
Special Effects by John P. Fulton
Art Direction by John G. Goodman and
  Martin Obzina

Set Decoration by Russell A. Gausman
  and A. J. Gilmore
Musical Score and Direction by Hans J.
  Salter
Sound by William Hedgcock and
  Bernard B. Brown
Makeup by Jack P. Pierce
Costumes by Vera West
Assistant Director: William Tummel
Edited by Philip Cahn
CAST: Boris Karloff, Lon Chaney, Jr., J.
  Carrol Naish, John Carradine, Anne
  Gwynne, Peter Coe, Lionel Atwill,
  George Zucco, Elena Verdugo, Glenn
  Strange, Sig Ruman, William Edmunds,
  Charles Miller, Philip Van Zandt,
  Julius Tannen, Hans Herbert, Dick
  Dickinson, George Lynn, Michael
  Mark, Olaf Hytten, Frank Reicher,
  Brandon Hurst
Karloff as Doctor Gustav Niemann.

1945

THE BODY SNATCHER

RKO–Radio
Executive Producer: Jack J. Gross
Produced by Val Lewton
Directed by Robert Wise
Screenplay by Philip MacDonald and
  Carlos Keith (Val Lewton) · From a
  story by Robert Louis Stevenson
Photographed by Robert De Grasse
Art Direction by Albert S. D'Agostino
  and Walter Keller
Set Decoration by Darrell Silvera and
  John Sturtevant
Music by Roy Webb
Musical Direction by Constantin
  Bakaleinikoff
Sound by Baily Fesler and Terry Kellum
Recorded by Terry Kellum
Assistant Director: Harry Scott
Costumes by Renée
Edited by J. R. Whittredge

CAST: Boris Karloff, Bela Lugosi, Henry Daniell, Edith Atwater, Russell Wade, Rita Corday, Sharyn Moffett, Donna Lee

Karloff as John Gray.

ISLE OF THE DEAD

RKO–Radio
Executive Producer: Jack J. Gross
Produced by Val Lewton
Directed by Mark Robson
Screenplay by Ardel Wray and Josef Mischel · Suggested by a painting by Arnold Böcklin
Photographed by Jack MacKenzie
Art Direction by Albert S. D'Agostino and Walter Keller
Set Decoration by Darrell Silvera and Al Greenwood
Music by Leigh Harline
Musical Direction by Constantin Bakaleinikoff
Sound by Jean L. Speak
Assistant Director: Harry Scott
Costumes by Edward Stevenson
Edited by Lyle Boyer
CAST: Boris Karloff, Ellen Drew, Marc Cramer, Katherine Emery, Helene Thimig, Alan Napier, Jason Robards, Sr., Ernst Dorian, Skelton Knaggs

Karloff as General Nikolas Pherides.

1946

BEDLAM

RKO
Executive Producer: Jack J. Gross
Produced by Val Lewton
Directed by Mark Robson
Screenplay by Mark Robson and Carlos Keith (Val Lewton) · Suggested by the picture "Bedlam" by William Hogarth
Photographed by Nicholas Musuraca
Special Photographic Effects by Vernon L. Walker
Art Direction by Albert S. D'Agostino and Walter E. Keller
Set Decoration by Darrell Silvera and John Sturtevant
Music by Roy Webb
Musical Direction by Constantin Bakaleinikoff
Sound by Jean L. Speak and Terry Kellum
Costumes by Edward Stevenson
Assistant Director: Dorian Cox
Edited by Lyle Boyer
CAST: Boris Karloff, Anna Lee, Billy House, Richard Fraser, Glenn Vernon, Ian Wolfe, Jason Robards, Sr., Leyland Hodgson, Joan Newton, Elizabeth Russell, Ellen Corby, Robert Clarke

Karloff as Master George Sims.

1947

LURED (PERSONAL COLUMN)

Hunt Stromberg–United Artists–Oakmont
Executive Producer: Hunt Stromberg
Produced by James Nasser
Associate Producer: Henry S. Kesler
Directed by Douglas Sirk
Screenplay by Leo Rosten · From a story by Jacques Companeez, Ernest Neuville, and Simon Gentillon
Photographed by William Daniels
Art Direction by Nicolai Remisoff
Associate Art Director: Victor Greene
Music by Michel Michelet
Musical Direction by David Chudnow
Sound by H. Connors
Makeup by Don Cash
Assistant Director: Clarence Eurist
Edited by John M. Foley and James E. Newcom

CAST: George Sanders, Lucille Ball, Charles Coburn, Boris Karloff, Sir Cedric Hardwicke, Alan Mowbray, George Zucco, Joseph Calleia, Tanis Chandler, Allan Napier, Robert Coote
Karloff as Charles Van Druten.

THE SECRET LIFE OF WALTER MITTY

RKO–Goldwyn
Produced by Samuel Goldwyn
Directed by Norman Z. McLeod
Screenplay by Ken Englund and Everett Freeman · From a story by James Thurber
Photographed by Lee Garmes
Special Effects by John P. Fulton
Art Direction by George Jenkins and Perry Ferguson
Set Decoration by Casey Roberts
Music by David Raskin
Musical Direction by Emil Newman
Songs by Sylvia Fine
Sound by Fredlau
Assistant Director: Rollie Asher
Edited by Monica Collingwood
Technicolor
CAST: Danny Kaye, Virginia Mayo, Boris Karloff, Fay Bainter, Ann Rutherford, Thurston Hall, Gordon Jones, Florence Bates, Konstantin Shayne, Reginald Denny, Henry Corden, Doris Lloyd, Fritz Feld, Frank Reicher, Milton Parsons, The Goldwyn Girls
Karloff as Dr. Hollingshead.

DICK TRACY MEETS GRUESOME (DICK TRACY'S AMAZING ADVENTURE)

RKO
Produced by Herman Schlom
Directed by John Rawlins
Screenplay by Robertson White and

Eric Taylor · From a story by William H. Graffis and Robert E. Kent and the comic strip by Chester Gould
Photographed by Frank Redman
Special Effects by Russell A. Cully
Art Direction by Albert S. D'Agostino and Walter Keller
Set Decoration by Darrell Silvera and James Attwies
Music by Paul Sawtell
Musical Direction by Constantin Bakaleinikoff
Sound by Jean L. Speak and Terry Kellum
Assistant Director: James Lane
Edited by Elmo Williams
CAST: Boris Karloff, Ralph Byrd, Anne Gwynne, Edward Ashley, June Clayworth, Lyle Latell, Tony Barrett, Skelton Knaggs, Jim Nolan, Joseph Crehan, Milton Parsons
Karloff as Gruesome.

UNCONQUERED

Paramount
Produced and Directed by Cecil B. De Mille
Screenplay by Charles Bennett, Frederic M. Frank, and Jesse Lasky, Jr. · From a novel by Neil H. Swanson
Photographed by Ray Rennahan
Special Effects by Gordon Jennings
Art Direction by Hans Dreier and Walter Tyler
Set Decoration by Sam Comer and Stanley Jay Sawley
Music by Victor Young
Sound by Hugo Grenzbach and John Cope
Second Unit Director: Arthur Rosson
Assistant Director: Edward Salven
Edited by Anne Bauchens
Technicolor
CAST: Gary Cooper, Paulette Goddard, Howard Da Silva, Boris Karloff, Cecil

UNCONQUERED (*continued*)

Kellaway, Ward Bond, Katherine De Mille, Henry Wilcoxon, C. Aubrey Smith, Virginia Campbell, Mike Mazurki, Robert Warwick, Marc Lawrence, Richard Gaines, Alan Napier, Gavin Muir, Victor Varconi, Virginia Grey, John Mylong, Oliver Thorndike, Nan Sunderland, Porter Hall, Jane Nigh, Lloyd Bridges, Dorothy Adams, Clarence Muse, Raymond Hatton, Julia Faye, Charles Middleton, Tiny Jones, Fred Kohler, Jr., Noble Johnson, Ethel Wales, Byron Foulger, Francis McDonald, William Haade, Jeff Corey, Lex Barker, Lane Chandler, Claire DuBrey, Inez Palange, Greta Granstedt
Karloff as Seneca Chief Guyasuta.

1948

TAP ROOTS

Universal International–Walter Wanger
Produced by Walter Wanger
Directed by George Marshall
Screenplay by Alan Le May · From a novel by James Street · Additional Dialogue by Lionel Wiggam
Photographed by Lionel Lindon and Winton C. Hoch
Art Direction by Frank A. Richards
Set Decoration by Russell A. Gausman and Ruby R. Levitt
Music by Frank Skinner
Sound by Leslie I. Carey and Glenn E. Anderson
Makeup by Bud Westmore
Costumes by Yvonne Wood
Assistant Director: Aaron Rosenberg
Edited by Milton Carruth
Technicolor
CAST: Van Heflin, Susan Hayward, Boris Karloff, Julie London, Whitfield Connor, Ward Bond, Richard Long,

Arthur Shields, Griff Barnett, Sondra Rodgers, Ruby Dandridge, Russell Simpson
Karloff as Tishomingo, a Choctaw Indian.

1949

ABBOTT AND COSTELLO MEET THE KILLER, BORIS KARLOFF

Universal–International
Produced by Robert Arthur
Directed by Charles T. Barton
Screenplay by Hugh Wedlock, Jr., Howard Snyder, and John Grant · From a story by Hugh Wedlock, Jr., and Howard Snyder
Photographed by Charles Van Enger
Special Effects by David S. Horsley
Art Direction by Bernard Nerzbrun and Richard H. Riedel
Set Decoration by Russell A. Gausman and Oliver Emert
Music by Milton Schwarzwald
Sound by Leslie J. Carey and Robert Pritchard
Makeup by Bud Westmore
Costumes by Rosemary Odell
Assistant Director: Joe Kenny
Edited by Edward Curtiss
CAST: Bud Abbott, Lou Costello, Boris Karloff, Lenore Aubert, Gar Moore, Donna Martell, Alan Mowbray, James Flavin, Roland Winters, Nicholas Joy, Mikel Conrad, Morgan Farley, Victoria Horne, Percy Helton, Clair Du Brey, Harry Hayden, Vincent Renno
Karloff as Swami Tapur.

1951

THE STRANGE DOOR

Universal–International
Produced by Ted Richmond

Directed by Joseph Pevney
Screenplay by Jerry Sackheim · From the
  story "The Sire de Maletroit's Door"
  by Robert Louis Stevenson
Photographed by Irving Glassberg
Special Effects by David S. Horsley
Art Direction by Bernard Herzbrun and
  Eric Orbom
Set Decoration by Russell A. Gausman
  and Julia Heron
Musical Direction by Joseph Gershenson
Sound by Leslie J. Carey and Glenn
  E. Anderson
Makeup by Bud Westmore
Costumes by Rosemary Odell
Assistant Director: Jesse Hibbs
Edited by Edward Curtiss
CAST: Charles Laughton, Boris Karloff,
  Sally Forrest, Richard Stapley, Michael
  Pate, Paul Cavanagh, Alan Napier,
  William Cottrell, Morgan Farley,
  Charles Horvath
Karloff as Voltan, a servant.

THE EMPEROR'S NIGHTINGALE
(CISARUV SLAVIK)

Czech State
Rembrandt Films
Live Action Direction by Milos Makovec
Animation Direction by Jiri Trnka
Screenplay by Jiri Trnka and Jiri
  Brdecka · From a story by Hans
  Christian Andersen
English Narrative by Phyllis McGinley
Photographed by Ferdinand Pecenka
Music by Vaclav Trajan
Agfacolor
CAST: Jaromir Sobotoa, Helena
  Patockova
Karloff as Narrator.

1952

THE BLACK CASTLE
Universal–International

Produced by William Alland
Directed by Nathan Juran
Screenplay and Story by Jerry
  Sackheim
Photographed by Irving Glassberg
Special Effects by David S. Horsley
Art Direction by Bernard Herzbrun and
  Alfred Sweeney
Set Decoration by Russell A. Gausman
  and Oliver Emert
Musical Direction by Joseph Gershenson
Dance Direction by Hal Belfer
Sound by Leslie J. Carey and Joe Papis
Makeup by Bud Westmore
Costumes by Bill Thomas
Assistant Director: William Holland
Edited by Russell Schoengarth
CAST: Richard Greene, Boris Karloff,
  Stephen McNally, Paula Corday, Lon
  Chaney, Jr., John Hoyt, Michael Pate,
  Nancy Valentine, Tudor Owen, Otto
  Waldis, Harry Cording
Karloff as Doctor Meissen.

1953

COLONEL MARCH
INVESTIGATES
(COLONEL MARCH OF
SCOTLAND YARD)

Eros-Criterion-Panda
Produced by Donald Ginsberg
Directed by Cyril Endfield
Screenplay by Leo Davis · From the
  stories by Carter Dickson
Photographed by Jonah Jones
Art Direction by George Paterson
Music by John Lanchberry
Musical Direction by Eric Robinson
Edited by Stan Willis
CAST: Boris Karloff, Ewan Roberts,
  Richard Wattis, Sheila Burrell, Anthony
  Forwood, John Hewer, Joan Sims,
  Ronald Leigh Hunt, Roger Maxwell,
  Patricia Owens, Dagmar Wunter,

Sonya Hana, Bernard Rebel
Karloff as Colonel March.

THE HINDU (SABAKA)

United Artists
Produced, Directed, Story, and
    Screenplay by Frank Ferrin
Photographed by Allen Svensvold and
    Jack McCoskey
Art Direction by Ralph Ferrin
Music by Daksnamurti
Sound by Eugene Grosman
Edited by Jack Foley
Eastmancolor
CAST: Boris Karloff, Nino Marcel, Lou
    Krugman, Reginald Denny, Victor
    Jory, June Foray, Jay Novello, Lisa
    Howard, Peter Coe, Paul Marion,
    Vito Scotti, Lou Merrill, Larry Dobkin,
    Jeanne Bates
Karloff as General Pollegar.

ABBOTT AND COSTELLO MEET DR. JEKYLL AND MR. HYDE

Universal-International
Produced by Howard Christie
Directed by Charles Lamont
Screenplay by Lee Loeb and John
    Grant · From the screen stories by
    Sidney Fields and Grant Garrett and
    the novel by Robert Louis Stevenson
Photographed by George Robinson
Special Effects by David S. Horsley
Art Direction by Bernard Herzbrun and
    Eric Orbom
Set Decoration by Russel A. Gausman
Musical Direction by Joseph Gershenson
Dance Direction by Kenny Williams
Dialogue Direction by Milt Bronson
Sound by Leslie I. Carey
Makeup by Bud Westmore
Costumes by Rosemary Odell
Edited by Russell Schoengarth
CAST: Bud Abbott, Lou Costello, Boris

Karloff, Helen Westcott, Craig Stevens,
    John Dierkes, Reginald Denny, Edwin
    Parker
Karloff as Doctor Henry Jekyll.

THE MONSTER OF THE ISLAND (IL MOSTRO DELL'ISOLA)

Romano
Directed by Roberto Montero and
    Alberto Vecchietti
Screenplay by Roberto Montero · From
    a story by Carlo Lombardo
Photographed by Augusto Tiezzi
Music by Carlo Innocenzi
CAST: Boris Karloff, Franca Marzi,
    Renato Vicario, Germana Paolieri,
    Patrizia Remidi, José Fierro, Carlo
    Duse
Karloff as a leader of a dope-smugglers'
    gang.

1957

THE JUGGLER OF OUR LADY

Twentieth Century Fox–Terrytoons
Producer by Bill Weiss
Directed by Al Kousel
Supervised by Gene Deitch
Story and Screenplay by R. O. Blechman
Animation by Gene Deitch and Al Kousel
Music by Philip Scheib
Technicolor/Cinemascope
    Karloff as the Narrator.

SILENT DEATH (VOODOO ISLAND)

United Artists
A Bel-Air Production
Executive Producer: Aubrey Schenck
Produced by Howard W. Koch
Directed by Reginald Le Borg
Story and Screenplay by Richard Landau
Photographed by William Margulies

Special Effects by Jack Rabin and
  Louis De Witt
Music by Les Baxter
Makeup by Ted Coodley
Assistant Director: Paul Wurtzel
Edited by John F. Schreyer
CAST: Boris Karloff, Beverly Tyler,
  Murvyn Vye, Elisha Cook, Jr., Rhodes
  Reason, Jean Engstrom, Frederick
  Ledebur, Glenn Dixon, Owen
  Cunningham, Herbert Patterson,
  Jerome Frank
Karloff as Phillip Knight.

1958

FRANKENSTEIN 1970

Allied Artists
Produced by Aubrey Schenck
Directed by Howard W. Koch
Screenplay by Richard Landau and
  George Worthing Yates · From a
  story by Aubrey Schenck and Charles
  A. Moses
Photographed by Carl E. Guthrie
Art Direction by Jack T. Collins
Set Decoration by Jerry Welch
Music by Paul A. Dunlap
Sound by Francis C. Stahl
Makeup by Gordon Bau
Assistant Director: George Vieira
Edited by John A. Bushelman
Cinemascope
CAST: Boris Karloff, Tom Duggan, Jana
  Lund, Donald Barry, Charlotte Austin,
  Irwin Berke, Rudolph Anders, John
  Dennis, Norbert Schiller, Mike Lane
Karloff as Baron Victor von Frankenstein.

THE HAUNTED STRANGLER
(GRIP OF THE STRANGLER)

MGM
MLC / Producers Associates / Eros Films
Executive Producer: Richard Gordon

Produced by John Croydon
Directed by Robert Day
Screenplay by Jan Read and John C.
  Cooper · From a story by Jan Read
Photographed by Lionel Banes
Special Effects by Les Bowie
Art Direction by John Elphick
Music by Buxton Orr
Musical Direction by Frederick Lewis
Sound by Peter Davies
Edited by Peter Mayhew
CAST: Boris Karloff, Jean Kent, Elizabeth
  Allen, Anthony Dawson, Vera Day,
  Tim Turner, Diane Aubrey, Dorothy
  Gordon, Peggy Ann Clifford, Leslie
  Perrins, Michael Atkinson, Desmond
  Roberts, Jessie Cairns, Roy Russell,
  Derek Birch, George Hirste, John G.
  Heller, George Spence, Joan Elvin, Max
  Brimmell, John Fabian
Karloff as James Rankin/Doctor Tenant,
  "The Haymarket Strangler."

1963

CORRIDORS OF BLOOD
(THE DOCTOR OF SEVEN DIALS)

MGM
Producers Associates
Executive Producer: Richard Gordon
Produced by John Croydon and
  Charles Vetter
Associate Producer: Peter Mayhew
Directed by Robert Day
Story and Screenplay by Jean Scott Rogers
Art Direction by Anthony Masters
Music by Buxton Orr
Musical Direction by Frederick Lewis
Photographed by Geoffrey Faithfull
Sound by Cyril Swern and Maurice Askew
Assistant Director: Peter Bolton
Edited by Peter Mayhew
CAST: Boris Karloff, Betta St. John, Finlay
  Currie, Christopher Lee, Francis

Matthews, Adrienne Corri, Francis De
Wolff, Basil Dignam, Frank Pettingell,
Marian Spencer, Carl Bernard, Yvonne
Warren, Charles Lloyd, Robert Raglan,
John Gabriel, Nigel Green, Howard
Lang, Roddy Hughes, Julian D'Albie
Karloff as Dr. Thomas Bolton.

THE RAVEN

American International
An Alta Vista Production
Executive Producers: James H. Nicholson
and Samuel Z. Arkoff
Produced and Directed by Roger Corman
Screenplay by Richard Matheson ·
Suggested by the poem by Edgar Allan
Poe
Photographed by Floyd Crosby
Special Effects by Pat Dinga
Photographic Effects by Butler-Glouner,
Inc.
Art Direction by Daniel Haller
Set Decoration by Harry Reif
Music by Les Baxter
Makeup by Ted Coodley
Costumes by Marjorie Corso
Raven Trainer: Moe Disesso
Assistant Director: Peter Bolton
Edited by Ronald Sinclair
Pathécolor and Panavision
CAST: Vincent Price, Peter Lorre, Boris
Karloff, Hazel Court, Olive Sturgess,
Jack Nicholson, Connie Wallace,
William Baskin, Aaron Saxon, Jim
Junior (a raven)
Karloff as Doctor Scarabus, an evil
sorcerer.

THE TERROR

American International
A Filmgroup Production
Executive Producer: Harvey Jacobson
Produced and Directed by Roger Corman

Associate Producer: Francis Ford Coppola
Story and Screenplay by Leo Gordon and
Jack Hill
Photographed by John Nickolaus
Art Direction by Daniel Haller
Set Decoration by Harry Reif
Music by Les Baxter
Sound by John Bury
Assistant Director: Monte Hellman
Costumes by Marjorie Corso
Titles by Paul Julian
Edited by Stuart O'Brien
Pathécolor and Vistascope
CAST: Boris Karloff, Jack Nicholson,
Sandra Knight, Richard Miller, Dorothy
Neumann, Jonathan Haze
Karloff as Baron von Leppe/Eric.

1964

THE COMEDY OF TERRORS

American International
An Alta Vista Production
Executive Producers: James H. Nicholson
and Samuel Z. Arkoff
Produced by Anthony Carras and
Richard Matheson
Directed by Jacques Tourneur
Story and Screenplay by Richard
Matheson
Photographed by Floyd Crosby
Special Effects by Pat Dinga
Art Direction by Daniel Haller
Set Decoration by Harry Reif
Music by Les Baxter
Sound by Don Rush
Assistant Director: Robert Agnew
Makeup by Charlie Taylor
Costumes by Marjorie Corso
Edited by Anthony Carras
Pathécolor and Panavision
CAST: Vincent Price, Boris Karloff, Peter
Lorre, Basil Rathbone, Joe E. Brown,

Joyce Jameson, Beverly Hills, Paul
Barsolow, Linda Rogers, Luree
Nicholson, Buddy Mason, Rhubarb (the
cat)
Karloff as Amos Hinchley.

BLACK SABBATH
(I TRE VOLTI DELLA PAURA)

American International
Emmepi/Galatea/Lyre
Presented in the United States by James
  H. Nicholson and Samuel Z. Arkoff
Produced by Salvatore Billitteri
Directed by Mario Bava
Screenplay by Marcello Fondato, Alberto
  Bevilacqua, and Mario Bava · From
  the stories "The Drop of Water" by
  Anton Chekhov, "The Telephone" by
  F. G. Snyder, "The Wurdalak" by
  Alexei Tolstoy
Photographed by Ubaldo Terzano
Art Direction by Giorgio Giovannini
Set Decoration by Riccardo Dominici
Music by Les Baxter (American) and
  Roberto Nicolosi (Italian)
Sound by Titra Sound Corporation
Makeup by Otello Fava
Costumes by Trini Grani
Edited by Mario Serandrei
Eastmancolor
CAST: Boris Karloff, Mark Damon, Susy
  Anderson, Michele Mercier, Lidia
  Alfonsi, Jacqueline Pierreux, Milli
  Monti, Glauco Onorato, Rika Dialina,
  Massino Righi
Karloff as Gorca, a vampire.

BIKINI BEACH

American International
Executive Producers: James H. Nicholson
  and Samuel Z. Arkoff
Produced by Anthony Carras
Directed by William Asher
Screenplay by William Asher, Leo

Townsend, and Robert Dillon
Photographed by Floyd Crosby
Special Effects by Roger and Joe Zonar
Art Direction by Daniel Haller
Set Decoration by Harry Reif
Music by Les Baxter
Dance Direction by Tom Mahoney
Edited by Fred Feitshans
Pathécolor and Panavision
CAST: Frankie Avalon, Annette Funicello,
  Martha Hyer, Keenan Wynn, Don
  Rickles, Harvey Lembeck, John Ashley,
  Jody McCrea, Candy Johnson,
  Danielle Aubry, Meredith MacRae,
  Dolores Wells, Janos Prohaska,
  Timothy Carey, Val Warren, Donna
  Loren, Paul Smith, James
  Westerfield, Little Stevie Wonder, The
  Pyramids, The Exciters Band, Boris
  Karloff
Karloff as the Art Dealer.

TODAY'S TEENS

Twentieth Century Fox/Movietone
Karloff as Narrator.

1965

DIE, MONSTER, DIE!
(MONSTER OF TERROR;
THE HOUSE AT THE END
OF THE WORLD)

American International
Executive Producers: James H. Nicholson
  and Samuel Z. Arkoff
Produced by Pat Green
Directed by Daniel Haller
Screenplay by Jerry Sohl · From the
  story "The Colour Out of Space" by
  H. P. Lovecraft
Photographed by Paul Beeson
Special Effects by Wally Veevers and
  Ernest Sullivan

DIE, MONSTER, DIE! (*continued*)

Art Direction by Colin Southcott
Music by Don Banks
Sound by Ken Rawkins and Robert Jones
Makeup by Jimmy Evans
Assistant Director: Dennis Hall
Edited by Alfred Cox
Pathécolor and Colorscope
CAST: Boris Karloff, Nick Adams, Susan
  Farmer, Freda Jackson, Terence De
  Marney, Patrick Magee, Paul Farrell,
  Leslie Dwyer, Sheila Raynor, Harold
  Goodwin, Sidney Bromley, Billy Milton
Karloff as Nahum Witley.

1966

THE GHOST IN THE
INVISIBLE BIKINI

American International
Executive Producers: James H. Nicholson
  and Samuel Z. Arkoff
Produced by Anthony Carras
Directed by Don Weis
Screenplay by Louis M. Heyward and
  Elwood Ullman · From a story by
  Louis M. Heyward
Photographed by Stanley Cortez
Music by Les Baxter
Songs by Guy Hemric and Jerry Styner
Sound by Ryder Sound Services
Edited by Fred Feitshans and Eve
  Newman
Pathécolor and Panavision
CAST: Tommy Kirk, Deborah Walley,
  Aron Kincaid, Quinn O'Hara, Jesse
  White, Harvey Lembeck, Nancy
  Sinatra, Claudia Martin, Francis X.
  Bushman, Benny Rubin, Bobbi Shaw,
  George Barrows, Basil Rathbone,
  Boris Karloff, Patsy Kelly, Susan Hart,
  Luree Holmes, Alberta Nelson,
  Andy Romano
Karloff as Hiram Stokeley, the corpse.

THE DAYDREAMER

Embassy Pictures
A Videocraft International Production
Executive Producer: Joseph E. Levine
Produced and Screenplay by Arthur
  Rankin, Jr. · From the stories "The
  Little Mermaid," "The Emperor's
  New Clothes," "Thumbelina," "The
  Garden of Paradise" by Hans
  Christian Andersen
Directed by Jules Bass
Animagic Sequences by Don Duga
Animagic Photographed by Tad Mochinga
Live Action Sequences by Ezra Stone
Live Action Photographed by Daniel
  Cavelli
Art Direction by Maurice Gordon
Music and Lyrics by Maury Laws and
  Jules Bass
Eastmancolor and Animagic
CAST: Paul O'Keefe, Jack Gilford, Ray
  Bolger, Margaret Hamilton, Robert
  Harter; *Voices*: Tallulah Bankhead,
  Victor Borge, Patty Duke, Sessue
  Hayakawa, Burl Ives, Boris Karloff,
  Hayley Mills, Cyril Ritchard, Terry-
  Thomas, Ed Wynn, Robert Goulet
Karloff's voice as the Rat, puppet.

1967

THE VENETIAN AFFAIR

MGM
Produced by Jerry Thorpe and E.
  Jack Neuman
Directed by Jerry Thorpe
Screenplay by E. Jack Neuman · From
  a novel by Helen MacInnes
Photographed by Milton Krasner
Art Direction by George W. Davis
Set Director: Henry Grace
Music by Lalo Schifrin
Edited by Henry Berman
Metrocolor and Panavision

CAST: Robert Vaughn, Elke Sommer, Karl Boehm, Edward Asner, Boris Karloff, Felicia Farr, Roger C. Carmel, Lucianna Paluzzi, Joe De Santis, Fabrizio Mioni, Wesley Lau, Bill Weiss

Karloff as Doctor Pierre Vaugiroud.

MONDO BALORDO

Crown International
Ivanhoe Productions/Cine Produzioni
Directed by Robert Bianchi Montero
Narrative by Castaldo and Tori
American Version by Ted Weiss
Music by Lallo Gori and Nani Rossi
Edited by Enzio Alfonsi
American Version by Fred Von Bernewitz
Eastmancolor and Stereorama
Karloff as the Narrator.

MAD MONSTER PARTY

Embassy Pictures
A Videocraft International Production
Executive Producer: Joseph E. Levine
Produced by Arthur Rankin, Jr.
Directed by Jules Bass
Screenplay by Harvey Kurtzman and Leo Korobkin · From a story by Arthur Rankin, Jr.
Music and Lyrics by Maury Laws and Jules Bass
Eastmancolor and Animagic
CAST: Boris Karloff, Phyllis Diller, Gale Garnett, Ethel Ennis, Allen Swift (voices)

Karloff as the Karloff puppet.

THE SORCERERS

Allied Artists
Tigon/Curtwell/Global
Executive Producer: Arnold Louis Miller

Produced by Patrick Curtis and Tony Tenser
Directed by Michael Reeves
Screenplay by Michael Reeves and Tom Baker · From a story by John Burke
Photographed by Stanley Long
Art Direction by Tony Curtis
Music by Paul Ferris
Edited by David Woodward
Eastmancolor
CAST: Boris Karloff, Elizabeth Ercy, Ian Ogilvy, Catherine Lacey, Victor Henry, Susan George, Dani Sheridan, Ivor Dean, Peter Fraser, Meier Tzelniker, Bill Barnsley, Martin Terry, Gerald Campion, Alf Joint

Karloff as Professor Monserrat.

1968

TARGETS

Paramount/Saticoy
Produced, Directed, and Screenplay by Peter Bogdanovich · From a story by Polly Platt and Peter Bogdanovich
Photographed by Laszlo Kovacs
Art Direction by Polly Platt
Sound by Sam Kopetsky
Pathécolor
CAST: Boris Karloff, Tim O'Kelly, Nancy Hsueh, James Brown, Sandy Baron, Arthur Peterson, Mary Jackson, Tanya Morgan, Monty Landis, Paul Condylis, Mark Dennis, Stafford Morgan, Peter Bogdanovich, Daniel Ades, Tim Burns, Warren White, Geraldine Baron, Gary Kent, Ellie Wood Walker, Frank Marshall, Bryon Betz, Mike Farrell, Carol Samuels, Jay Daniel, James Morris

Karloff as Byron Orlok.

· · ·

1970

THE CRIMSON CULT
(CURSE OF THE
CRIMSON ALTAR)

American International/Tigon
Executive Producer: Tony Tenser
Produced by Louis M. Heyward
Directed by Vernon Sewell
Story and Screenplay by Mervyn Haisman
 and Henry Lincoln
Additional Material by Gerry Levy
Photographed by Johnny Coquillon
Art Direction by Derek Barrington
Music by Peter Knight
Makeup by Pauline Worden and
 Elizabeth Blattner
Costumes by Michael Southgate
Eastmancolor
CAST: Boris Karloff, Christopher Lee,
 Mark Eden, Barbara Steele, Michael
 Gough, Rupert Davies, Virginia
 Wetherell, Rosemarie Reed, Derek
 Tansey, Michael Warren, Ron Pomber,
 Denys Peek, Nita Lorraine, Carol Anne,
 Jenny Shaw, Vivienne Carlton, Roger
 Avon, Paul McNeil, Millicent Scott,
 Vicky Richards, Tasma Bereton,
 Kevin Smith, Lita Scott, Terry Raven
Karloff as Professor Marshe, occultist.

ISLE OF THE SNAKE PEOPLE

Azteca-Columbia
Produced by Henry Verg (Enrique
 Vergara) and Jhon Ibanez
Directed by Henry Verg (Enrique
 Vergara) and Jack Hill
Screenplay by Jack Hill
Photographed by Austin McKinney
Music by Alice Uretta
Color
CAST: Boris Karloff, Julissa, Charles East,
 Ralph Bertrand, Judy Carmichael,
 Tongolee, Quentin Miller

Karloff as Doctor Carl Van Boulder, a
scientist.

1971

BLIND MAN'S BLUFF
(CAULDRON OF BLOOD;
THE SHRINKING CORPSE;
EL COLECCIONISTA DE
CADAVERES)

Cannon Films/Hispamer Films
ıA Robert Weinbach Production
Produced by Robert D. Weinbach
Directed and Story by Edward Mann
 (Santos Alcocer)
Screenplay by John Nelson, José Luis
 Bayonas and Edward Mann (Santos
 Alcocer)
Photographed by Francisco Sempere
Art Direction by Gil Parrondo
Music by José Luis Navarro and Ray
 Ellis
Songs by Edward Mann (Santos Alcocer)
 and Bob Harris
Makeup by Manolita Garcia Fraile
Edited by J. Antonio Rojo
Eastmancolor and Panoramica
CAST: Boris Karloff, Viveca Lindfors,
 Jean-Pierre Aumont, Jacqui Speed,
 Rosenda Monteros, Ruven Rojo,
 Dianik Zurakowska, Milo Quesada,
 Mercedes Rojo, Mary Lou Palermo,
 Manuel de Blas, Eduardo Coutelen
Karloff as Charles Badulescu.

THE INCREDIBLE INVASION
(INVASION SINIESTRA)

Azteca-Columbia
Produced by Enrique Vergara and Jhon
 Ibanez
Directed by Enrique Vergara and Jack
 Hill
Screenplay by Jack Hill

Photographed by Austin McKinney
Music by Alice Uretta
Color
CAST: Boris Karloff, Enrique Guzman,
Christa Linder, Maura Monti, Yerte
Merute, Toni Valdez, Sango Alemez,
Marca Flores, Griselda Mina,
Rosalanga Balbo, Tito Navarro
Karloff as a malevolent scientist.

THE FEAR CHAMBER

Azteca-Columbia
Produced by Enrique Vergara and
Jhon Ibanez
Directed by Enrique Vergara and
Jack Hill
Screenplay by Jack Hill
Photographed by Austin McKinney

Music by Alice Uretta
Color
Karloff as a benevolent scientist.

1972

HOUSE OF EVIL

Azteca-Columbia
Produced by Enrique Vergara and
Jhon Ibanez
Directed by Enrique Vergara and
Jack Hill
Screenplay by Jack Hill
Photographed by Austin McKinney
Music by Alice Uretta
Color
Karloff as a menace.

A NOTE ON THE TYPE

The text of this book was set on the Linotype in Janson, a recutting made direct from type cast from matrices long thought to have been made by Dutchman Anton Janson, who was a practicing type founder in Leipzig during the years 1668–87. However, it has been conclusively demonstrated that these types are actually the work of Nicholas Kis (1650–1702), a Hungarian, who most probably learned his trade from the master Dutch type founder Dirk Voskens. The type is an excellent example of the influential and sturdy Dutch types that prevailed in England up to the time William Caslon developed his own incomparable designs from them.

The display type used in this book is Broadway, a type designed by Morris Fuller Benton for American Type Founders in 1929.

Composed by Maryland Linotype, Baltimore, Maryland
Printed and bound by Halliday Lithograph, West Hanover, Massachusetts

Typography and binding design by Virginia Tan